Analysis and Visions for Europe

Josef Langer

Analysis and Visions for Europe

Theories and General Issues

PETER LANG
Frankfurt am Main · Berlin · Bern · Bruxelles · New York · Oxford · Wien

Bibliographic Information published by the Deutsche Nationalbibliothek
The Deutsche Nationalbibliothek lists this publication in the Deutsche Nationalbibliografie; detailed bibliographic data is available in the internet at http://dnb.d-nb.de.

Cover Design:
© Olaf Glöckler, Atelier Platen, Friedberg

Published with the support of the Forschungsrat
of the Alpen-Adria-Universität Klagenfurt.

ISBN 978-3-631-60135-8

www.peterlang.de

Contents

Chapter III

Knowledge Europe

Chapter IV

Enlargement And Borders

Chapter V

Reality Difficult To Grasp

Foreword

This book is part of a series of publications about European issues, which derived from conferences organized by the Department of Sociology at the Alpen-Adria-Universität Klagenfurt, Austria. It contains a selection of the proceedings of the 4th International Symposium on European Issues ("What will be? Analysis and Visions for Europe"). The meeting took place on the 25th and 26th of September 2009 and assembled around two dozen scholars and experts from academic and political institutions around Europe. The book is meant as a twin to a previous publication on "Forces Shaping the EU" (2008), which explored how different social science paradigms contribute to better understanding the European Union. This time the emphasis is on anticipating the future. Where can future studies reasoning lead us? How could Europe look in two or three decades? The book contains eight presentations from the symposium plus five additional articles, including an introduction by the editor. Five participants in the symposium did not submit for publication. Their input was still essential for this book, because of the intriguing ideas these participants fed into the discussions during the symposium. In particular, I would like to mention Franck Biancheri, the founder of the French think tank LEAP (Laboratoire Européen d'Anticipation Politique), Gertrúd Kendernay-Nagyidai (Brussels), Zlatko Tišljar (Maribor) and Laura Dib (Helsinki).

A specialist stream ("Convergence/Divergence in the Visions of Europe: Focus on Social Practice") within the framework of the 4th International Symposium on European Issues took place in collaboration with the Department of Information and Communication Sciences at the University of Zadar (Croatia), on September 4th and 5th, 2009.

My thanks go to the Alpen-Adria-Universität Klagenfurt, which provided the main material prerequisites for the symposium and this publication. The administrative side of the symposium was managed by Karen Meehan and Anna Mattila. Special thanks go to Karen Meehan who supported the technical side of the editing work. Last but not least, I would like to mention Božena Krce Miočić, Nikša Alfrević, Jurica Pavičić and Goran Vlašić who provided the link to the special stream in Zadar.

Klagenfurt, February 2011

J. L.

Introduction

Josef Langer

European Union Post-Lisbon Perspectives

According to the official stance of EU policy makers it is the Lisbon Treaty, which is taking Europe into the Twenty-First century.[1] After the European Convention had completed drafting a treaty establishing a Constitution for Europe on the 10th of July, 2003 after more than a year's work, it took another six years and a number of political casualties until this legal framework in a slightly revised version entered into force on December 1st, 2009. The main casualties visible to the public were represented by the referenda in France (May, 2005) and The Netherlands (June, 2005), which rejected the "Constitution", and an Irish referendum (June, 2008), which rejected the Lisbon Treaty, also known as Reform Treaty. With this treaty, it is believed, Europe will be better able to tackle such challenges as globalization, demographic shifts, climate change, the need for sustainable energy sources and new security threats. But, what we have seen so far from the Lisbon Treaty is the appointment of a "President" of the European Union, the Belgian Herman van Rompuy, and an EU "Foreign Minister", the UK's Baroness Catharine Ashton. All the other promises still have to be seen. And not only this, but all the assumptions on which this treaty is based need closer scrutiny and discussion. It is convictions like that on which the contributions in this book are based. Europe is too important to be left only to politicians and lobbyists.

It has to be mentioned that this book is a follow-up of a previous publication entitled "Forces Shaping the EU"[2], which raised questions about the historical, political and theoretical foundations of European integration. In the centre of discussions stood the ambiguous identity of the EU, which obviously can serve quite diverse and often incompatible expectations. Is it an empire in disguise, a federation, a *sui generis* cooperation of states, a neo-colonial project or the seminal leaf of a European nation. Besides such crucial questions the book dealt with problems of supranational communication ("Tower of Babel"), the role of nations in the integration process, the legitimacy of borders, the leaching out of democracy and legal fictions in EU law. "Inspired by Modernity", "On Uncertain Ground", "Ambiguous Cultures" and "Legitimacy from the Periphery" were the main chapter headings circumscribing the various themes. As a

---

1 [http://europa.eu/lisbon_treaty/index_en.htm] retrieved on 18.10.2010.
"The Treaty of Lisbon amends the EU's two core treaties, the Treaty on European Union and the Treaty establishing the European Community. The latter is renamed the Treaty on the Functioning of the European Union. In addition, several Protocols and Declarations are attached to the Treaty."

2 Langer, Josef (2008), Forces Shaping the EU, Frankfurt a.M./New York (Peter Lang).

matter of course, many of these themes will be dealt with in this book too. But the main thrust will be on the question of anticipating the future. How could EUrope look in 2030? Although readers will find this concern primarily in the three contributions of Chapter I ("A Bird's Eye View"), clues can be found more or less explicitly in the contributions to "Institutional Aspects" (Chapter II), "Knowledge Europe" (Chapter III) and "Enlargement and Borders" (Chapter IV) as well. Finally, two contributions deal with the EU as a "Reality Difficult to Grasp" (Chapter V).

The discussion is opened by Józef *Niżnik* who raises the question whether existing theories on European integration have any value in predicting the future of the EU. For this purpose, he provides a short reflection on the future as a subject of scientific research in social sciences in general. He concludes that, given the epistemological character of sociology and political science, such expectations are totally unfounded. Nevertheless, to reflect matters of future in these disciplines is indispensable. Then he turns to the most prominent theories of European integration, i.e. to the neo-functionalist, functionalist and intergovernmentalist interpretation of the process. He concludes that existing theories are unable to grasp the full specificity of EU integration. Not least, due to their *ex post facto* approach. It is also this, which makes such theories inadequate to predicting the future. In this situation of limited theoretical capabilities we have to rely on the wisdom of the Europeans. Here, scenario design could be an appropriate avenue. Although not as stringent as scientific theories, similar to wisdom it can contain elements of intuition, emotion and even foolishness, while at the same time applying knowledge, reason and cleverness.

Josef *Langer*, in his contribution, looks first into a number of EUropean scenarios from the past and what was left when they hit reality. Intriguing discoveries can be made in doing so. Although none of the investigated scenarios ever became full reality within the time perspective they tackled, sometimes rather unlikely visions did come true. In this tradition Langer sketches several scenarios about the future of nations in the EU context, its final borders and EU societies in 2030. His guiding assumptions are that market economy, private property, social inequality and technological progress (i.e. capitalism) as basic parameters of EU societies will still be in place in two or three decades. Everything else would be an even greater surprise than the collapse of the Soviet Union with its satellites, in the Eighties and Nineties of the last century. Hence, any medium and short term future will have to be imagined in the frame of such assumptions. On the other hand, Europe as a geopolitical concept has pulsated throughout history. At times it contracts, at times it expands, at times it completely disappears in order to give way to competing concepts such as feudal empires or nations.

The future of Europe will, to a large extent, depend on the cognitive map of its inhabitants and rulers. This is what concerns Hans-Peter *Meier-Dallach* when he analyses the European landscape from an *organic* point of view. Europe, metaphorical seen as a very old body, is somehow alienated by the *systemic* and *utilitarian* narrowing of the EU approaches, which threatens to standardize places across the continent and increasingly exhausts living species. He develops his ideas by walking in the metropolitan area of Zurich, where he recognizes EUrope developing in a nutshell, although Switzerland is not even a member of the Union. Still, it cannot escape from the metropolitan strategies the EU subjects its own members to. Mutating more and more into a mega system it encircles the personality of Europe with adverse consequences. This mutation is becoming increasingly visible in the natural, settlement, traffic and communication landscape of metropolitan areas, where everything is put under a "users" perspective. Meier-Dallach's contribution describes a controversy between Europe as a historical body, organism and personality, and Europe as a utilitarian system moving towards a totalitarian future. Europe's faces are becoming more complex. Are they still Europe's faces?

This leads to a discussion by Thomas *Döring*/Eithne *Knappitsch*/Birgit *Aigner* of economic approaches regarding the assignment of political functions and competences between the European Union and its Member States. The contribution outlines the economic theory of federalism and the development of the European Union budget. Subsequently, a critical analysis of the existing structure regarding the division of political competences within the EU is attempted. Finally, the authors ask whether these economic considerations provide arguments for an alternative assignment of political functions between the EU and its Member States. Are economic theory and EU practice compatible? Not really, the current allocation of tasks within the EU is partly inconsistent with normative criteria. This is then further explained by the authors. In the following contribution Lojze *Sočan* discusses theoretical issues of the current evolution of global development systems. He puts forward an international comparison of the EU development concept, the structural changes, and the role of governance in the process of upgrading globalization. Sočan criticizes the EU 2020 developmental programme as too conventional and not ambitious enough in the face of increasing competition from the BRIC (Brazil, Russia, India, China) countries. As one of the handicaps of the EU he points to the huge difference between its Member States in terms of economic and institutional development. However, Sočan is particularly complimentary about what he calls "consensus societies" in Europe, which he suggests as developmental benchmarks for everybody else.

How can women lawyers' voices be heard and adequately considered on any EU level in the future? This is the question, which Vittorio *Olgiati* tackles in his contribution, which reaches far into the historical and professional dimensions of the European legal systems and the difficulties with attempts to arrive at a common EU scope. After introducing empirical evidence about the limits and potentials of women lawyers' standing in the current professional arena, he offers insights for a prospective gender-oriented professional agenda in four scenarios: a) impact of legal polycentricity, b) the defensive EU law-policy making, c) assessment of *ratio juris* as issue of legal education and d) the post-national question of European intellectuals. This question of a European knowledge society is approached from a slightly different perspective by Franc *Mali* in his contribution on the impact of the European Research Area (ERA) on output, structure and organisation of the scientific community in Slovenia, for which globalization and Europeanization mean not only challenges but also opportunities. He discusses several issues connected with the openness of science in a small state to the international arena. As with Olgiati the role of principle agents and emerging intermediary structures is discussed. But also how local knowledge and differences matter in a globalised world. Whether outward-looking and receptive to international cooperation, or sticking with further consolidating domestic scientific traditions, the main challenge for the small state appears to raise the quality and international visibility of researchers.

Vlado *Sušac*/Tomislav *Krpan* get their teeth into the European language policy starting with the basic question "What is a language?". Having experienced the disintegration of Yugoslavia with the accompanying appearance of "new" languages on the international political landscape the two seem particularly suited to dealing with this complex issue. They discuss the political dimension in the delimitation of languages, providing examples from South Eastern Europe. The contribution partly uncovers the ambiguity inherent to EU language policy. A diligent analysis of the Yugoslav experience can to some extent help to anticipate the future of multilingual regimes like the EU. For example, that privileging one language does not guarantee cohesion.[3] Concerning the latter, Reis *Mulita*, who discusses the future of enlargement and migration in Europe, is rather optimistic, provided the process is properly engineered by the EU. Both phenomena he sees as somehow natural, given the everlasting human inclination towards power over nature and society. Following this strand of thoughts the EU will not only receive Turkey as a member but also countries, which have no membership perspective for the time being. More arguments about anticipated consequences of Turkey's EU membership can be found in the contribution by Nuri Ali *Tahir*. This author discusses in particular the progress Turkey has made during the last decade in getting closer to EU standards but also the rise of this country as a regional power since the demise of the Soviet Union.

The last chapter of the book contains two contributions dealing with the ambiguous but difficult to grasp communication of the EU with its citizens. Anna *Mattila* investigates the attempt of the EU Commission to take advantage

---

[3] For language policy and EU future see also Cajvaneanu, Doina (2008), The Tower of Babel Revisited – The European Union as a Failed Speech Community, J. Langer (ed.), Forces Shaping the EU, Frankfurt a. M./New York (Peter Lang), pp. 175 - 184.

of the internet in getting in touch with the broader public. She demonstrates how the ambitious goals backed by the powerful interest to get the "Constitution" into force were effectuated over several years. The main emphasis of her analysis is on *Debate Europe*, an online platform the Commission launched in March 2006. The contribution contains statistics from an observation period of six month and corresponding interpretations. Variables like user activity, language distribution, spamming patterns etc. are investigated. It has to be mentioned here that *Debate Europe* was terminated and archived by the Commission in February 2010, shortly after the Lisbon Treaty ("Constitution") had overcome all political resistance and got into force. This raised not only eyebrows but also anger among the *Debate Europe* community, and not only among it. Milan *Jazbec* carries this thread on by discussing the role of political jokes in an imperial context. Is the EU an empire in search of a joke? He bases his analysis on political jokes from vanished Yugoslavia, which although smaller in size had some structural similarity with the current much larger EU. Jazbec explores the various social, emotional and cognitive functions of political jokes. When make comparisons with the EU factors like the intermediary role of multilevel governance come into sight. The consternation of the EU by political jokes and its attempt for direct communication with citizens seem to be shaped by similar factors.

Chapter I

A Bird's Eye View

Józef Niżnik

Theories of Integration and the Future of the European Union

Confronted with the ambitions of the students of European integration to develop its theory one has to ask why European integration should need a theory? Or, what such theory could be used for? After all, European integration is a process that started in international politics in post-war Europe with quite specific intentions, goals and measures, which have been explicitly formulated by appropriate actors, and concrete steps to achieve them have been undertaken. In other words, we are talking about political reality, which had its initiators (e.g. R. Schumann, J. Monnet, K. Adenauer and others), has emerged in effect of political decisions and has materialized in the form of international treaties. Does such a process require a further explanation to be supplied by "theory"? Should we not limit our interest just to the history of European integration? There is also a problem with justifying attempts to formulate a general theory of the European Union (EU). Simon Hix, cited by Ben Rosamond, formulated objections to such ambitions quite clearly: "We do not have a general theory of American or German politics so why should there be a general theory of the EU?" (Rosamond 2000, p. 17). Developing a "theory" of European integration may be perceived as a way to turn a specific flow of events, that is, political decisions and their consequences, into an autonomous "object", detaching it from the will of the people and placing it above the real current of politics. In other words, European integration might appear as a Hegelian force (spirit), directing the activities of people. Among a variety of possible answers to the question formulated at the beginning there are two, which seem to be especially relevant in the present discussion. First, European integration can possibly be used as a pattern for regional integration, which could be followed in other parts of the world. Therefore, the theory of European integration could serve as a general theory of regional integration. Although such a role may seem to be confirmed by integrative initiatives on other continents there are serious objections, which point out to the specificity of the European context and its process of integration (Wallace 1994). Also, the cases of integration elsewhere have achieved nowhere near the European level of integration. Another answer to the question "why should we need a theory of integration" might be that such a theory would help us to predict the future of European integration, which means also the future of the European Union.

Here I would like to show that such expectations are totally unfounded. Let me start with some initial reflections devoted to the future as a subject of scientific research in social sciences.

The future, as an object of research, is a case of a clearly unscientific subject (since the future does not exist at the time of reflection), which scientists are reluctant to give up. Also, popular expectations addressed to science would not allow them to give up. The reflection on the future of Europe seems to be an especially good illustration of the peculiarity of the theoretical status of future-oriented research. Social scientists undertaking so called "future studies" are in a particularly difficult situation because, in addition to the peculiarity of their subject (the future), they also have to face the specificity of their disciplines, sociology, political science etc. The specificity of social sciences includes theoretical problems as well, with meanings of the basic epistemological categories as with ontological distinctions. For example, the opposition "objective-subjective" must take into consideration the dual position of human beings in the process of cognition of social reality (Berger/Luckmann 1966). However, despite theoretical problems with reflection about the future in social and political matters, such reflection is indispensable for current decision-making and for the justification of the corresponding actions.

It is quite natural that in dealing with questions about the future we expect to profit from the relevant theories. In social sciences, however, such expectations may appear groundless because of the very limited predictive potential of social theories. One should not be confused by the idea of predictive capability which, according to methodology, is supposed to be one of the main features of any theory, along with capabilities to describe and to explain. First, those characteristics have been formulated with natural sciences in mind, and – second – in philosophy of science the understanding of prediction usually has a very "technical" meaning, which can not necessarily be suitable for the social matters, which usually have a more complex nature than the subjects of natural sciences. Therefore, for most philosophers of science it is clear that the "theory" in social sciences is of a very "soft" category. Jonathan Turner, sociologist, puts this in the following words: "Any analysis of sociological theory should begin with a blunt admission that, from the perspective of ideal scientific theory, sociological theorizing has a long way to go" (Turner 1974, p. 8). The theorizing of political science seems to be in exactly the same situation. Theories of integration as a possible support for reflection about the future of the EU appear to be still more complicated, because those theories are even more distant from the ideal of scientific theory than most social theories.

In the following I will briefly analyze the process of cognition in social sciences focusing on the theoretical status of theory and the nature of knowledge obtained in those disciplines. My aim at this point is to show that – if certain basic methodological requirements are observed – different social theories, even those competing for the status of the most correct ones, may in fact be complementary rather than rival. Epistemological arguments for this thesis are usually either neglected or deliberately missed due to the variety of interests, which are usually involved in social matters. European integration studies represent an especially good area of political science to illustrate such a situation. I will attempt to show that different theories of integration are just forms of "theorizing *ex post*", that is theorizing about a process that has been accomplished. Such work might be justified if the aim of a theory would be merely to provide an explanation. However, "theories of integration" are also used to formulate visions of the future of Europe. Therefore, it is important to stress that such theorizing mostly serves predefined views on the future of an integrated Europe and are built on the basis of presumptions, which reflect specific interests and preferences. In consequence, different theories can claim cognitive validity while offering competing ideas of European integration. Therefore, theories of integration are of little help in the reflection on the future of the EU. In order to explain how is it possible that two competing theories may both be correct, I have proposed to distinguish an object of investigation (which may be common for different theories), and an object of knowledge (which may be different in the case of different theories).

Epistemological consideration helps to explain how is it possible to study the same object (an object of investigation) and to obtain knowledge, which corresponds only to some of the possible aspects of this object. My suggestion is that the object covered by the acquired knowledge and explained by the relevant theory should be identified as an object different from the intended object of investigation. It is what I want to call an object of knowledge. Therefore, different theories of the same object of investigation (in our case it is European integration) may be, actually, instances of theorizing about different objects of knowledge. (Kuhn 1970; Niżnik 1979; Wittgenstein 2000, pp. 298 - 299)

Let me now move to European integration, a subject, which has become an object of investigation for a number of political scientists conducting EU studies, which have resulted in different theories. These theories usually compete with each other, although attempts to integrate their differences are also present in some of the theoretical proposals (Peterson 1995, Richardson 1996). With all limitations and restrictions that make the term "theory" in social sciences a kind of overstatement (if compared to the theory in natural sciences), the situation with theories of integration seems to be still more problematic. It has been shown in a number of analyses (Rosamond 2000, p. 189; Eilstrup-Sangiovanni 2006) and further on will be also argued in the present text that theories of integration have a definite contextual character. This means that they have originated in specific historical circumstances, reflect specific approaches to politics and especially represent quite a clear stand with regard to the role of a nation state.

Political scientists discussing "theories of integration" are far from unanimity in their understanding of what should be counted as theorizing about European integration. Depending on the scope of their analysis they either present numerous theoretical approaches to integration (Rosamond 2000; Eilstrup-Sangiovanni 2006) or concentrate on just a few major positions in this area, which correspond to the most intensely debated answers to the question of what kind of political entity the European Union is (Pollack 2005). Probably the best known and, indeed, an excellent book on the topic is Ben Rosamond's book on Theories of European Integration (Rosamond 2000). Rosamond, unlike most other specialists on European integration, demonstrates a high level of awareness of a variety of factors determining the nature and the content of so called "theories of integration". He has adopted a reasonable distance to the very use of the concept of "theory" in the context of European integration. Also, his extensive references to sociology of knowledge make his discussion of theories of integration a fascinating excursion into the methodology and philosophy of social sciences. At the same time, however, in a relatively concise text Rosamond in a very readable way builds quite a comprehensive landscape of conceptualizations of European integration. Concentrating on the first line of controversies in this area, which have appeared in the debate between neofunctionalism and intergovernmentalism, Rosamond also discusses a number of other theoretical attempts, which show that the coexistence or even complementarity of those dominant rivals in the theory of integration is possible. Speaking for myself, I was especially attracted to this book because I discovered that more than twenty years after my book "Object of Knowledge in Social Sciences" was published (only in Polish, which makes it impossible for Rosamond to have known it) someone presented an almost identical view of the nature of social sciences, referring to the same constitutive factors and using the same arguments.

Let me now recall the basic ideas of those major "theories of integration". One should notice that the conceptualizations used can be quite misleading. For example, the term "neofunctionalism" suggests close links to functionalism. Only more detailed analysis of Ernst Haas ideas, which provided the basis for neofunctionalism, and comparing it with the works of David Mitrany, the leading figure in functional theory of integration, can show that their views on the nature of European integration are radically different. One of the main differences has been well pointed out by Rosamond, who suggests that "Functionalism was primarily a theory of *post-territorial* governance, whereas neofunctionalism was an early theory of *regionalism*" (Rosamond 2000, p. 69).

Another source of confusion can be found in the term "intergovernmentalism". In the current European debate this term most often refers to one of the general approaches to European integration. It can serve as description of the EU governance system stressing its (supposedly) basic mechanism of decision-making. In its other use it can indicate intentions of political leaders with regard to the preferable – or in some cases exclusively acceptable – form of relations between the EU Member States, which exclude or radically limit the role of supranational authority in these relations. However, the works on "theories of integration" use the word "intergovernmentalism" as a "theory", which attempts to answer the question of what the nature of European integration is or, in other words, of what European integration (or European Union) is.

I would now like to move to a more systematic, albeit very brief presentation of the main "theories of integration". European integration from the very beginning, that is since the European Coal and Steel Community (ECSC) was founded (1951, Treaty of Paris) – by its very idea – undermined the state-centred approach to politics. The tension between this most established view on international politics and new forms of political relations, which were initiated with the beginning of European integration, is probably the most important factor in the development of theories of integration and in the theoretical dispute over the nature of the whole process. With the progress of integration the simplest and most basic distinctions became problematic. For example, what is "domestic" and what is "international". Ben Rosamond quite extensively discusses the basic question whether International Relations (IR) is the proper discipline for studying European integration (Rosamond 2000, p. 157). There is no doubt that EU studies located on the ground of IR have been most often framed into an intergovernmental approach, because the main subject of this discipline is relations between the states. Some authors believe that IR might be the right discipline for studying the process of integration and especially its initiation but must be replaced by comparative politics when the analysis of the EU system is taking place. Indeed, intergovernmentalism reflects a state-centric approach and its main problem is the position of the state and its role within an integrating totality. Within such an approach the problem of the nature of the EU political system seems to have been falsely formulated since the only recognized actors in the politics of the EU are the Member States.

Neofunctionalism – on the other hand – concentrating on the process of integration itself, has from the very beginning focused on the supranational powers and competences of the emerging political system. This is why neofunctionalism used to be, sometimes, identified with federalism.

It should be noted that what have been accepted as theoretical ideas on European integration was, in fact, an instance of theorizing *ex post* about an empirical process that was already in progress. Ernst Haas' first book on European integration – published after the first years of experience of the European Coal and Steel Community, at the moment when the next step of integration had been initiated – had an immediate reference to practice with the start of the European Economic Community (EEC) (Haas 1958). Also, it has appeared to be a correct theory because the initiation of the EEC had been perceived as a confirmation of the idea of a spill-over which, according to neofunctionalism, was a crucial mechanism of integration.

The next observation that can be made at this point is that representatives of different theoretical orientations start with different premises while seemingly attempting to answer the same or similar questions. However, if formulated on the ground of different premises, the same questions usually open quite different areas of possible answers. For example, Rosamond pointed out that Stanley Hoffmann, who presented an early critique of neofunctionalism and opened a theoretical venue for an intergovernmental view on integration, had perceived economics and politics as quite separate. On the other hand, the strong linkage of the two has been the basic assumption of the neofunctional approach taken by Haas, Lindberg, and others. Therefore, theorizing on the basis of different assumptions will most likely lead to different theoretical positions. As will be shown later, such different theoretical positions address, in fact, different objects of knowledge. In other words, from the very beginning those authors aimed to prove some of their initial theses, which were different and – as long as the dissimilarity of their objects of knowledge was not noticed – might appear contradictory.

The initial success of neofunctional reasoning could be attributed to its fundamental premises, which relied on common beliefs and observations. For example, neofunctionalists suggested that economic integration would inevitably lead towards political integration. There are enough everyday observations, which may assure us that there is no such thing as purely economic process, completely detached from politics. Therefore, such assumption must have looked quite convincing. The same applies to the idea of "spillover", the fundamental mechanism which, according to neofunctionalism, has been pushing integration further on. In fact, this idea has been so much a part of common knowledge that in many languages it is expressed in proverbs. For example, in Polish there is a proverb saying: "If you give him a finger, he will grab the hand". According to the "spillover hypothesis" integration in one sector of the economy – due to the obvious functional links – would inevitably push forward integration in other sectors, and the integration in the economy would spill over into politics. The beginnings of European integration looked exactly like the implementation of this rule. Within six years the initial six partners in the ECSC moved from coordination of steel and coal production toward further economic cooperation within the European Economic Community. Also, the political aspirations of this next Community were quite explicit despite the "economic" name of the new organization. Although economic spillover is supposed to work by itself, it needed some measures of coordination, which made necessary the emergence of a supranational authority with clear political competences. Moreover, the process of integration affects the mentality and attitudes of important figures in Member States leading to "loyalty transference", which is necessary if the new supranational institutions are to function properly. Such loyalty transference can be easily explained and justified by the neofunctional belief that the main aim of the process is the welfare and wellbeing of people involved, which can be better secured by a new form of international coexistence and cooperation. In this situation the distinction between what is "domestic" and what is "international" had to fade out. Of course, empirical research, for example those studies on national identity, made the criticism of neofunctionalism an easy task. But the careful analysis of the rival "theory" shows that the main reason for opposing neofunctionalism can be found at the level of the initial assumptions, political beliefs and values. In another word, those who reject the neofunctional perspective on European integration are looking for such a "theory of integration", which develops their different presumptions and supports their specific value structure.

The intergovernmental opposition to neofunctionalism, best represented by the works of Stanley Hoffman (1964; 1966), has been stimulated by assumptions and questions, which did not bother representatives of neofunctionalism. First of all is the question, which later acquired the French expression of "*finalité*", that is the question of where the whole process of integration is heading to, or what the final form of a new political system might be. The intergovernmental view from the very beginning was determined by a strong realist position regarding the nature of international politics in which the leading role is supposed to be played by the states. Therefore any development, which might change this role was rejected as unrealistic. In the background one can find a strong attachment to the value of the state's sovereignty. With such a starting point it is easy to find arguments pointing to the weaknesses of the spillover hypothesis or to question the idea of the dependence between the economy and politics. In consequence, the intergovernmental approach was not so much interested in integration as a way to weaken or even only modify the role of states, but in integration as a new environment for the state's actions in which Member States remain the basic actors. In other words, both "theories" pretending to grasp the same subject – European integration – have been referring to the knowledge about its different aspects, which at the end reflected different objects of knowledge. While neofunctionalism, indeed, tried to look for a new quality in this international experiment, intergovernmentalism was interested in the challenges, which this experiment created for the states and any hypothesis that would take into consideration the transfer of power to a supranational authority was rejected.

Andrew Moravcsik, with his liberal intergovernmentalism, added still more complications to the understanding of this concept. Moving his attention from the decision-making process of the EU to the factors that decide about Member States' positions in intergovernmental bargaining, Moravcsik stressed the importance of domestic matters for common decisions in the EU. His liberal intergovernmentalism simply takes into consideration the impact of the domestic politics of Member States on the process of European integration. Moravcsik suggests that "An understanding of domestic politics is a precondition for, not a supplement to, the analysis of strategic interaction among states", (Moravcsik 1993, p.

481). Putting "European integration" into the place of "strategic interaction among states" opens a very useful venue for explanations of a variety of episodes in the history of European integration, which have been possible only because of the impact of the domestic issues of the Member States. One recent example is the failure of the ratification process of the European Constitution in France and the Netherlands in the 2005 referenda. What makes Moravcsik's idea still more confusing is the fact that, depending on the way his arguments are used, liberal intergovernmentalism can also be read – probably against the intentions of its author – as a support for neofunctionalism. For example, it is quite possible that sometimes domestic pressure can be in favour of spillover, if extending integration into further sectors of the economy or public life would seem to be beneficial for the particular state. Also, Moravcsik's opinion on the democratic legitimacy in the European Union can serve as a kind of support for neofunctional logic: He believes that there is no problem of democracy deficit in the EU because, after all, decisions in the European Council are made by representatives of Member States who are democratically elected in their countries. In fact, the idea of a "two-level game" – gaining domestic support for the actions that are instrumental for the integration (international dimension), which can then stimulate a behaviour of the electorate, which is favourable for the domestic politicians – can also be perceived as an argument useful for bridging the gap between neofunctionalism and intergovernmentalism (Putnam 1988).

Therefore, those "theories" should not be perceived as competing paradigms. In their backgrounds we can easily find different leading questions ("What is the role of the nation state in the integrating Europe?" vs. "Why and how is the process of integration progressing?"), which stem from different conceptions of acceptable political settings ("Member State's position must not be undermined by supranational institutions" vs. "Common interest of integrated Europe reflects best interests of Member States"), referring to different structures of values (Westphalian vs. post-Westphalian). Of course, this last difference, indeed, indicates competing views on main political objectives. But those views are not the results of different theories but initial premises, which determine political preference, and in consequence lead to separate "theories". Therefore, Ben Rosamond is right when he states that "intergovernmentalism is a *political preference* held by a range of actors within the EU" (Rosamond 2000, p. 153).

In order to better see the differences in theoretical aims of both approaches one can simply ask questions about certain theoretical or logical inconsistencies. One such question, addressed to intergovernmentalism, is: "Why do states participate in an activity, which limits their autonomy?" Of course, there are a number of possible answers, which may refer to quite different theories. The "two-level game" discussed earlier is one of them. The very question, however, as well as possible answers, show that intergovernmentalism also needs other approaches, not excluding those that have been declared rival theories, in order to solve different puzzles that have been created by the process of European integration. In the case of this particular question a supporter of intergovernmentalism might simply answer that the states participate in the process of integration only as far as their autonomy is not threatened. Such an answer would not be satisfactory because the limits imposed by the process of integration on the states' autonomy are too visible even if decision-making procedures seem to be based on intergovernmental bargaining as a fundamental mechanism. More satisfactory would be an answer which, in fact, needs a neofunctional approach to integration; the states participate in integration for reasons, which may be in each case different but in every case this participation serves their particular goals in some way.

The way European integration is conceptualised in the intergovernmental approach indicates a kind of "conceptual inertia" (Niżnik 1979, p. 106). The deep-rooted concepts – like "state" or "sovereignty", for example – have been redefined because of the pressure of current political reality but remnants of their old, outdated meanings are still present.

The problems with the conceptualization of the current political reality in the integrating Europe led to some terminological inventions, which took for granted what had been observed in the EU and on the basis of the current political practice created conceptual and theoretical novelties. This is the case with the idea of Multi-Level Governance (MLG) or with an Open Method of Coordination (OMC) (Niżnik 2006, p. 8). Both ideas fit well into a new approach to the developing political reality in the EU, which had been diagnosed as a "governance turn" in the EU studies. The first one clearly intends – within the so called "governance turn" in EU studies – to pacify the controversy over federal (neofunctional at the background) or intergovernmental course of EU development. The latter offers a solution in such cases of policy-making when there is a need for a common policy but existing legal provisions leave the right of decision to the Member States' governments. The development of such conceptual inventions shows that existing "theories of integration" are unable to grasp the full specificity of the European process of integration. Therefore, we should not expect that such inadequate "theories" would be helpful in predicting the future of the European Union, which will be determined by a variety of factors both of internal and external origin.

What is the meaning of the "governance turn" in EU studies? This was not a turn in theorizing style or a turn in theoretical preferences, but the move toward a different problem area. And the reason for this move was not theoretical dissatisfaction with one or other theory but the opening to the different aspects of the process of integration that came together with the Treaty on the EU. At the same time, however, this turn – with the MLG idea – created an alternative for the state-centred perspective of the intergovernmental approach to European integration. In this way MLG has sometimes been perceived as the replacement of neofunctionalism, which certainly is not the case. The governance turn reflects only the change of the object of knowledge in the EU studies, and not the replacement of one theory of integration with another one. In fact, such a "turn" could be understood as an empirical solution of at least one dilemma in the theoretical debate over European integration, which is the question whether the European Union is one of the known forms of political phenomena (e.g. an international organization) or a "*sui generis*" political system. Moving to the centre of the EU studies the phenomenon of governance seems to confirm the idea of the European Union as a "*sui generis*" political entity. In fact, such confirmation may also be found in the views of the informed politicians. Denis MacShane, a former British minister for Europe, commenting on the 2009 election of President of the European Commission, characterized this position in the following words: "In theory it's one of the most powerful jobs in the world. But this is Europe, where the normal rules don't apply" (MacShane 2009).

Therefore, speculating about the future of the EU on the basis of existing "theories" – which are mostly *ex post* rationalizations of some aspects of the integration practice – does not look very promising. The phenomenon of the European Union calls for genuinely creative ideas, which go beyond the current controversy over federalism versus intergovernmentalism (Niżnik 2007). The future of the EU seems to depend mostly on the wisdom of Europeans. Unfortunately, so far, there are no signals of a surplus of wisdom in Europe. On the contrary, in the Member States' public debates European matters most often appear in the framework of local politics for which European interest is too abstract an idea. It is clear that the lack of thinking in terms of "European interests" makes us blind to many opportunities that European integration may open up. Although global challenges made their way into the public discourse there is no common awareness of the fact that global threats can be more easily controlled by common policies and institutions. There are more elements in the most acceptable vision of contemporary politics and social life, which are basic and important but their role in the discourse about European integration is misunderstood. For example, the elevation of the ideal of democracy to the position of an absolute value and an organizing element of the whole European discourse made it very difficult for people to accept the role of elites. Also, the paramount importance of democracy has imposed on the European discourse a very specific structure of sense, which pushed to the side other values, which at the beginning of the European integration served as the leading ideals (Niżnik 2008). Probably most important of them is solidarity, which is still present in the European discourse but most often on a lip service basis only.

Concluding, I would like to recall Michael Burgess' reference to Spinelli suggesting that the European Union "is the product of the interaction between what exists and what must exist" (Michael Burgess 2000, p. 280). Everything indicates that we underestimate the role of "what must exist" and what probably will be a decisive factor in the future development of the EU, e.g. global reshuffling of the world scene, which will force Europeans to move toward a deeper unity. Therefore, although theories of integration might be only a kind of intellectual exercise and offer very little to predict the future of the EU, we certainly need further theorizing in order to get the best from what is inevitable anyway: a more integrated Europe, proud of its diversities but also with a stronger common identity of Europeans.

References

Berger, Peter/Thomas Luckmann (1966), *The Social Construction of Reality*, Anchor Books, Doubleday & Company Inc., Garden City/New York.

Burgess, Michael (2000), *Federalism and European Union: The Building of Europe*, 1950 - 2000, Routledge, London.

Eilstrup-Sangiovanni, Mette (ed.) (2006), *Debates on European Integration*, Palgrave, New York.

Haas, Ernst (1958), *The Uniting Europe. Political, Social and Economic Forces, 1950 - 1957*, Stanford University Press, Stanford.

Hoffmann, Stanley (1964), 'The European Process at Atlantic Cross-purposes', in *Journal of Common Market Studies*, Vol. 3, No. 1, pp. 85 - 101.

Hoffmann, Stanley (1966), 'Obstinate or Obsolete? The Fate of the Nation State and the Case of Western Europe', in *Daedalus*, Vol. 95, No. 3, pp. 862 - 915.

Kuhn, Thomas (1970), *The Structure of Scientific Revolutions*, University of Chicago Press, Chicago.

McShane, Denis (2009), 'The Accidental Head of Europe', in *Newsweek*, 21.09.2009 [http://www.newsweek.com/2009/09/10/the-accidental-head-of-europe.html] retrieved on 4.1.2011.

Niżnik, Józef (1979), *Przedmiot poznania w naukach społecznych*, PWN, Warszawa.

Niżnik, Józef (ed.) (2006), *Multilevel Governance: Patterns and Degrees of Political Integration. The EU Eastern Enlargement Challenge*, IFiS Publishers, Warsaw.

Niżnik, Józef (2007), 'On Imperative of Creative Thinking about European Integration', in *Dialogue and Universalism*, Vol. XVII, No. 12/2007, pp. 95 - 100.

Niżnik, Józef (2008), 'Discourse and Social Communication. The Case of "Democracy" in the European Integration Discourse', in Josef Langer (ed.), *Forces Shaping the EU. Social Science Approaches to Understanding the European Union*, Peter Lang, Frankfurt a. M./New York, pp. 215 - 228.

Peterson, John (1995), 'Decision–making in the European Union: Towards a Framework for Analysis', in *Journal of European Public Policy*, Vol. 2(1), pp. 69 - 93.

Pollack, Mark (2005), 'Theorizing EU Policy Making', in H. Wallace/W. Wallace/M. A. Pollack, *Policy-Making in the European Union*, 5th edition, Oxford University Press, New York, pp. 13 - 48.

Putnam, Robert (1988), 'Diplomacy and Domestic Politics', in *International Organization*, No. 42, pp. 427 - 460.

Richardson, Jeremy (1996), 'Policy-making in the EU: Interests, Ideas and Garbage Cans of Primeval Soup', in J.Richardson (ed.), *European Union: Power and Policy-Making*, Routlege, London, pp. 4 - 30.

Rosamond, Ben (2000), *Theories of European Integration*, St. Martin Press, New York.

Turner, Jonathan (1974), *The Structure of Sociological Theory*, The Dorsey Press, Homewood, Illinois.

Wallace, William (1994), *Regional Integration: The West European Experience*, Brooking Institution, Washington D.C.

Warleigh, Alex (2006), 'Learning from Europe? EU Studies and Re-thinking of "International Relations"', in *European Journal of International Relations*, Vol.12 (1) , pp. 31 - 51.

Wittgenstein, Ludwig (2000), *Philosophical Investigations*, Polish edition: Dociekania Filozoficzne, PWN Warszawa.

Josef Langer

Europe 2030: Anticipating Nation, Border and Society

The desire to predict the future appears to be a never-ending fascination for human beings, albeit most of the time in vain. Then again, there is Cassandra from Ancient Greek mythology to whom, due to his interest in her beauty, the god Apollo granted the ability to "hear the future". However nobody believed her when she foresaw the destruction of Troy. With the emergence of modern science, the ability to meet prognostic desires became more realistic, although as it turned out mainly in the natural sciences. For the prediction of future states of social organisations August Comte's famous instruction for the social sciences from the early Nineteenth century, "*Savoir pour prevoir, prevoir pour prevenir*", has barely ever been met with success. It is rather assumptions like those by Stefan Zweig (1942/2005), an Austrian writer, that contemporaries are denied a recognition of the beginning of great historical movements, the future is not ours to see. Or, as Mark Steyn pointed out in his book *America Alone* (2006), that, "to a five-year-old boy waving his flag as Queen Victoria's Diamond Jubilee procession marched down the Mall in 1897, it would have been inconceivable that by the time of his 80th birthday the greatest empire the world had ever known would have shrivelled to an economically moribund strike-bound socialist slough of despond […]"[1] It was also hardly imaginable, when belligerent Germany lay in smoke and ashes in 1944, and plans were made on the side of the Allies for her complete deindustrialisation (Morgenthau Plan), that this country would again become the main European economy a few decades later.

And yet, in hindsight (*ex post factum*) historical developments and events often appear to be plausible, particularly in the field of economics where elaborated theoretical instruments are available. In the meantime we know at least that capitalist economies go through cycles and produce severe crises from time to time. Still, valid predictions are rare. As the proverb has it: "An economist is an expert who will know tomorrow why the things he predicted yesterday didn't happen today." Political and social predictions are even more contingent as can be demonstrated by the demise of the Soviet socialist system at the end of the Eighties. If there were any such predictions (e.g., von Mises 1951/1922; Amalrik 1970) they remained remote and were neglected by the political and scientific mainstream. The fact that predictions in the social sciences "fail" is obviously linked to the nature of human conduct. Any information can change its direction. Hence, the awareness of predictions by relevant actors can easily

---

1 Quoted from [http://article.nationalreview.com/428996/tattered-liberty/mark-steyn] retrieved on 11.5.2010.

thwart the predicted results (if not cause the opposite). Additionally, predictions in the social sciences are often bound to certain (dominant) interests, a kind of wishful thinking, neglecting undesirable variables. A lot of media communication today is to bring about futures desired by certain dominant interests. Further, there is no undisputed social theory on which predictions could safely build, not to speak of the fragile methods on which the collection of relevant information has to rely. Such dilemmas exist when trying to predict the consequences of individual or group behaviour, but more so when it comes to the future of whole societies or groups of societies.

Hence, statements about the future in social sciences[2] are more or less *anticipations* rather than reliable *predictions*. Although numerous methods and instruments (Delphi, scenario method, trend analysis, simulation etc.) are available today to back up anticipatory thinking, the most we can expect from such undertakings is a stronger awareness of uncertainty and its variables, particularly in the case of whole societies or groups of societies (e.g. emerging countries, the West, EU, East Asia). This explains to some extent the numerous visions and scenarios circulating about the future of EUrope besides those to which the EU institutions stick programmatically by themselves. Understandably, like any bureaucracy with its internal division of labour, EU decision makers are first of all producing scenarios of sectoral relevance (economic growth, financial redistribution, immigration etc.). But, every now and then so called "reflection groups" get assigned to speculate on the future of the EU as such.[3] Comparing global scenarios of this kind, the first issue which leaps to the eye is the influence of group composition and *Zeitgeist* on the content of the scenario. Whereas in the late Nineties when the *Internet boom* was still promising long lasting economic growth a "Forward Studies Unit" in the Commission suggested five scenarios for the EU in 2010, which considered a broad range of economic, cultural, social, political and international variables, a similar attempt recently to reflect on EUrope in 2030 restricts itself almost entirely to economic or economy-related variables. The impact of the *financial crisis*, generally assumed to have been kicked off by "subprime poison" in the US, on the thinking in this reflection group chaired by the former prime minister of Spain, Filipe Gonzales, peeps out behind almost every sentence of this report, when trying to look ahead into 2030.[4]

Any scenario of this kind is more or less subjective and contingent upon the client. The more powerful the client, the more vested interests can be ex-

---

2 About the essential dividedness of the social sciences in anticipating the historical course of society see Prisching (2005).

3 For more on this see Langer (2008b).

4 Project Europe 2030 – Challenges and opportunities, A report to the European Council by the Reflection Group on the Future of the EU 2030 [http://www.reflectiongroup.eu/wp-content/uploads/2010/05/reflection_en_web.pdf] retrieved on 16.8.2010.

pected in the forecast. This does not mean that it could not contain significant variables, which will unfold in the future. However, which of them will prevail remains a provisional assumption. It can well be that variables which appear dominant to the futurologist will become insignificant or even vanish over the course of time, whereas others will become strong and influential. But the reverse is also possible. I will try to demonstrate this briefly with an example by Hans Magnus Enzensberger, an eminent German intellectual and writer, who in his book "Ach Europa!" (Oh, Europe!) (1987) anticipated in the Eighties of the last century a Europe of 2006. Enzensberger's "Ach Europa" (1987) is a collection of seven country essays[5] dated between 1982 and 1986, plus an epilogue (1987), where he tries to imagine Europe in 2006. The country reports are based on visits, observations and conversations with people of the respective countries, frequently intellectuals like Enzensberger himself. Although the main forward looking efforts are in the epilogue, the country reports already contain observations, which in hindsight appear of prognostic relevance, whereas for the author they were only minor matters at the time.

One example are the nationalistic potentials in countries of Central Europe, which were at that time still communist. It is not the Yugoslav secession wars and the accompanying atrocities a couple of years later – Yugoslavia was not part of Enzensberger's reflections –, but his observation of the Hungarian opposition in the mid-Eighties (131 pp.), which stick out. Unlike most Western observers he noticed that this opposition was fundamentally divided: *cosmopolitans* versus *populists*. It is obvious that for him the cosmopolitans were the more significant opposition, although he notices their entanglement with the ruling Communist Party[6], but this may be because of his belief. The *populists*, those who object to the *Treaty of Trianon* (1920), and want to protect Hungarianness etc., he considers parochial. He sees their political relevance, if at all, mainly in Hungary's relation to the Romania of Ceausescu, because of the two million-strong Hungarian minority in that country in 1985. However, a quarter of a century later, the populists dominate the Hungarian parliament, with more than a two thirds majority. Who would have thought in 1985 about such a "scenario" for Hungary a quarter of a century later? Not to speak about the sudden return of nationalism in the violent demise of Yugoslavia.

In the epilogue (1987) to his country reports he himself dabbles in suggesting a scenario for Europe in 2006. As this time line has already passed we can check where he hit the bull's eye and where he erred. For his vision Enzensberger comes up with a fictitious American journalist, Mr. Taylor, who reports for *The New New Yorker* about different places in the Europe of 2006. Mr. Taylor's first

5 Sweden, Italy, Hungary, Portugal, Norway, Poland and Spain.

6 "Between the regime and us is a division of labour. The Party needs us … If we did not exist, the Party would have to invent us." (p. 134; author's translation).

stop is Ramstein, the US Army base in Germany where he served as an officer until 1994. Here we learn that the US Army has left Germany (Europe?) in the Nineties, with the exception of two hundred men in Berlin. The "Alliance" (NATO) still exists in 2006, but more on paper than in reality. Ramstein, once a major US military base has fallen into ruin. The European Community ("Europäische Gemeinschaft") is a chicken-coop of ever more but smaller Member States with shared economic interests only, no real global power but obsessed with the protection of its minorities and its alleged complexity. The character invented by Enzensberger experiences European cities still as crowded, despite the declining population. Immigrants he meets are recognized by their food preferences, old kinds of "guest workers" ("Yugoslavs") still remain in large numbers, not necessarily to compensate the declining population. The European Community is still a community of "twelve languages" only in 2006, but has made it to a common currency. Towards the end of the Eighties the author does scent the advent of a profound change in Europe but he does not imagine the implosion of the communist East Block, the end of the post-World War II Yalta order.

Germany is still divided into a West and an East German state in Enzensberger's 2006, although with open borders and officially friendly neighbourly relations. Together with Austria and Switzerland it has developed into a European core of a kind of *ecotopia*, where trains seem to have replaced cars as major means of traffic. The melt-down of a nuclear reactor in France in 1991 made the implementation of environmentally friendly policies easier. By the way, smoking in the public is prohibited in 2006. The *Berlin Wall* has turned into a green belt of nature protection with all kinds of rare fauna and flora, cared for in a brotherly manner by scientists from both German states. But, when visiting Berlin, Mr. Taylor also learns that despite friendly official relations, under the surface *Ossis* and *Wessis* cannot really bear each other. Reunification of Germany didn't take place, because the Germans, like all other Europeans, with the exception of the French, prefer to live in small states. They recognized that the empire-building of the Nineteenth and Twentieth century was a mistake. New motto: "Divide, but don't rule." Then, in Helsinki Mr. Taylor looks for Erkki Rintala, the long-term European Community president who gave up his job a couple of months before. When he finally finds him in his dacha-like residence in the Finnish wilderness, he learns of the reasons for the president's resignation. Brussels is an ape house, a supranational hydrocephalus. Those who have a say, have no democratic legitimation and those who have been elected have nothing to say. In comparison with the president of the USA, the president of the European Community is a nobody[7]. Europe is without power in 2006. Its armies

7 It is mind-boggling to compare this vision from 1987 with an address of the British MEP Nigel Farage towards the first EU "President" Herman van Rompuy in 2010. [http://www.youtube.com/watch?v=bypLwI5AQvY] retrieved on 19.8.2010.

have been ablated; the still super powers USA and USSR have withdrawn. Europe has enjoyed sixty decades of continued peace, war has become unthinkable. There are no unresolved border questions and threatening minority problems have completely disappeared.

However, it turns out that Enzensberger's Europe of 2006 is not ruled to any great extent by Brussels anymore. The attempt to transform the European Community into an "ever deeper union", into a strongly integrated and centralized super state has failed. The resignation of president Rintala is a symptom of this failure. He calls activities of bygone years towards building a European state a "Brussels idiocy", which had to lead to a gigantic and costly bankruptcy. Nobody has ever managed to homogenize Europe and unite it politically. What he dreams of is a united Europe without unification. Europe like a fractal object, too irregular in its micro structures to be united under one rule. Chaos is Europe's most important resource. Enzensberger's scenario for Europe in 2006 doesn't reveal much about the economy, but is obviously a capitalist market regime on both sides of the former Iron Curtain. There was a crisis as a consequence of the nuclear melt-down in France in the Nineties. Now, German and French companies are fiercely competing with Americans for business in the Balkans. High rise buildings are clustering capitals like Bucharest, whereas in the countryside things remain the same. Corruption in the Balkans is still strong. Amazingly, in 1987 Enzensberger anticipated that Romania's communist ruler Nicolae Ceausescu will be murdered by his own apparatchiks. Implicitly the text tells us that the post-Soviet satellites are not members of the European Community yet. European societies appear as places of queer individualism, cultural experimentation and absurd life styles. At least it is this impression, which Mr. Taylor takes with him when he returns to the USA from Prague.

Although the predictions of this German man of letters are based on many tacit assumptions and are somewhat arbitrary, in hindsight the content appears no less informative than any scientific forecast from that time about the year 2006. Enzensberger's main failure was probably that he did not anticipate the impending reunification of Germany. But then, who did? Obviously, when anticipating the future of society, social relations and institutions, which appear "natural", are least expected to change. And "natural" in this context appears to be what is under the control of the most powerful. The division of Germany after World War II was practically a consequence of the two emerging super powers – the USSR and the USA. After some decades for many this was just "natural", for left-leaning intellectuals in particular. What is considered "natural" today? The EU? Capitalism? Market economy? Globalization? This deserves special attention when speculating about tomorrow. On the other hand, Enzensberger didn't say anything specific about communism in 2006, except not including the former Soviet satellites in the western political hemisphere. Maybe he sympathised with a "third way" between capitalism and socialism ("communism with a human face"), or believed in the "convergence" of the two systems, once a serious theoretical approach. The variables and realities that a scenario disregards are at least as telling as those it makes explicit.

Another problem of macro scenarios like those about the EU is the ambiguity of the object itself. Enzensberger expects the European Community (now: EU) to be bankrupt in 2006, its president resigned and Europe's people stubbornly longing for "small is beautiful" political entities. And indeed, the "Constitution" for a more coherent and powerful EU had just failed referenda in France and The Netherlands. On the other hand, since the Eighties the European Community had developed into the European Union (1992) and enlarged three times (1995, 2004 and 2006). Did this increase or decrease its overall power? The answer probably depends on the perspective from which one looks upon it. Institutionally it was most likely more powerful in 2006 than in the Eighties, despite the negative referenda. However, the writer prophet seems to have a strong personal dislike for any centrally ruled Europe, so it is maybe wishful thinking that the striving of some for an "ever deeper union" should fail in the end. With regard to his expectations about ecological Europe, however, it is mirror-inverted: the ecological transformation of Europe in 2006 was in reality less progressed than he envisioned. And finally, such concrete prophecies as the assassination of a president like Nicolae Ceausescu, how could anybody "know" that years in advance? A bold guess drawn from hermeneutics, emotions and speculation?

Whereas what appears "natural" and stable in society can unexpectedly change or even disappear, inversely what is considered to be fluid, in transition or disintegrating, might remain quite stable, resilient or changing less strongly than expected. It is the latter to which I want to turn in the following: a) the fate of the nation state in the EU framework, b) the question of Europe's geography and borders and c) EU related trends in European societies. All three issues appear to me momentous for the future of the EU but usually attract little attention in official scenarios. And if, then, for example, the nation is looked at as outdated or hostile, an answer to the question of the final EU borders has so far been denied and the development of European societies is seen almost entirely through economic glasses. Besides that, official EU future scenarios usually lack considerations of *path dependence*. It is not much exaggerated to claim that from the perspective of EU elites and their brain trusts the history of Europe begins with EU integration. The socio-political dimension is preferably covered by complexity-reducing opinion surveys, with the imminent risk of basing decisions on artefacts. Whereas anybody watching the political process in EU institutions carefully, will notice long-term historical patterns at work. In any case, not to be blind towards historical constellations, coagulated institutions and different intellectual (ideological) traditions should be beneficial to any forward-looking attempt.

A post-national era?

Understanding nation as an "imagined community" and "human invention" (Anderson 1983) is a shared idea today, far beyond the narrow circle of political scientists. It has replaced earlier ontological concepts defining nation as common roots groups. It is obvious that the new "constructivist" approach is politically intriguing, because it suggests all kinds of interventions from "nation-building" to post-nationally designed communities. The EU is usually mentioned as an example of the latter. But will the nations disappear in the frame of the EU, or will they only abandon their own state and sovereignty, or is all of this just wishful thinking? Is nation unavoidable? (Greenfeld 1999) Does the talk about the "post-national" state hit a reality? The transfer of sovereignty to the EU and the submission of nation states under international agreements and rules are usually given as an indication for the erosion of the nation state. On the other end, it is the revival of ethnic minorities, usually favourably treated and supported by the EU and international organisations, run by a new meritocratic global-minded "aristocracy", which threatens the integrity of existing nation states. The regionalisation of Europe, which could replace the nation states is a long-standing discussion. Spain (Catalonia), Italy (Lega Nord) and particularly Belgium appear to be early candidates for such a development. The latter with its two parts, French-speaking Wallonia and Flemish-speaking Flanders, seems to be farthest in the erosion process in 2010, with a separatist party leading Flanders in the Belgium elections. In the face of this the Flemish Belgian sociologist Geert van Istendael asserts in an interview that all countries are disintegrating, the difference is just that the Belgians know it.

However, when looking at states, which are showing an inclination to fall apart, these are not classical nation states but entirely those where – due to certain historical reasons – different ethnic groups have been bound together by force. In Europe the causes for multiethnic nation states were always certain external constellations of power. In Atlantic Europe the ruling aristocracy imposed its own "nationhood" (language, education, culture etc.) on other ethnic groups in its territory of rule in the course of the transition from feudalism to a modern state. This did not happen without fierce oppression and violence as the numerous uprisings and civil wars in early nations like France or Great Britain show. Some of these conflicts kept their violent character up to modern times, e.g. those surrounding the Basques in Spain, the Irish in Great Britain or the Corsicans in France. In the Europe of the Holy Roman Empire (HRE), nation states emerged in three waves. The first wave (a) created Italy (1859) and Germany (1871). Although the HRE had already been terminated by Napoleon in 1806, it took another half a century to further deplete the power of its most prominent rulers, the House of Habsburg, so that nation states could succeed. In the course of this, what was left to Habsburg turned into the Austro-Hungarian Monarchy (1867). The defeat of this monarchy allied with Germany in World War I (1914

- 1918) led to its dissolution and a second wave (b) of nation states emerging, a belt of new states[8] between Germany and the revolutionary Russia (1917), also known as Soviet Union (SU). World War II did not basically change this situation from the perspective of nation state building, with the exception of the three Baltic States, which became part of the SU after 1945. With the end of the Soviet Union almost another half a century later the third wave (c) of births of nation states occurred. Now, almost every major ethnicity between Germany and Russia proper has its own state.[9] Among them finally also those people, whom Marx/Engels considered as "unhistoric", because they lacked, for a long time, an indigenous power and intellectual elite; e.g. Slovenia and Slovakia.

However, this third wave seems to have taken place in an era, which some consider already as post-national, a political environment where the nation state is eroded. Its sovereignty to a great deal transferred to supranational entities like the EU, or, less obvious but practically with similar effects to international organizations (WTO, UNO, IMF etc.). If this process were to continue, a fourth wave of nation states could be expected, where in the frame of the EU the rest of those European ethnicities, which have not yet reached "statehood" (Basques, Catalans, Flemish et al.) could celebrate independence. But this "independence" would most likely be depleted to a kind of linguistic and cultural autonomy in the relation to the super-state EU. At least, if the logic of supra- and post-nationalism stays path bound. In that case the EU could soon reach a politically more complex shape, though very similar in design to what was suggested for the survival of the Austro-Hungarian Monarchy (Popovici 1906) in the decade before the outbreak of World War I. No later than at this point history would have drawn a circle – the nation culturally autonomous but politically bound by a "union". The Hungarian social scientist, historian and politician Oscar Jászi in his retrospective analysis of "The Dissolution of the Habsburg Monarchy" (1929), which also contains thoughtful assumptions about the evolution of nationalism and the nation state, gives plausible reasons why the project of transforming the Monarchy into a supra-national state – a kind of proto EU – with linguistic and cultural autonomy for its constituencies failed. "… the real problem of the former monarchy was not the annihilation of all historical individualities and constitutions in the unity of a nationless super-state […], but to give fair opportunity to the nations to build up their own states according to their historical traditions and to combine them as equal members of a confederation." (Jászi 1929/1966, p. 246)

In a nutshell: Jászi sees the Habsburg dynasty in a centuries-long battle with *feudal nationalism* (Hungarian, Czech, German et al.) about hegemony, but

---

[8] Yugoslavia, Hungary, Czechoslovakia, Poland, Lithuania, Latvia, Estonia and Finland.

[9] The new ones include Slovenia, Croatia, Bosnia, Makedonia (FYROM), Serbia, Montenegro, Slovakia, Czech Republic and Moldavia.

when the hydra-heads of feudal particularism were finally cut down in the course of Enlightenment and the Nineteenth century, a new threatening force appeared – *democratic nationalism*. "And, whereas, the Habsburgs triumphed with comparative ease against the feudal nationalism, which represented a lower type of economic and political organization (based on anachronistic privileges and the exploitation of the bondsmen), the new popular and democratic nationalism, which tried to reconstruct the crowns on the basis of popular sovereignty against the nationless absolutism of the Habsburgs, signified a higher principle of political organization, which the dynasty could not conquer." (ibid.) What Jászi is claiming, is that the nations and nationalities of the monarchy at the end were not satisfied with some sort of federation promising cultural autonomy but desired full sovereignty, i.e. territorial integrity and supreme lawmaking authority. This was particularly the case for those nationalities who had an own elite narrating a heroic foretime and bemoaning the loss of institutional independence at some point in the past. Unfortunately, for many of the eleven nationalities of the Habsburg Monarchy national aspirations including sovereignty remained unfulfilled when the monarchy vanished in 1918. The successor states either remained strongly multiethnic (Czechoslovakia, Poland, Yugoslavia and Romania) or harboured at least some pockets of smaller ethnic groups (Austria, Hungary). And, above all, their external sovereignty turned out to be limited, depending on alliances with larger powers in Europe. All in all, the emphatic concept of nation and nation state as the ultimate home for the liberated individual remained mutilated in reality when the supranational feudal dynasty had disappeared from central Europe.

World War II put the national question into a kind of deep freeze for almost five decades. It remained overshadowed by "system competition" (Cold War) between the capitalist West (USA et al.) and the communist East (Soviet Union et al.). Only when the Soviet Union gave a free hand to its satellites and itself vanished, did the national question pop up again. The reasons why had it remained under wraps from 1945 onwards seem having been twofold: a) the destruction, suffering and exhaustion of Europe by World War II and b) the division of the continent into a capitalist (West) and communist (East) block, each dominated militarily and ideologically by a hegemonic power – America (USA) in the west and Russia (USSR) in the east. As adversative as the two powers appeared, both were promoting universal ideologies (capitalism versus socialism) and the convergence of national policies by some sort of inter-/supranational institutions (NATO, IMF, Warsaw Pact, COMECON, OECD, EEC, EFTA etc.). This regime prevented military conflicts between the European nation states, while the self-understanding and identities of the nations as born out of the Nineteenth and early Twentieth century remained more or less untouched, with a few variations. Under Soviet supervision the concept of "socialist nation" was introduced, whereas in the West talk about "patriotism" attenuated the aggressive nationalism common until World War II. The West responded to the dwindling of the communist block and the related disappearance of "system confrontation" with forceful "globalization" and the expansion of supranational structures, particularly in Europe with the transition of existing supranational institutions (EEC etc.) to a more tightly integrated European Union (1992).

However, the release of Eastern Europe from Soviet hegemony, unexpectedly lead to a new blaze of nationalism and a number of new nation states through secessions. And it was not the post-World War I political geography which re-emerged, but something similar to World War II when Slovakia and Croatia were separate states for a short period, or even better the political map suggested by reformers of the late Habsburg monarchy (Popovici 1906). More than in the interwar period national aspirations of the smaller people could be realised when the Soviet grip loosened, with the dissolution of Czechoslovakia peacefully, in the case of Yugoslavia with a lot of pain and victims. Somehow paradoxically, none of the post-communist states wanted to enjoy, at least for some time, sovereignty in the classical sense of nation state, but all immediately decided to join the supranational/intergovernmental (NATO, EU etc.) institutions of the West. While Eastern Europe was in transition from a state-planned economy and one party political system, Western Europe was changing from a nation-centred thinking to post-national ideologies justified with "globalization". The EU offered both a seemingly new identity – universalistic values and institutionally backed individualism (Münch 2008).

Pertti Joenniemi (2002), in an essay on Finland's perspective in the EU, has put this national dilemma convincingly between the poles of Herderian and Hegelian thinking. He believes in the benefits of the internationalisation of state functions (Hegel) by the EU, and Finland's advantages due to its historical experience within the Russian Empire: "[…] the leap from being linked with a multinational empire having its centre in St. Petersburg to a Brussels centred European Union is, after all, not that large." At the same time Joenniemi hopes that Finland as a nation with its particular language, culture and people (Herder) will not only survive but the EU will "provide Finland with increasing room to express what could be comprehended as its true and original nature … However, a European Union resting on a joint identity would be perceived as quite problematic." (ibid., p. 209) This seems to be the main difference between the national question in Europe at the turn to the Twentieth century and today. National (popular) sovereignty appeared to be urgent at that time, whereas a century later the survival (equality) of one's own language and culture (identity) seems to suffice, a mode of government already reflected as an offer to the people by the rulers of that time, World War I prevented its realisation. However, there was and is a big question mark in such reasoning whether national identity without sovereignty will work. As Jászi in his assessment of a reformed proto-EU Habsburg in 1929 pointed out, in this federation of "Larger Austria" German would have superimposed all other languages as *lingua franca*. Similarly today with English in the EU, despite all the political acknowledgements of the other 22 languages, it is practically the only negotiating language. And not only this, English has penetrated all European societies to an extent German never achieved in central Europe. Was it the EU or globalization, or both, since about the Nineties English has been pushed as language of all relevant parts of society, in business, academia, science and technology in particular. There is barely an invention of any kind, which is not introduced in English (of the American variety) words.

So, what about nation, nation state and national identity in 2030 and beyond? It could well be like in the past, a kind of historical *déjà vu*, this time as a success. The EU is building on where the medieval order of Europe finally ended, World War I and the break-down of the multiethnic monarchy of the Habsburgs in central Europe. The EU is trying to accomplish, and this time for a much larger territory, what the Habsburgs had in mind for central Europe but failed: a supra-national political entity, now made up of almost all European nations. However, the outcomes of these efforts might not be as intended. The question lingers on whether, in comparison to the imperial monarchies of the past, a modernized supra-national entity like the EU signifies a higher principle of political organisation than the sovereign national states, or not. Hence several scenarios are imaginable for the nations and nation states, not only a post-national order (Scenario 1).

Scenario 1 (**"post-national Europe"**) After transferring most legislation and decision making to the supranational EU institutions the nation states remain empty shells. A new generation of European leaders, among them many with migratory background, identify first of all with EU institutions and cosmopolitan ideas. For them "European" is identical with EU. Member States have lost their national connotation in favour of simply being locations for economic activities with specific profiles of strength and weaknesses. By 2020 enlargement has reached Turkey, Ukraine, Belarus and the Caucasus Republics. EU citizenship replaces national citizenship. Anybody worldwide is entitled to apply for it. This background is the base for identity formation in education. Objective: a highly specialised, individualized and mobile workforce. Any remaining need for collective identity is served by either commercially designed or politically suggested artificial identity offers. English is not only the *lingua franca* of the EU but is becoming so influential that national languages turn into pidgin, limited in relevance to private and life world situations. All systemic communication (transport, science, technology, government etc.) is dominated by English. This particularly affects German and French. The small languages resist longer, because of their lesser significance for the unification process. Political parties are superseded by NGOs, representative democracy by participative consultations (surveys, citizens' movement etc.). Europe is ruled by a cosmopolitan meritocracy with its power base in inter- and supranational institutions.

Scenario 2 (**"national-revival"**) The enlarged EU of 27 and more does not fit under one roof. Inequalities between as well as inside Member States are growing. Whoever can, migrates to the better off Member States. This leads to depletion of eastern and southern Member States in terms of human resources. In countries like Hungary, Greece or Portugal basic services like health, education and security can no longer be provided. The attempt to fill the empty spaces and places with people from even poorer regions outside the EU leads to cultural and ethnic conflicts with the remaining domestic population. To counter this decline the richer Member States transfer huge amounts of financial resources to the depleting fringes, with few sustainable results. The giving countries already battle with overpopulation due to immigration pressure from inside and outside the EU, causing ethnic and social conflicts, the tensions inside the EU system increase. In this critical situation, nationalistic leaders in France, The Netherlands, Flanders[10] and Austria come into power and first stop the transfer of financial resources to the crisis states, border controls are reintroduced and immigration is strictly controlled. In the receiving countries, which are already governed by right wing coalitions, people go to the streets and demand governments of "national unity" and a return of decision making power (sovereignty) from the EU to the national parliaments. Hungary is the first to stop paying membership fees to the EU and other international institutions. The EU is in a state of dissolution. Brussels, Germany, Sweden and Finland make last attempts to save what can be saved. After forays into supranationalism lasting for decades, European elites recognize that their real power derives from the people. Democracy on nation state level is refreshed again. National parliaments regain power.

Scenario 3 (**"Europe of fatherlands"**) With the entry into force of the Treaty of Lisbon in 2009 the EU has reached its highest degree of integration. From then on, step by step it loses grip on the continent, tasks are gradually returned to the Member States, or simply interpreted in their favour when implemented. First indications for such a development are the appointment of low profile politicians to the new positions of "President" and "Foreign Minister" of the EU, a severe crisis of the Euro zone and resistance of some Member States against the mobility of people inside the Treaty territory. Additionally, the UK, Poland and the Czech Republic join forces to sabotage any further "deepening" of the greater Union. Finally, a number of policy areas have been moved back to Member States, or groups of them. For example, the Euro zone is divided into a northern and southern currency; the Schengen-free travelling is limited to states with similar economic levels etc. National citizenship has regained some of its

---

[10] Belgium no longer exists in 2030. Flanders became independent a decade earlier and Wallonia joined France.

relevance. The enlarged EU in 2030 is basically a common market and free trade zone. A revised Lisbon Treaty framework remains intact, although its day to day implementation is fuzzy and ambiguous. Despite this lowering of overall integration Turkey is not part of the Treaty but gets a separate arrangement. The same applies to Ukraine and Belarus, which remain as a buffer between the EU and Russia. Europe is ruled by obscure but dynamic relationships of national-, inter- and supranational elite circles. The EU structures keep some coordinating and mediating functions but are less monolithic than at the time of the Lisbon Treaty. It is a Europe of variable geometry. Strategic decisions remain with the Member States.

Scenario 4 ("**Europe of proximity**") In the course of the post-Lisbon Treaty process the EU fails to reach economic and political cohesion between its members. During the negotiations about the budget period 2014 - 2020 regional groupings emerge stronger than in previous periods as single actors. Foremost it is the *Visegrad Group* of Poland, Slovakia, Hungary and the Czech Republic. These countries throw their voting weights together to counter first of all German and French interests. The Scandinavian members also find common grounds in the battle for chunks of the EU budget and lifestyle questions, so does the southern tier Italy, Greece, Spain and Portugal. In the further development some of these coalitions turn out to be more permanent, others less. Among the more stable co-operations are France (with Walonia), Flanders, The Netherlands, Germany, Austria and Switzerland[11], which form a centre group of the EU. Scandinavia with the Baltic States is another cluster with coordinated policies towards the EU. The *Visegrad Group* has been extended by the inclusion of Croatia and Slovenia. Greece is coordinating policies with Bulgaria, Romania, Serbia and Macedonia. Although formal structures of these groupings remain weak, they suffice to allow their recognition as distinct actors inside the EU. Geographic proximity, some shared history, similar culture and economic status turn out to be the main parameters for the formation of such alliances by proximity. Gradually peoples and national elites identify with these intermediary groupings. EU identity remains low, national identity strong but extended by a macro regional identity, which is viewed favourably.

European territory

"Any European State […] may apply to become a member of the Union." This is how the Treaty of Lisbon (Art. 49, Consolidated Version of the Treaty on European Union) defines the circle of potential Member States. Unfortunately, there is no further definition of "European State" or Europe, except one under-

[11] Switzerland joins the EU in the Twenties of the Twenty-First century.

stands the reference to the values in Article 2[12] as a definition for "European". Only, in that case, membership in principle would be open to any state globally, as long as it respects and is committed to promoting predefined "European values". In such a reading of the EU project something like "World Union" would be the last consequence. However, there is no hint from any of the major documents informing the public about the course of European integration that such a far reaching objective was ever intended. But, if "Europe" is not meant synonymously to cover the whole world, it must have a border. The common sense approach to find this border is certainly to consult geography. In 1887 Austria-Hungarian geographers declared a spot near the village of Dilove – today western Ukraine, south of the town of Rakhiv – as the geographical centre of Europe. Whereas, about a century later, the National Geographic Institute of France using the method of gravitation centres (marginal points: Spitsbergen [N], top of the Urals [E], the Azores [W] and Canary Islands [S]) identified the geographical centre of Europe in Lithuania, near the village of Purnuskes. However, by and large Europe's geographical delimitations are not contested today. An exception is the south-eastern border of the continent in Russia. Here we find sometimes the crest of the Caucasus or the Kuma-Manych[13] Depression north of it mentioned as the continent's border to Asia[14]. To opt for one or the other version has consequences, for example, for the question of which is the highest mountain in Europe. In the first case it would be Mt. Elbrus (5642 m) in the Caucasus, in the second Mont Blanc (4810 m) in the Alps.[15]

Hence, from the viewpoint of geography and given Article 49 of the Treaty, it should be no problem to define the members eligible for EU membership, respectively its final border. Albeit, there have been a number of political decisions since World War II, which challenge the relevance of a geographical definition of Europe for the EU project. The Council of Europe, for example, expanded from ten founding members (1949) to 47 today, including practically all republics of the bygone Soviet Union, except Belarus and the "-stan" coun-

---

12 Art. 2 "The Union is founded on the values of respect for human dignity, freedom, democracy, equality, the rule of law and respect for human rights, including the rights of persons belonging to minorities. These values are common to the Member States in a society in which pluralism, non-discrimination, tolerance, justice, solidarity and equality between women and men prevail."

13 That the Manych Depression and the Caucasus are a kind of frontier is also indicated by the long history of conflicts between its people and Russia as a European power.

14 The Kuma-Manych Depression was suggested by the Swedish geographer Philip J. von Strahlenberg in 1730.

15 It is my guess that a great majority in the EU would still name Mont Blanc as the highest mountain in Europe when asked. It is a question, which is not irrelevant when dealing with enlargement. So far, it was only a short glimpse of history when the Elbrus became politically relevant for Europe: On the 21st of August, 1942 German mountain troopers (Gebirgsjäger) raised the Third Reich's war flag on its peak.

tries in the south east. Another case is the European Song Contest, for which all countries are eligible, which fall within the European Broadcasting Area (EBA). The EBA follows a mere technocratic definition and includes North African and Near Eastern countries as well as those in the Caucasus. Or, the UEFA European Football Championship, where countries like Georgia, Azerbaijan, Armenia, Kazakhstan, Turkey and Israel take part. It is geographically undisputed that of this group, Israel is not in Europe, whereas the others have either a very small chunk of territory in Europe (Kazakhstan, Turkey) or are located at geographically controversial boundaries. From these examples it appears that being recognized as "European" depends on a mix of geographical, political, economic, cultural and situational criteria. With Israel, for example, it is probably cultural and political considerations, which legitimate its stakes in European organizations, among them the EU, with which this country is already closely associated[16]. Then there are Kazakhstan and Turkey, which are similarly related to Europe in geographical terms, but Turkey is already a member of most European organizations whereas Kazakhstan is not, not even of the Council of Europe.

Turkey's attempts to move from its long time participation in European politics, perceived in history more often than not as an external invader, to become part of a European identity by acceding the EU, delivers excellent material to reflect the territorial limits of Europe and European integration. First of all, EU membership is not like membership in those other "European" organizations mentioned before, which have much narrower functions and less power. Hence, the public concern about their affairs and membership is low. With the EU it is different. Throughout its existence it has continuously expanded its power over Member States and their citizens to an extent where everybody can feel affected. In this process people turn from low committed onlookers to part of a polity with associated identity concerns. As a consequence, new members are judged whether they are compatible with the pack or not by a broad public, not only by officials of corresponding formal organizations. It is obvious, the further the EU is expanding beyond its founding members and the deeper it is integrating, the stronger the public resistance is getting, particularly in net paying countries such as France and Germany. Whereas the expansion from the EC6 to the EU15 could practically still take place behind the public's back, the accession of the post-communist east central Europe in 2004/2007 (EU10) was already met with considerable suspicion. Now, with the accession process concerning Turkey, the public resistance appears to be gaining strength so that several national leaders in the EU are suggesting a "special relationship" instead of full membership for Turkey. Although the populations in the new Member States seem to be in general more

---

16 [http://www.eeas.europa.eu/israel/index_en.htm] retrieved on 7.9.2010.

pro enlargement than those of the EU15, average support for Turkey is in the clear minority, among the EU15 it is less again by a considerable percentage.[17]

Turkey seems to be the case that will somehow clarify the content of Article 49 (TEU), which so far remains a black box. As boundary is just the other side of identity, and Article 49 implies a definition of Europe, with the outcomes of the accession negotiations with Turkey we will know more about the identity of the EU as well as beyond conventional geography the territorial limits of Europe. Should Turkey at the end be accepted as full member, Europe will have expanded across the Bosporus into Asia Minor. The question about its final borders will remain open. Otherwise, Turkey not gaining full membership, an understanding of Europe as defined by today's geographers will be confirmed. So much about Europe. On the other hand, the proceedings leading to Turkey's inclusion in the EU will reveal the true nature of the EU. Given the concerns and resentments against full membership of Turkey visible from opinion polls[18] and public discussions in major EU countries, it will be crucial how this membership will be legalized after the closing of all negotiation chapters. For example, will the referenda promised in France and Austria take place? Will the German conservatives insist on a "special relationship" only, a pledge made to its electorate in several national elections? Or will Turkey be accepted by elite decision only? Should Turkey be welcomed by a broad democratic agreement then not only the EU but also Europe as we know it geographically would have expanded. The EU would have demonstrated that its talks about democracy are more than empty phrases, but this also applies if Turkey is rejected. Otherwise, its intergovernmental character would be confirmed and hence, the legitimacy of the extent the EU encroachments into individual and collective life seriously questioned.

Europe is the only continent without geological justification. It owes its existence entirely to the will and ability of the posterity of those tribes who overwhelmed and inherited the Roman Empire. Without the Visigoths winning over the Huns (Battle of the Catalaunian Plains, 451 AD), the Frankish knights against the Arabs (Battle of Tours, 732 AD), the Mongols shrinking back from the Germans in the Thirteenth century and Renaissance armies beating off Ottoman advances into central Europe (siege of Vienna 1529 and 1683), Europe as a concept most likely would not exist today. It would simply be a part of Asia, as its geological formation suggests. Europe as we know it today emerged when migrating Barbarian invaders ("Völkerwanderung") took over a tumbling and dissolving Roman Empire and gradually from its remaining pieces built a new civilisation by their own nature over centuries. In a first millennium cautiously

17 See, for example, Public Opinion in the European Union (EUROBAROMETER) [http://ec.europa.eu/public_opinion/archives/eb/eb66/eb66_en.pdf] retrieved on 7.9.2010.

18 See, for example, Eurobarometer 66, where only 26% of population in the EU15 is in favour of Turkey's membership, 37% in the NMS.

recovering what was left from Rome and the earlier *axial age* (Karl Japers, "Achsenzeit"), then from the Fifteenth century onward in an unprecedented historical pace in increasing exchange with civilisations and cultures outside the European system.

Until far into modern times Europe was more or less identical with the dense networks of aristocracy genealogically rooted in the age of Barbarian migration. And only when Russia became part of this system the mentioned division to Asia was openly drawn. Although Europe is no proper continent, the territory in which this post-Roman civilisation developed could have been decisive for the direction of its evolution. Europe has a heavily structured coast line, which is three times as long as the coast line of Africa, while that continent has a three times larger area. Such a structure divides by enabling diverse cultural and political subsystems ("competition") but also connects by the short distance to the neighbour's coast line ("cooperation"). Besides, all people living west of the large Slavic plains are more or less close to the sea, and its opportunities.[19]

The evolution of Europe as a system rather than being a fixed territory is the main reason why its definition remains variable and situational. With the invitation offered to Turkey to become a member of the EU the geographic definition of Europe has been tacitly questioned again. And yet, it was only a situational decision, which might suit certain circles of interests in the Euro-Atlantic sphere. On the other side, when the Soviet bloc collapsed at the end of the Eighties there was often talk about a "return to Europe" in the former Soviet satellites. In this case the definition of Europe confined itself to Western Europe and the EEC, respectively. In recent decades it has become increasingly custom to use the terms "EU" and "Europe" synonymously. The consideration of the countries west of the former Iron Curtain, in particular the city belt from southern England down to the Alps and northern Italy, as the European "heartland", is obviously widely shared. In this case the limits of Europe can be expected where the rule of this heartland ceases.

When the Iron Curtain was removed and Soviet power contracted to Russia proper in the Nineties, the cosmopolitan Norwegian sociologist and peace researcher Johan Galtung imagined five scenarios for the eastern borders of the European Union: a) EU12 plus Austria and Hungary, b) a border dividing Poland, Czechoslovakia and Yugoslavia, c) EU12 plus Finland, the three Baltic states, Poland, Czechoslovakia and Yugoslavia, d) an eastern border dividing Belarus, Ukraine and c) a pan European "house" including the ex Soviet Union and Turkey (Galtung 1993, 131 pp.). For Galtung as a cosmopolitan universalistic thinker scenario five was the option to be preferred, a Europe from the Atlantic to the Pacific. The Nineties as a time of radical change were, of course, prone to all kinds of speculations about Europe's (the EU's) future borders, especially

[19] See the inspiring book by Rolf Edberg (1988) on how Europeans "kept on sailing".

with respect to the east. The Austrian historian Otto Molden, for example, suggested on the ground of rich historical and cultural arguments the eastern border of a European polity along the following line: eastern Finland – Vyborg – Narva – Daugavpils – Pripjet swamps – Tarnopol – Hotin – Dnjestr estuary (Molden 1990, 57 pp).

Europe as a geopolitical concept has pulsated throughout history. At times it contracts, at times it expands, at times it completely disappears in order to give way to competing concepts like feudal empires or nations. Throughout the Nineteenth century Europe was seen as a system of big powers, (Ottoman) Turkey included. Most of these were dynastic and held huge colonies around the world. Europe was expanding. European elites, British and French first of all, ruled the world. The interweaving of nation and empire created forces of expansion unprecedented in history. From World War I Britain emerged as the greatest empire ever seen, but the forces of contraction were already at work, however hardly recognized by contemporaries. Some, like Coudenhove-Kalergi[20], at least had a foreboding of Europe's political decline, which he tried to avert by suggesting a pan-European governance. The colonies of the continental powers would have become a constitutive part of this empire ("Europäisches Reich") (Coudenhove-Kalergi 1934, pp. 195 - 198), the British Empire remaining a separate European power. Decolonization as conducted in the decades after World War II was not on the agenda yet. On the contrary, the colonies were planned to be settled and further developed by surplus European populations, similarly to the way Australia or the Americas were settled. A great deal of boundaries of such a European polity would have been on other continents. Together with the British Empire most of the world would have become "European", completely ignoring the geographical definition of Europe. Things turned out differently, as we now know. In 1945 Europe was on its knees and Britain bankrupt, its overseas properties sold off or awaiting independence. Albeit, the vague Art 49 (TEU) together with the universalistic accession criteria laid down at a summit in Copenhagen (1992) leave the impression, as if for some this interwar idea of a united Europe including parts of Asia and Africa is still lingering on.

When Coudenhove-Kalergi propagated this extended European empire in the interwar period he suggested Vienna in Austria as its capital (Coudenhove-

[20] Count Richard Nikolaus von Coudenhove-Kalergi was the founder of the Pan-Europa Movement (1922). He was a descendent of a European aristocratic family serving the Austrian House of Habsburg. His mother Mitsu was Japanese. Nikolaus' father Heinrich became acquainted with her while serving a term of duty at the Austro-Hungarian Embassy in Tokyo. But the family soon moved back to Europe where Nikolaus and his brother received an international education. As a member of the European aristocracy with global views and linkages Count Richard Nikolaus von Coudenhove-Kalergi became an early promoter of a united Europe along the lines of an elitist blueprint.

Kalergi 1934, pp. 201 - 206). His reasoning was that this city – due to politics, economy, culture, geography and history – is more predestined than any other city in Europe to become its federal capital. Geographically, Vienna is the most central capital, its European mission is symbolized by keeping in safe custody the regalia of Charles the Great (742 - 814 AD) and culturally, Vienna could be regarded as more European than German due to its mixture of people. Besides that, having once been the capital of a formidable empire, Vienna is in need of a mission appropriate to its still available imperial infrastructure. But, in 1934 Coudenhove-Kalergi identified three European states as basically not being nations and hence these were in need of a different mission: Belgium, Switzerland and Austria. Of this choice of three he suggested a European mission for Austria with its capital Vienna.[21] In case of a German-French rapprochement, which he did not see in 1934, he could also imagine a city in the German-French border region (e.g. Basel, Luxemburg) as European capital. Similar his stand towards Brussels: in case Great Britain were to join a European union, Brussels would be the ideal capital due to its geographic location. However, like Winston Churchill in his famous speech at the University of Zurich in 1946, Coudenhove-Kalergi foreclosed the possibility of a British membership. When after World War II European integration began to unfold institutionally it was a different Europe than in the interwar period, divided by the Iron Curtain and at the frontline of a Cold War. As France and West Germany were the most significant actors the locations for the integrationist institutions had to be somewhere in their vicinity. The main competitors were and still are Luxembourg, Strasbourg and Brussels. At the end, these cities became the places, which still host most of the EU institutions today.

Coudenhove-Kalergi's Vienna did not come into consideration, not only due to its peripheral post-World War II location but because Austria did not even take part in the integration process at the beginning. But Brussels proved to be a perfect fit when a downsized Britain became an EEC member in 1973. However, with the "reunification" of Europe after the demise of the communist bloc, and especially after the massive enlargement of the EU towards the east and south east the question about its institutional locations could be asked anew. The UK is not the British Empire, hence its weight might not justify Brussels and a re-allocation of main EU institutions appears plausible, considering that the EU has changed so much since the Nineties. Actually, demands to concentrate the European Parliament in Brussels and to give up its second location in Strasbourg come up from time to time, but without any broader discussion with regard to the new situation in an enlarged EU.

---

[21] The mission for Belgium would have been to civilize the Congo and for Switzerland to promote the idea of freedom, Geneva with the seat of the League of Nations, a predecessor of the UNO, as the capital of the world.

One exception is Franck Biancheri, an unconventional thinker from the French think tank "europe2020". However, interestingly, he does not see any reason in enlargement to move the institutional centres of the EU further east, because the East "will not affect the demographic, economic, financial and scientific balances. Thus the centre of gravity of the enlarged EU will remain in effect in the Euroring 1 area."[22] With "Euroring 1" he basically means the north western city belt of Europe, located in a mysteriously prosperous backbone stretching from southern England to northern Italy. In this limited space EU institutions should be reshuffled. London: European Council, Brussels: European Parliament, The Hague: European Court of Justice, Paris: European Commission and Frankfurt: European Central Bank. This suggestion raises the question whether political and economic capitals must be the same, particularly as the EU due to its history has an economic bias. It could well be that a shift of the main EU institutions closer to its geographical centre would be more favourable for its development than insisting on keeping everything at the Atlantic rim.

Ever since its foundation, but particularly since the big enlargement to post-communist Europe, the world is wondering about the precise content of Article 49 (TEU), which implies the final territorial limits of the EU. As identity and boundary are in principle just two sides of the same coin, the lack of clarity about the extension of "Europe" in Article 49 also indicates a lack of clarity about what kind of political "animal" the EU is. The Lisbon Treaty ("Constitution") does not seem to have changed much in this dilemma. Events like the handling of the financial crisis (2008/09) and unwanted migration, questioning appeals for solidarity and the blockade of international agreements by individual Member States all show that the identity of the EU and thus its boundaries are still uncertain. Hence, any attempt to anticipate its future territorial boundaries must simultaneously reflect the likely future political identity of the EU. A post-national imperial EU (Scenario 1, above) would press for wider borders and membership and is sure to exceed the geographical borders of Europe moving towards Asia and Africa. Theoretically, the size and external border of the EU would only depend on the ability of its bureaucracy to enforce regulations and control of the expanded territory. Although strong economic and bureaucratic circles to pursue such a course seem to exist, the realization appears rather unlikely, given the already existing public resistance to expanding to Asia Minor with Turkey. A complete revival of the classical nation state (Scenario 2), which would imply a reintroduction of permanent check points at state borders is not likely either in the next three or four decades. More likely for 2030 is an EU within the current borders (Scenario 3) plus the territory of former Yugoslavia and Albania. In a "Europe of proximity" (Scenario 4), which is not so visible yet as an option, the boundary question would be decided case by case according to

---

22 [http://www.europe2020.org/spip.php?article363&lang=en] retrieved on 13.9.2010.

the perceived security needs of a country or group of countries. Only Scenario 1 would push the EU beyond the known geographical borders of Europe and give Article 49 (TEU) an entirely political meaning. As a rule of thumb: The more democracy in the Member States, the smaller the EU will remain. With the European Parliament it might be different. But in this case the question of a common demos and legitimacy would have to be raised. There is no such thing as a European people in sense of a "demos" yet.

Anticipating European societies

Apart from politics, how will people live in Europe in a few decades? What kind of society can our children look forward to? Commonly shared views today usually expect a greying population, a shortage of human and natural resources, increasing social inequality, conflicts between immigrants and natives, a stagnating or even declining economy, and the like. All in all, rather unpleasant expectations. The only exception seems to be an unbroken belief in technological progress. On the other hand, we know from the past that the future never looks like the present and, even more unsettling, it rarely unfolds as imagined. With respect to "society" not only the future but the concept itself is at stake. Within classical sociology "society" is usually understood as institutions and social relations within the confines of a (nation) state. But what if state boundaries like in the EU visibly disappear, what understanding of society applies then? Are national societies replaced by a meta-level "European society", or does society as such "evaporate" as some seem to fear (e.g. Bach 2008)? How much "European society" do we see after about two decades of the EU and more than 50 years of European economic integration (EEC)?

There are undeniable institutions in place, which appear "European" (Commission, EP, Council etc.) and we see people interacting with the help of these institutions, mainly the upper echelons of Member States. Then there are larger and smaller companies doing business across borders. Some of the bigger companies operate within a global range (BP, Deutsche Bank, Siemens, Renault, and many more). However, with the latter the real European character (ownership, decision making etc.) is not always easy to decipher. Then we witness all kinds of cross-border, if not global NGOs, and numerous EU mobility programmes. But that is about all. The EU by and large is still a playing ground for elites first and foremost (Haller 2008). For the overwhelming majority of its population the Member States' societies remain the most visible point of reference, the most essential basis for social life and survival. Even more, there are signs that the top down elite-lead attempt to integrate Europe has provoked processes of closing rather than opening society in some if not all Member States. This has not been well researched yet, but there are sporadic reports[23] particularly about what was once the Iron Curtain, that *Schengen* has reduced rather than stimulated cross-border activities in the immediate vicinity. Aggregated economic data might not show this yet, but there are conspicuous signs in the micro-sphere of society that such processes of closure are underway. Not least in the political sphere, where protecting one's native country's interests seems to be on an upswing.

However, the analysis of what is really going on in European societies has been hampered by a paradigm shift in the social sciences, which probably obscures more than frees our look at society. A shift, which has been identified as the "cultural turn". It is a turn away from understanding society as a reality defined by something like structure, function, power, relations and interest, now "problems of meaning, discourse, aesthetics, value, textuality, and narrativity, topics traditionally within the humanists' purview" (Friedland/Mohr 2004, p. 1) are coming to the fore. It was the USA where this "turn" first emerged. And, astonishingly, it took shape and developed somehow in parallel with neoliberalism, getting stronger with what was called the "Reagan Revolution" in the late Seventies of the last century. In Europe its real time did not come until the Nineties, when Soviet supremacy ended in the east and the EU emerged as a politically deepened and extended continuation of the European Economic Community. Although, the EU did not invent this idealistic intellectual reorientation of Western social sciences, it influenced and was influenced by this "turn". I have yet to see any deeper investigation into this matter, studying the connection between this paradigmatic shift and the emergence of the new order in Europe. But it is obvious that views as expressed in talking about the EU as "post-national" or as a "non-imperial empire" contain traces of the "cultural turn". Without this the EU would most likely look different today, in many ways. The necessities of power and interests would be more clearly envisaged and displayed.

"Cultural turn", simply put, means not to expound a social phenomenon in its "vertical" dimension, i.e. with respect to social inequality, for example, not to interpret it as a problem between property or income classes (e.g. working class versus capitalists, lower middle class vs. upper middle class) but foremost in its "horizontal" aspects, i.e. focusing on implications of meaning. Here, again as example, social inequality gains attention mainly as a difference of meanings. Consequently, what was once seen as "class conflicts" (vertical) is now obscured, instead potential social aggression directed to be kept on the same social level (horizontal), i.e. between men and women, native and foreign, old and young, gay and straight etc., differences which appear "cultural" first of all. The view of differences through the "vertical" lens of social inequality has not com-

23 [http://diepresse.com/home/spectrum/zeichenderzeit/593813/index.do?_vl_backlink=/home/spectrum/zeichenderzeit/index.do] retrieved on 30.9.2010.

pletely disappeared but now it is only one among several perspectives, it lost conceptual and political priority. Some call this transformation of the theoretical mind in the social sciences "post-modernism", others speak of "late modernity", "second modernity" and so on. All in all a picture of conceptual fragmentation and arbitrariness in the social sciences emerges. The EU is a powerful engine in this intellectual transformation not only by "agenda setting", defining areas of research and signalling problems, which it considers worth being intellectually dealt with, but also by emitting more tacit expectations concerning scientific and academic organisation (e.g. "Bologna process"), methodology and theories. Any forward looking attempt, particularly if commissioned by EU institutions, will have to face the limits of this new intellectual framework.[24]

If we take, for example, the recent 'Project Europe 2030' report[25] to the European Council by a high brow reflection group, the intellectual "turn" (cultural and neo-liberal) of the last three or four decades with its limitations is quite visible. What is eye-catching is its one-dimensional approach and politically affirmative selection of dimensions and variables. The report does not reflect alternative scenarios for the EU in 2030, except a dualistic view of success and failure. Whereas drafting scenarios basically means painting pictures of possible futures, this report is content with demanding actions in view of current threat perceptions. From this perspective Europe's future is melting down to how we deal with ageing, migration, integration, knowledge, energy security, climate change, security and whether the EU manages to become an "assertive" global player, everything under the premise of competition. Although it belongs to the essence of every scenario that it is more bound to the present than to the future, with this one it is particularly strong. Its dimensions and variables can be easily collected by browsing Western "quality" media. There is simply no surprise in it, but several hidden assumptions and empirical evidences, which need scrutiny. For example, the unquestioned adoption of international university rankings, although it is obvious that these are horribly skewed toward English speaking countries. Or, elsewhere, that the EU "needs" to grow its population "pro-actively". The assumptions behind this remain obscure. On the whole, this report, which is supposed to be an intellectual compass for EU policies, does not say anything that has not been said before. Emphasis is on the Single Market, common migration rules concerning legal migration and better actions against clandestine migration, encouraging skilled migration, investing heavily in R&D with the 2020 goal of three per cent of GDP, and better tertiary education. It also states that even if the Union has the network and institutions required, it is up to the member countries to utilize them.

24 For more about this see my introduction to 'Forces Shaping the EU' (Langer 2008b)

25 Project Europe 2030 – Challenges and Opportunities, May 2010; [http://www.reflectiongroup.eu/wp-content/uploads/2010/05/reflection_en_web.pdf] retrieved on 13.9.2010.

This "Project Europe 2030" in its affirmative and one-dimensional orientation stands in interesting contrast to an attempt from 1999 when a Commission internal *Forward Studies Unit* painted five scenarios for Europe 2010.[26] That the EU cannot survive without its bond with citizens is an explicit assumption of that study. Social values and trends, technological advances, demography, social relations and the like come into view. What makes the five scenarios particularly interesting is that their time perspective 2010 is our present and we can judge how close they come to reality. In "Triumphant Markets" (Scenario 1) the EU is "basically an increasingly unified and ever-growing European economic area." There is no "ever deeper union" in sight. Scenario 2 ("The Hundred Flowers") assumes that by 2010, due to an "explosion of micro-activity" enabled by new Information and Communication Technologies (ICT), traditional political systems will fall apart. The EU is hit by a crisis of confidence, absenteeism, tax evasion and civil disobedience, social and regional differences are getting wider. Europeans are falling back on local life. Actually, there is something true in this picture, albeit the situation is not yet as dim as imagined. In contrast, in face of the recent financial crisis some could well have the impression that the governing elites are acting with "Shared Responsibilities" (Scenario 3). The fourth scenario ("Creative Societies") pictures the EU in 2010 as a champion of new social and ecological values. "Inspired by a radical different approach to wealth, production and welfare, the new political elites carry out a reform of the very basis of industrial society." Finally, Scenario 5 suggests the EU in a "Turbulent Neighbourhood" for 2010. The EU is turning into a besieged citadel and security has become the number one public concern.

Although none of the five scenarios precisely match the reality Europeans are facing in 2010, they do contain elements of what has or is occurring, even if for entirely different reasons to the ones they posited. After all, the authors did underline the fact that these scenarios were not 'visions', 'strategies' or 'policies', which is probably just as well. The scenario that appears closest to our actual experience is probably 'Turbulent Neighbourhoods' (Scenario 5) with the description of Europe as a besieged citadel that, combined with the global financial crisis, somewhat inhibits the continuation of large-scale neo-liberal policies and the downsizing of the welfare state, at least in some parts of the EU. At the same time, the nation state mentality is stronger again than a decade ago. Scenario 1 ("Triumphant Markets") also has some elements of recognition for the present. The EU in the meantime has gone through two major enlargements, it has adopted a kind of "Constitution", the Lisbon Treaty, which equipped it with a legal personality, a 'foreign minister' and a 'president'. What is completely

[26] Gilles, Bertrand/Anna Michalski/Lucio R. Penchi, Scenarios Europe 2010 – Five Possible Futures for Europe, Working Paper, July 1999 [http://www.mcrit.com/transvisions/documents/scenarios_europe_2010.pdf] retrieved on 10.8.2010.

absent, however, from this future "painting" is the poignant financial crisis towards the end of the anticipated time span. With Scenario 3 ("Shared Responsibilities") to claim that the EU is carrying out a "wide-ranging reform of its system of government at all geographic levels" would also be a rather illusive conclusion. Although, we hear a lot of talk about climate change and notice the emphasis on energy efficient technologies, there is no "radical change" in economy and social organisation in sight ("Creative Societies"). There are, if we dare to look matters squarely in the face, some fairly unpleasant things going on in Europe at the moment. The growing gap between rich and poor for instance. Or, the intrusion into the privacy of citizens, justified by pointing to "terrorist threats".[27] But Scenario 2 ("The Hundred Flowers"), which expects a dramatic response of citizens towards such effects of EU policies, is still far from becoming a reality.

The future of the EU as a supranational political system is one thing, the future of the European society something else, although both are undeniably related. If society is defined as the most comprehensive system of social relations to which an individual naturally belongs, which in modern times is the state society, then it is still problematic to speak of a "European society". Assigning EU citizenship to citizens of Member States does not make a European society, nor does the abolishing of regular border controls or introduction of mobility programmes for the young. A European society would require a feeling of commonness, a common language of some sort to enable unhindered communication, a common culture and common institutions. So far the EU has only provided the latter and it is doubtful that it will ever be able to initialize the other three. However, a European society is not totally illusory, if we look at the elite stratum. The emerged EU institutions do provoke pan European social relations on a regular basis, relations which show the features of a societal system. In colloquial terms this could be called the European high society. But this includes only a very small part of the EU population, even if we count secondary impacts of EU institutions like NGOs, international business organisations etc. The overwhelming majority of Europeans live and feel under nation state conditions. Hence, one forward looking question could be, whether 2030 will a) see a broader and more established European society, or b) will remain an elite circle, or, and this is also not completely impossible, c) the elites will even retreat again to their national base, and give up exercising society on a European level. Here we should remember that the aristocracy were part of a European society for centuries, until the evolution of the nation state bound it back to tribal origins.

Whether European society or not, the equally or even more important question is, what kind of society Europeans will be part of in a few decades. From

---

[27] In this course, the delegation of domestic security matters (e.g. SWIFT, access to DNA data bases) by the EU as well as some Member States to the USA is particularly irritating.

the scenarios discussed, what could be found ten years later corresponding to reality were mainly economic and security dimensions. In general, predictions are probably most reliable, when assuming the defining and central elements of a system to stay in place, also in the future, anything else would belong to the rare instances of revolutionary change. An example of such a revolution was the abrupt collapse of the communist Soviet Union and its satellites by the end of the Eighties and beginning of the Nineties, when all basic coordinates of these "real socialist" societies changed. The scenario constructors of the EU *Forward Study Unit* in 1999 did not assume something comparable in their pictures for the EU 2010, nor does this 'Project Europe 2030'. To imagine that market economy, private property, social inequality and technological progress (i.e. capitalism), which are the parameters of EU societies, will similarly disappear as "real socialism" did in the past, appears rather unrealistic for the next two or three decades; it would give any scenario a surreal touch, because there is barely any indication that EU societies will no longer be capitalist in two decades or so. Hence, scenario building will realistically variegate inside this framework, which still leaves enough room for the imagination. To link to rather persistent variables from previous scenarios, i.e. security, demography, environment, market intervention, would appear natural.

Under such premises two main scenarios come into focus for 2030; pictures, which are well known from the history of capitalism, but are adapted here to a different global and technological constellation.

Scenario 1 (**"Globalized Society"**) – The EU Single Market is firmly in place. In a number of branches (e.g. finance, environment, transport), European "global players" have emerged. The interests of these economic actors increasingly shape EU and national policies. As a consequence, economic inequality inside each member state but also between them dramatically increases. Distributive policies have improved infrastructure in the eastern and southern periphery, but failed to close up ranks in wealth with the prosperous core. Millions of Europeans from the eastern and southern belt of the EU have moved to its more productive and prosperous centres, leaving empty spaces back home. The generation EU2030 has been raised and educated as highly individualized, mobile, specialised and politically correct knowledge workers, fully dedicated to keeping the economy growing. Birth rates continue to fall. The EU has become the most competitive knowledge-based economy in the world. Millions of highly skilled individuals from outside the EU take advantage of the "blue card" and immigrate. In this way the rapid decline of the indigenous population, which is threatening economic growth, can be effectively compensated. However, despite massive immigration EU societies remain culturally rather coherent. What has emerged is a single culture of consumption and production, which marginalizes any immigrant as well as traditional domestic cultures. Nevertheless, to prevent conflicts originating in a social inequality, comparable with Nineteenth century capitalism, technologically sophisticated methods of surveillance and control are in place. Whereas cultural conflicts, which were the cause of so much apprehension at the beginning of the century, have been successfully dealt with by educational means.

Scenario 2 (**"Return of the Natives"**) – The recovery of EU economies after the financial crisis of 2007/2008 was short-lived. Tight austerity measures cause slow growth, stagnation and in some states even a decline of the GDP. The attempt to implement a common economic policy in the Euro zone creates stiff resistance among the population of the richer Member States who fiercely oppose sharing their taxes with economic laggards. Finally Greece, Portugal and Ireland go bankrupt. Social inequality is increasing all over the Union. Although, the recurring economic crisis has slowed down immigration, some of Europe's big cities are haunted by clashes between ethnic Europeans and the immigrant population, particularly from the Islamic world. Most of the post-communist new members turn away from the EU and try to find individual solutions for their misery left by the supra-national experiment of EU membership: population depleted, social structure distorted (no middle class) and with a foreign-owned economy. Although, the initial thrust for "own folks first" policies comes from right wing parties, main stream politicians also begin leaning towards this. Local economies try to replace long-distance trade, which is suffering under increasing energy costs. Attempts to replace declining crude oil with a similarly efficient substance have failed so far. A significant number of people question the dominance of economic values and instead identify more strongly with their life world (e.g. family, community, neighbourhood, nation). This leads to a pick-up of birth rates once more. The attempt to impose "European values" top down has failed in the face of the great variety of values in Member States. Related to this was the abandonment of the idea of a common EU social policy in favour of national welfare traditions. Hence, social inequality can adapt to what is seen as legitimate in individual Member States. Supranational solutions, which measure everybody with the same yard stick are replaced by tailor-made policies for each country. Although the EU of the Lisbon Treaty has long lost its credibility, certain supranational structures remain in place (e.g. Customs Union, External Action Service) and new ones even emerge (e.g. common defence). Otherwise, there are strong signs of national and regional renaissance, leaving the picture of a great variety of societies.

Looking ahead

When people speculate about what will be, they usually extrapolate from the present, adulterate it with their wishes, anxieties and interests, and the result is an image of the future. With experts this is not much different, except that they can draw on a more systematic knowledge of the present. Another point is taking account of the past when looking forward. The general public tends to glorify the past and sometimes longs for its return, whereas in many scientific attempts it is simply neglected, although its presence in the present can hardly be denied. I have tried to argue that the EU offers its Member States an identity, which a century ago was already on the brink of becoming reality in the Austro-Hungarian monarchy, but was not welcomed by the political leading circles. This time it seems to be different, although the results could be the same: reducing political nations to nothing but cultural entities. Or, even less, into economically competing regions instead of nation states. The European Union as a peace project, replacing violent conflicts by consensus, trade and cooperation? Again, history could provide us with baffling food for thoughts. For example, since the Thirty Years' War, the periods between wars among great powers have become longer and longer in Europe.[28] But these periods were not all linked with free trade. On the contrary, times of free trade were often much more violent than those of economic protectionism. After all, this is true for the two decades before and after the turn of the Twentieth century.[29] This should make us think twice about the EU as a provider of peace in the future. Equally, the case that supranationalism is a better principle of political organisation than nation states, has not yet been convincingly asserted.

The factor neglected too often in forward-looking studies is *path dependence*: What can be decided rationally and what will be determined more or less unknowingly by structures of the past. In the different scenarios suggested here, I have tried to consider this factor, although in most cases it remains implicit. The four scenarios about the future of the nation state in the frame of the EU emphasise different and often conflicting forces in Europe's history. Basically, these are forces of expansion ("empire") and contraction ("nation"). The underlying assumption is that these forces do not act consecutively but simultaneously. What kind of EU we will see in 2030 will depend on the resultant of these historical forces. The scenarios suggested are rough sketches of how this could be imagined today. The final borders of the EU will be closely linked to this outcome, because border is always only another side of system identity. In any case, Europe's political territory is of a more fragile character than that of any other continent. Although, the political shape of the EU will be of some relevance for our future society, its character appears in my arguments less uncertain than that of the EU itself, because this society will still be capitalist in my assumptions. Anything else would appear highly implausible, after the demise of communism. Finally, with capitalism we have more than 200 years of experience. The question is only whether it still can surprise us with social constellations we have not seen yet. What will remain, however, are the surprises immanent in a changing technology.

---

[28] World War I and World War II are the exception, if we do not view the whole period as one continuous war.

[29] See Mulligan, William (2010), The Origin of First World War, Cambridge (Cambridge UP).

By 2030 we will know more about the medical, social, political and psychological consequences of the all-embracing adoption of information technology (mobile phones, internet etc.) in our societies. Also the mist around the availability of energy sources and what climate change really means will clear up. This will significantly influence what scenarios will finally unfold. The European Union today is an excellent political frame for the utilisation of capital. This is a major drive for its enlargement. And probably the main reason why business circles in particular refuse to commit the EU to a final border. However, this advantage simultaneously attracts all the problems historically known from capital accumulation (social/economic inequality, migration, destruction of nature etc.). In this respect the situation today appears structurally similar to the late Nineteenth century. Hence, it is important how the relations between those who hold the power in the EU ("elites") and the population on Union and state level will develop. We know from history that when accumulating capital comes under threat in Europe the political response can easily be social repression inside and military aggression outside. The technological level we have reached provides enhanced possibilities in this respect (surveillance society etc.). Given the assumption that the basic characteristics of this relationship will be the same in 2030 as today, all the above-mentioned scenarios will have to take account of this.

References

Anderson, Benedict (1983), *Imagined Communities – Reflections on the Origin and Spread of Nationalism*, Verso, London.

Amalrik, Andrej Alexejewitsch (1970), *Kann die Sowjetunion das Jahr 1984 erleben?* Diogenes, Zürich.

Bach, Maurizio (2008), *Europa ohne Gesellschaft*, VS Verlag, Wiesbaden.

Brzezinski, Zbigniew (2007), *Second Chance*, Basic Books, New York.

Cameron, Fraser (2004), *The Future of Europe – Integration and Enlargement*, Routledge, Abington.

Cooper, Robert (2004), *The Breaking of Nations – Order and Chaos in the Twenty First Century*, Atlantic Books, London.

Coudenhove-Kalergi, Richard Nikolaus von (1934), *Europa erwacht!*, Paneuropa Verlag, Zürich/Wien/Leipzig.

Darwin, John (2008), *After Tamerlan*, Bloomsbury, New York.

Driakhlov, N.I./V.B. Sevko/I.V. Gulchenko (1992), 'The Outlook from Moscow – Perception of Europe by Moscow Students', in *International Journal of Sociology*, Vol. 22, Nos. 1 - 2, pp. 90 - 109.

Edberg, Rolf (1988), *... und sie segelten weiter*, Klett-Cotta, Stuttgart.

Enzensberger, Hans Magnus (1987), *Ach Europa!*, Suhrkamp, Frankfurt a. M.

Friedland, Roger/John W. Mohr (2004), 'The Cultural Turn in American Sociology', in R. Friedland/J.W. Mohr (eds.), *Matters of Culture: Cultural Sociology in Practice*, Cambridge University Press, New York, pp. 1 - 68.

Galtung, Johan (1993), *Eurotopia – Die Zukunft eines Kontinents*, promedia,Wien.

Greenfeld, Liah (1999), 'Is Nation Unavoidable? Is Nation Unavoidable Today?', in H. Kriesi, K. Armingeon, H. Siegrist, A. Wimmer (eds.), *Nation and National Identity – The European Experience in Perspective*, Rüegger, Chur, pp. 37 - 54.

Haller, Max (2008), *European Integration as an Elite Process*, Routledge, New York.

James, Harold (2001), *The End of Globalization*, Harvard University Press, Cambridge Mass.

Jászi, Oscar (1929/1966), *The Dissolution of the Habsburg Monarchy*, University of Chicago Press, Chicago/London.

Joenniemi, Pertti (2002), 'Finland in the New Europe - A Herderian or Hegelian Project', in L. Hansen/O. Waever (eds.), *European Integration and National Identity*, Routledge, London/New York, pp. 182 - 213.

Kriesi, Hanspeter/Klaus Armingeon/Hannes Siegrist/Andreas Wimmer (eds.) (1999), *Nation and National Identity – The European Experience in Perspective*, Rüegger, Chur/Zürich.

Langer, Josef (2008a), 'Path Dependence of Future Scenarios for the European Union', in J. Langer (ed.), *Forces Shaping the EU*, Peter Lang, Frankfurt a. M./New York, pp. 119 - 130.

Langer, Josef (2008b), 'Where does the European Union go? Social Science Questions and Answers', in J. Langer (ed.), *Forces Shaping the EU*, Peter Lang, Frankfurt a. M./New York, pp. 12 - 22.

Mises, Ludwig von (1922/1951), *Socialism: An Economic and Sociological Analysis*, Yale University Press, New Haven.

Münch, Richard (2008), *Die Konstruktion der europäischen Gesellschaft*, Campus, Frankfurt a. M.

Molden, Otto (1990), *Die europäische Nation*, Herbig, München.

Popovici, Aurel C. (1906), *Die Vereinigten Staaten von Groß-Österreich – Politische Studien zur Lösung der nationalen Fragen und staatsrechtlichen Krisen in Österreich-Ungarn*, B. Elischer, Leipzig.

Prisching, Manfred (2005), 'Interpretative Muster von Zeitdiagnosen', in R. Hitzler/M. Pfadenhauer (eds.), *Gegenwärtige Zukünfte - Interpretative Beiträge zur sozialwissenschaftlichen Diagnose und Prognose*, VfS, Wiesbaden, pp. 205 - 236.

Rokkan, Stein/Derek Urwin/Frank H. Aarebrot/Pamela Malaba/Terje Sande (1987), *Centre-Periphery Structures in Europe*, Campus, Frankfur a. M./New York.

Zweig, Stefan (1942/2005), *Die Welt von Gestern*, Fischer, Frankfurt a. M.

Hans-Peter Meier-Dallach

The European Union Hitting Europe's Birds: The Future of Landscapes[1]

"The living thing is superior to a non-living one;
nothing is better than the cosmos;
so the cosmos is a living being."
Posidonios, Greek philosopher of Stoa

Birds and books

On the 4th of March 2009 the BBC World Service surprised me by reporting on the living perspectives of birds in Europe in a contribution entitled "Climate hitting Europe's Birds". In the last decades during the rise of European Union 75 per cent of the species has been declining, losers, while a quarter has profited and is winning under the new regime. Bird populations are very old dwellers of Europe; they lived here long before us. A critical sociological lecture of the event was stimulated:

The threatened species loved Europe as a living body of landscapes, niches, villages, towns and diverse cultures: All in all the earth can be seen as a giant maybe, like Rabelais described it at the time of the Renaissance. They remember having been small brothers and sisters of a Europe made from blood, meat, sweat, toils, passion, work, poetry – shortly an organic paradise. What can the imminent loss of diversity contribute to my exploration into the future of the European Union (EU)?

I guess the winners would appreciate being members of the EU and welcome its performance. They can profit from the divorce of the two Europes: the Europe as a living body as opposed to the EU, which is on the road to becoming a system. The surviving species would accept having to live in a system. The loss of three quarters of the ancient species, of diversity, could even be advantageous for the survivors; it facilitates coordination and compliance to norms and history can be rewritten by forgetting that of previous times.

During the past years, I have learned much by walking through landscapes, villages, towns and metropolises. Walking gives space to dissident lecture. What I felt in nature led to a new walking through the libraries; very quickly I passed the displays occupied by the current books about the "Future of EU". My steps slowed down along the gallery of books written by the older species of science. Why did they disappear during the period of progress of the EU and the increasing endangering of birds' diversity? In my spare time, when I am not absorbed

---

1 In collaboration with the WORLD_DRIVES association.

by projects, I read such old books, for instance, Braudel, Elias, Walicki, Gurjewitsch, A. Weber, Simmel, Schopenhauer. Later on Paracelsus, Herodot, Latin and Greek writers such as Posidonios attracted me. In fact the benchmarking with birds delivers a huge contrast: the older species of books seem to be already dead while the current books are expanding to nearly 90 to 100 per cent.[2]

Visiting tour to metropolitan areas

Evidently birds do not study social or human sciences. But they are masters of reading societal changes in space. This may be the reason why birds have played a major role in myths and religions in nearly all cultures. The earth and its territories are their living partners including the air space. I guess that birds are more sensitive to the changes of landscapes than planners using Geographic Information Systems (GIS), maps and plans, because birds have to search for the living beings and elements; the small things and particularity of territories are essential for survival. Simultaneously birds perceive the borders where the body is losing vitality, becomes a green relict at the margins of a system or disappears under roads, platforms for houses or new towns.

We have studied social sciences or are well-certified planners but, nevertheless, we could learn from birds. Changes of landscapes are such of men, of societal mentalities or conducts. Many sites of construction are societal ones raising questions like who will live in this new settlement? Which birds are expelled before and will be abolished in a district? Walking brings an advantage along; instead of looking over all sites of Europe one follows a particular, but typical route. We undertake a visiting tour to the most relevant construction site of the EU's future – the metropolitan areas. Everywhere the first ranked master plans in spatial affairs concentrate on the creation of metropolitan areas. It seems that the period of "cohesion" strategies looking mainly to the peripheries in Member States has passed[3]. Also in Switzerland the metropolitan dream is flourishing; four metropolitan areas have been defined and compete to advance

---

[2] This essay looks forward against the background of previous papers where insights into periods shaping the EU and its images confirm the shifts from Europe as an organic model to a systemic construction (Meier-Dallach 2009 a/b). The periods "new technological and consumer styles", "governance by joint policy", "transformation through norms" pushed the EU as a system. They impacted the EU significantly more than the periods linked to Europe as a personality through "pacification by market" (after World War II), "agora and round tables" (the fall of the Iron Curtain) or "efforts for diversity" (federalist trends). Evidently the expansion of the EU imposes a fatalistic constraint and works as pressure for systemic logics as well as rationality. Europe as personality would need more time and could evoke "romantic" dreams and movements in an era of global competition.

[3] The strategies for the promotion of metropolitan areas could displace the policies of rural developments in peripheral areas also in new Member States of the EU and widen the urban-rural gaps. Such fears are articulated in Poland for instance and seem to be growing.

to the best mega-system of the Confederation, namely Zurich, Geneva-Lausanne, Basle and Berne like Washington as capital region. Let us make a visit to the area around Zurich.

As many others, the first drive of Zurich as a metropolis has the earth as donor. The lake of Zurich favoured the creation of a port in Roman times, which facilitated the founding of a town and settlements on both sides of the Limmat. In the Nineteenth century the railway began to dominate as traffic system and marginalised the port at the lake. The imposing architecture of Zurich's main station attests this change until today. But since the Nineteen Fifties, the airport has become the transnational and intercontinental gate of the metropolitan area (Picture 1). Metropolitan dimensions in Switzerland are small and short, struggling with the hills and mountains of the Alps, which reduce available space for buildings. So one can reach Zurich main station from the port through the Bahnhofstrasse in twenty minutes by foot and from here the airport can be reached in 20 minutes by train.

Picture 1 The generators of Zurich as metropolitan area

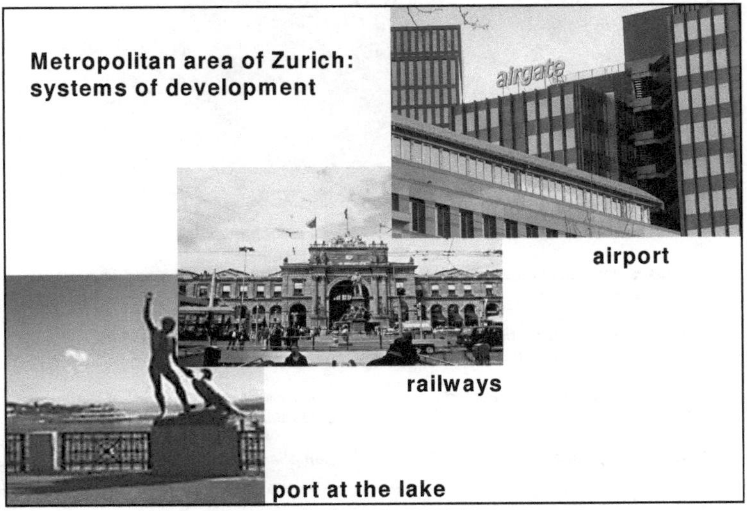

However, our trip does not follow the official tour. According to this, the primordial drives would still be the power and dynamics located in the City of Zurich. Although the City, for instance Paradeplatz, is a very important site for decisions in financial terms, the metropolitan area is driven by the surrounding areas and locations, municipalities, new towns and booming zones, the "coasts" of the City.

We start our tour in these coast regions. We collect impressions from two kinds of pictures, actual ones of the coast, territories surrounding the City, and such of the City, which go back to the Nineties. Behind the coast zones between airport and the City of Zurich one can see hills and in the distance the skyline of the Alps. The hills are like atolls where rich “birds” have landed, for instance Roger Federer, but one detects there still the nice rural villages typical for Switzerland. The excursion to the dialectics of metropolitan areas compares landscapes of the coast zone around Zurich (2009) with pictures specific for Zurich in the Nineties, 15 years ago, before the new wave of metropolitan strategies started. The new emerging corpus of landscapes in the surrounding area of the metropolitan space will be compared with the old city-body, i.e. “what is?” is challenged by “what was?”. Thereby a first level of interpretation looks at the landscape as a physical body. In the pictures of the traffic landscape (Picture 2a) one detects the relicts of earth, trees and woods besides the road-systems where surely birds are present.

Picture 2a Traffic landscapes – metropolitan and city type

We are missiles in the flux....	*We are inhabitants of vehicles in flux...*
The flux is absolutely determined from outside...	*There are bifurcations and freedom for choice in flux...*
The rhythms of flux are the pulses of centres and its attraction...	*The rhythms of flux are felt as rational decisions...*
The traffic behaviour is delegated to GPS...	*The style of driving is part of my character...*
Absolute obedience is automatic...	*Compliance to regulations is internalised...*

But our concept of landscape is substantially interested in the human birds living in the traffic landscape, here in the vehicles and cars on the roads. This societal and human level of interpretation is key to our comparative analysis. How are they feeling and living in the corpus of traffic landscape? How do they feel and conduct themselves in the coast situation compared with the city? Are the two landscapes, two specific “giants”, steering the conducts of people by shaping a metropolitan against a classic urban personality?

The metropolitan and urban traffic landscapes are significantly different. The coast pattern is characterised by flux, determined from the outside and steered top down. In terms of Linton (1945) one could say that two contrasting types of basic "traffic-characters" are created. In the urban type (Zurich in the Nineties) drivers felt that they were inhabitants of the car, capable of deciding, as a pilot with character. And surely the stream of traffic through the cities has been rather like living snakes than a track for missiles. In the coast pattern the basic treats are opposite – persons are determined from the outside, by centres as destinations, GPS and strict obedience is absolutely binding.

Traffic systems produce specific landscapes of communication (signaletic systems with direction signs). The coast pattern in the airport works without memory while the city pattern tells stories (Picture 2b).

Picture 2b Communication landscapes (signaletic) – metropolitan and city type

The city signaletic system animates the physical setting of tables while the coast pattern delivers only information. Very different are the time-givers (Zeitgeber) steering the behaviour in space. The coast pattern cuts duration, frees it from past and future, commanding the rational move to destination while the city pattern invites us to use more time in order to move in space.

At a first glance the settlement landscapes are quite different in their surroundings compared to those in the city (Picture 2c). The coast body of settlements shows a lot of isolated, provisional and outside oriented or chaotic objects, which surprise and produce specific sentiments. The city body stresses rather an integrated pattern, mostly on the level of architectural features. It evokes feelings of admiration, the configuration of built landscapes as a specific corporate identity, a personality revealing the character of the town. Such aristocratic gestures explain why nearly all tourist routes lead first to the holy districts of cities. The "law of nostalgic bias in aesthetic perception"[3] is linked to the strong personality of built landscapes in earlier periods of urban (and rural) development.

Picture 2c Settlement landscapes – metropolitan and city type

The configuration of objects is provisional, hazardous...	*The configuration of buildings is intended and reflecting a longue duration...*
The objects do not have any relation to the site (nature, environment)...	*The buildings shape the wider space as a context and surrounding...*
The climate is felt as ordered disorder at the margins of region...	*The climate is felt as ćholy worldŅ..*
All things are for something else for/ or from outside...	*The buildings regard each other, are communicative...*
Men behave like in a zero- or grey-zone without any commitment...	*The configuration expresses a kind of aristocratic gesture with links to aesthetic values...*

Natural landscapes in the coast area are richer than it seems at first glance – there are remains of natural landscape or even reserves of woods and grazing land for cows. But the situation in Picture 2d selects the natural landscape of an intersection to a new town, for example Glattpark (in picture). The physical characteristics have not yet created intimate sentiments like uniqueness, duration and attachment. The design is too strong to become a sign. And there is one interesting observation – the designed landscape is a person contrasting to wild zones of rests of nature and to the chaotic body of settlements.

---

[3] Empirical studies illustrate this observation: People assess the traditional patterns of landscapes as much more beautiful than the modern ones even if they are far from its meaning in present life. This symbolic pattern of conduct can be shown including natural, settlement and traffic landscapes (Meier-Dallach et al. 2003, pp. 164-165).

Picture 2d Natural landscapes – metropolitan and city type

The natural setting is constituted and made for us; the trees are too young as they could know us...	*We are embedded into nature and a part of it...*
The sentiments are fluid: we could sit down at another place...	*The sentiments are stable: there is no other place; it is rather unique...*
Arriving here and leaving the place is like to go to a shop...	*Arriving and leaving the site is a special passage of space and time...*
We respect the design and rules of the surrounding...	*The nature binds us together and steers our conducts...*

In Swiss cities natural landscapes play a significant role. Nearly all settlements are embedded into valleys or hills, i.e. they form an inverted panorama where one looks like from the scene to the elevated arenas for spectators, the pre-Alps, peaks of the Alps or the hills of Jura. This specific city pattern contrasts with situations in the surrounding zones of Zurich, where a quite large area is going to be built on, the new settlement of Glattpark.

Landscapes of men and societies are differently shaped in agglomeration and city zones. In agglomerations the societal body is dispersed; one detects singular individuals, who during commuting time are concentrated around stations. The bodies of traffic, settlements, landscapes and electronic communication absorb individuals and groups, i.e. their spatial availability as societal aggregations. Physical proximity has to struggle in vast areas (Picture 2e). But such contrasts could shape intensive sentiments of belonging together within small perimeters or oases of intimacy. The personality of societal landscapes is different from that observed in city areas. As in the example of leisure activity the pattern relies on density, concentration and public motivation and feelings.

Picture 2e Societal landscapes – metropolitan and city type

Distance of density: the vastness creates an oasis for us...

Joint life is intense, if it contrasts und responds to the built skylines...

Please stay away - we are a private island of intimacy in a flat world...

Take it easy and use that what we have...

We are a communitarian body ...

Neighbourhood is funny; water binds us together...

Public space has to be used like our houses and homes...

Please take part and submerge in the group...

Landscapes – from person to system

The observations collected from our tour in a metropolitan area can be summarised. Landscapes around the city, traffic, settlements, societal and communication patterns and natural settings form a mega-body. But it takes another quality than that put forward by Rabelais. The giant becomes de-personalised. It seems like a mega-system without qualities of living beings. Its components and drives result from planimetric logics – business plans following the most efficient routes, channels and means. The human beings and social groups disappear from the bodies, infrastructures and spaces, maybe they remain visible but they are steered by a new time rhythm and new spatial conditions.

In most metropolitan areas the city-body is encircled by mega-systems of the surrounding territories; they look very similar, the road- and traffic-systems, big settlements or luxury houses and districts, communication infrastructure, parks and rests of natural landscapes. But it is not only a kind of enclosing of the city body. Its outlook and design assimilates specific features of the surrounding system; it is mostly visible in districts and buildings where the historical architecture and forms have disappeared. The de-personalisation of the city districts is experienced by those inhabitants who have been dislodged to the agglomerations. The new giant from outside devours the same groups that are expelled from the city and have to seek a new living place within his corpus. Indeed the loss of basic groups of population – of its societal landscape – is the dramatic turn of the mutation from a city as a person to a part of a system. Often this process is accompanied by a face lifting of the districts concerned by new forms of architecture and design or restorations of traditional buildings and artefacts. So the new city body looks nice but vast and freed of human beings, the species of birds living there before.

I have walked through different metropolitan areas of Europe and since the EU concentrates the efforts to transform its members by metropolitan strategies it is not only legitimate but necessary to raise radical questions. Europe looks back at a past (and present) as a rich body of landscapes shaping significant characters. One could say that Europe's essential feature is its personality rooted in diversity between the Mediterranean and Northern Sea, between Oceans at the Atlantic and Ural, the Alpine formations and the endless plains. The EU is a very young partner of Europe – but it does not behave as a partner. The observations overwhelmingly suggest an opposite picture, even around Zurich as a metropolitan example of a country that is not a member of the EU. The EU mutates more and more into a mega-system encircling Europe as a personality. Far from the main issues prioritised by the EU, like financial, policy and juridical affairs, this mutation is mostly visible in the landscapes.

Theory of landscape revisited

I am aware that such walks through metropolitan regions triggered a change of my lectures in spatial sociology. Further my love for the personality theory of landscapes goes back to impressions from my childhood. I was born in a valley surrounded by an Alpine skyline of high mountains mirrored in a deep lake; so the conception of landscapes as a living body was convincing and survived all my positivist training in empirical and quantitative methods, cybernetics and system theory at the university. The most recent observations refer to the relevance of this view. How to revise the theory of landscape while taking them into account?

I illustrate the different approaches, landscape as person versus landscape as system, by using two Figures (3a/b). One can read the two approaches like frames of reference for discerning the differences in the observations made during the walk through a metropolitan area. The quintessence of the system approach is defined as "*divide et impera*". The four landscapes, natural, settlement, traffic, communication, are separated as systems[4] and treated as distinct objectives.

---

4 In a system-model, the parts are discrete but linked, while in an organism all parts are interconnected among each other. The division of labour in an organism is more "organic" – the borders are not well defined and diffuse. The organism creates an interplay of all actors (organs) within its territory according to a time rhythm. In an organism the elements and

Figure 3a Landscapes – the system paradigm as basics for the planimetric approach

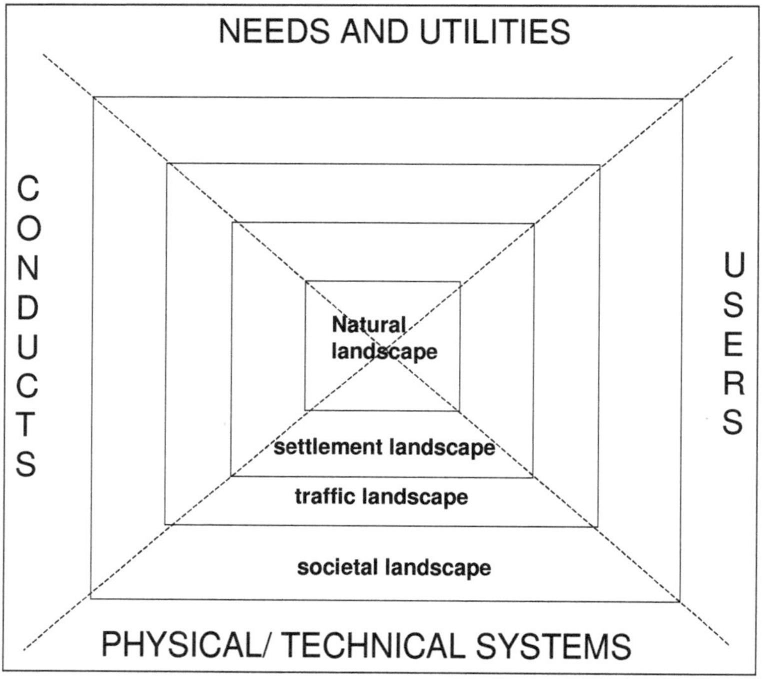

A further level of separation is relevant: the corpus of the landscapes is a physical system independent and freed from cultural, socio-psychic and mental spheres, i.e. the essential features of a human being. This divide frees science and planning from human, cultural and mental disturbance. Landscapes are cleaned from other aspects and disciplines like sociology, cultural and human science. There is a kind of economic advantage evident in this position: the landscapes are reduced to pure facts of natural or technical sciences facilitating the use of quantitative codes. The mind of planimetric methods becomes the all-inclusive-way for dealing with landscapes. Often this philosophy is inherent to the planning language; one speaks about "hard" factors (planimetric features)

functional units are neighbours with a trend to act by a synergetic mode. In border regions of the EU contrasts between the EU as a system and Europe as an organism, the logic of system borders and system time against the rhythms of organic boundaries and time are visible. Often the resistance against systemic models, anti-EU sentiments are transported by religious symbols and practices or cultural patterns rooted in tradition. Europe as an organism or as a personality reveals a multitude of treats and faces sharing them with non-European ones.

against "soft" factors in which some remnants of a bad conscience remain, showing that they are present but excluded from the planning business.

Figure 3b Landscapes – the person paradigm as basis for the human (poetic) approach

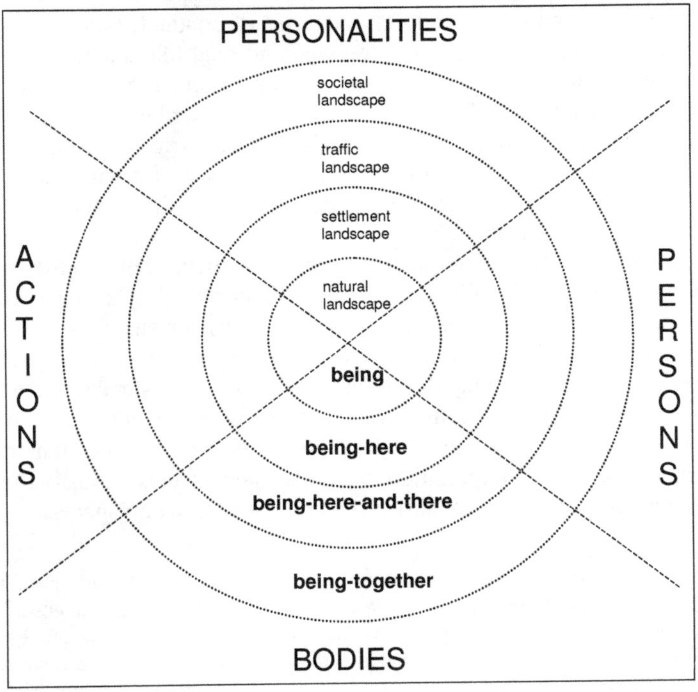

The system-model does not exclude sociology from the field and many planning strategies include societal, cultural and socio-psychic aspects. But a body without cultural meanings is a false approach at the beginning. The landscapes are biased by misplaced abstractions, by pure physical and technical facts missing the human factors. The human beings are reversed to "users" with some "needs or utilities" and actors of more or less determined conducts. According to my experiences as sociologist in planning processes these abstractions lead notoriously to the term of the "hard" factors. Landscapes are treated as abstract issues free from human factors, which are assigned later on to the category of "soft" factors. But soft means often fall out of decisions. The humanisation of planning is, if not excluded, postponed and displaced into secondary or last rankings. The planimetric approach defines time and space of landscapes as physical, technical and quantitative systems.

The opposite principle "*coniunge et redintegra*" guides the person-paradigm. Landscapes are taken as existential bodies and not reduced to their physical or technical elements. Planning is used as a means to integrate and not as the end to which beings are the means. Beings, human as well as animal ones, are integrated actors in the different landscape bodies. A car is not a physical object or vehicle but a casing of living beings. Landscapes exist as cultures, assigning meanings, emotions and defining spaces of conduct. Landscapes reveal specific characters and permit to be perceived and read like a person or personality. The ontological notion stimulated spaces of imagery and imagination through history. This "poetic" approach has been described and used, for instance, by Bachelard (2003, pp. 7 - 29). The planimetric mainstream tries to overcome it, but at the latest in a museum, for instance of traffic vehicles, one feels that the exhibited objects are correlated with specific human and cultural modes of being "here-and-there".

The concepts of the person-paradigm speak of "being-here-and-there" (Da-und-Dort-Sein) instead of traffic landscape, of "being-here" (Da-Sein) instead of settlement landscape, of "being-together" (Mit-Sein) instead of societal landscape. The natural landscape is conceived as "being" (Sein), i.e. the primordial setting embracing and shaping the human and animal existence. – One could define natural landscapes as shimmer of being, the most fundamental experience of living beings of the "*en kai pan*" (the unity in the whole). The change of notions is an ontological interpretation of landscapes as existential bodies with characteristics, persons or personalities shaping specific action spaces.[5]

[5] The organic or person paradigm has its roots in the European history of ideas and theories of society. The antique tradition of Stoa was very relevant in recovering the cosmos as living entity in the time of Renaissance for instance, by Spinoza, Giordano Bruno, Paracelsus and others, who were influenced by the idea of the organic character of the cosmos. Social theory was divided later into rationalist or positivist streams against organic theories, which tended to be promoted by romantic (also conservative) groups. In general the positivists often occupied the description of the present reality while the romantics tried to recover the past or the forward oriented searched romantic models for the future (regeneration of social reality as specific body of history (Szacki 1981, 151pp.). Very crucial was Schopenhauer's turn from the concept of world as a divine whole (*pan theos*) to that of "*macranthropos*", i.e. instead of god the human energy (the will) of human beings becomes the creator of the cosmos and of its landscapes. It is evident that the empirical, descriptive as well as speculative social theories have always used anthropomorphic metaphors and terms for interpreting social and cultural phenomena, like for instance Frobenius looking for explanations of ancient African culture or Alfred Weber who outlines a Sociology of culture. After the experiences of World War II he compared the history of Europe using terms like "historical body" (A. Weber 1950, pp. 17 - 26 and pp. 475 - 494), "organism" or "personality". In general the German sociology of culture has taken the cleavages between cultural mind, social religions, and technical rationalisation as an essential condition for the future. Alfred Weber predicted an overwhelming role of the "fourth man", the system-trained vehicle of a totalitarian future in the Fifties of the last century. It erodes the model of the "third man" characterised by the cultural mind of social religions promoting an overall responsibility for members of societies as well as for society *vis-à-vis* itself.

Chthonic time in metropolitan areas

Evidently the traffic systems have expanded enormously in the last decades on the surface, in the air space and underground. The traffic corpus of metropolitan areas is three-dimensional. Thanks to this fact unexpected meetings are probable. In Zurich near the opera, bordering the lake, a big underground parking complex is under construction. But some time ago the relicts of a very old landscape of Europe stopped the construction monsters – those of crannog settlements going back to the Stone and Bronze Ages. The most dynamic vector of system change detected one of the oldest "being-here" and "being-together" of early history. It is the *chthonic* face of European personality, the archaic form of being. Its body was a part of nature, of being; its person was a being-here, settlements in cottages on platforms over the sea, some places and routes for being-here-and-there, traffic landscapes. Being-together was embedded and characterised by cosmic myths and cults. This pre-historical face looks to us like a shadow from the past. It remembers the chthonic patterns as described by Frobenius (1933, pp. 10 - 43) in regard to ancient Africa. The trove evoked a stop of construction engines for some months. Zurich will preserve all these witnesses covered by the lake, reclaiming to become part of an UNESCO heritage area. The mega-system seems to fall in love with the chthonic personality of the old Europe.

Rembrandt was an ingenious painter of portraits; as models he preferred older people. But shaping the traits he succeeded to insert the faces of earlier life periods, of childhood, of the middle of life, into the present aging face. The whole biography of a person is present in his portraits; Simmel (1916, pp. 130 - 140) has taken Rembrandt as prototype for this organic shaping of reality, in our terms of interpreting societal bodies complying with the person paradigm.

Are there still traces of the chthonic time in modern Europe's personality? Outside of museums we will not find many hints, but increasing trends for buildings made from local materials provided by nature can be stated, also the estimation for the embedding of settlements into natural bodies, for instance valleys, terraces, highlands, islands, as a kind of cosmic feeling and strengthening local attachment and identity is growing. Examples of tracks of chthonic patterns can often be found in architecture, which tries to recover cosmic figures and sentiments. Traces are evident also in popular culture[6]. The designation of surrounding nature, for instance hills, mountains or peaks with ancient field names articulates a chthonic identity and a kind of being-together, a societal landscape. Evidently

[6] In empirical studies including preferences and sentiments of inhabitants, strong trends are found that the local attachment to communities is first ranked (Meier-Dallach et al. 2009c, p. 164). The attachment to family and to natural settings as well as tradition dominates the identification with national or transnational bodies; it is quite interesting that these local roots are predominant in the so called transformation countries in Middle-East and Eastern countries, mainly on rural sites and in peripheries. These local anchors maybe linked to chthonic patterns still persisting in modern societies.

even in modern times the focus on "being" in nature as guideline for housing, travelling or communication is visible in many trends of movements, sentiments and turns of lifestyles; authors even speak of a neo-chthonic trend.

Figure 4 Europe's faces between past and future, recession and dominance

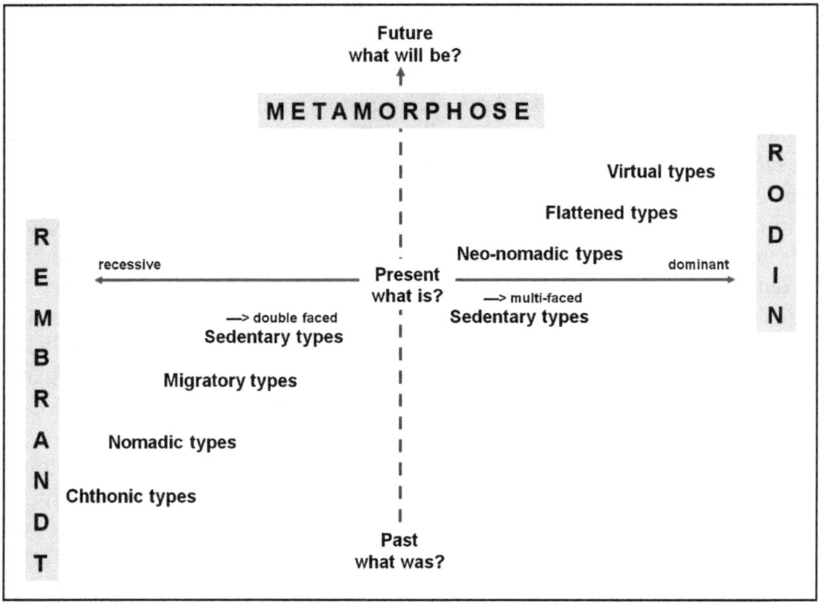

Which are the faces of Europe's personality in its different parts? In Figure 4 (above) the cardinal ones are assigned to a diachronic axis of diversity between past and future and to a horizontal axis mapping whether they are rather recessive or dominant in present time.

There are a lot of various types and examples of *nomadic* faces of Europe's landscape. Rembrandt's art of portraying are readable in many variations. But essential is its difference to the present. The "being-here-and-there" contrasts with modern concepts of traffic. In the early periods spatial mobility was not a transport from point A to point B, but rather a staying here at the residential location and there at the temporary place. Further, the movement was linked strongly to the "being-together"; nomadic societies strengthened the societal ties in order to fill deficits of cohesion due to seasonal separation of sites. To confirm the societal body it was necessary to hold together, here as well as being a member of there. Let us consider an example from Alpine transhumance. The Alpine cottages are dispersed in the highlands above the villages in the valleys. The paths to and from have the meaning of "here-and-there", i.e. a kind of difference within the same, like a Russian puppet. In summer time the dispersed pattern of cottages was the embracing puppet of the inner one which was the village in winter time, in the most intimate period of Christmas.

Europe's faces are shaped by *migration* periods, very dramatic ones during "barbarian migrations". They changed the faces of Europe many times and it is evident that these periods have had the character of convulsions. The traces of these periods and events are not strongly engraved into settlement, traffic or communicative landscapes. They were forgotten or displaced by the stakeholders of *sedentary* types. The sedentary patterns of landscapes are the most characteristic features of Europe. In fact the "being-here" developed the impressive diversity of Europe's personality shaping the outlooks and quality of life in nature, villages and towns as well as traffic structures during the Antiquity, Middle Ages and more recent periods – maybe enduring until the time after World War II. It is no exaggeration to say that the landscape of settlements and habitation has been the existential as well as cultural capital of the old continent[7]. But this (positively assessed) diversity contrasts to strong cleavages between urban and rural sites, Western and Eastern European, Southern and Northern patterns. Significant styles differentiated the settlement landscapes in towns and capitals from the countryside, where poor or chthonic and nomadic forms still survived – mainly in peripheries.

What does the sedentary pattern distinguish in comparison to the other ones? Here-being meant that the built body was a map of societal and cultural differentiations articulated by the character of houses and its grouping to a whole. It is noteworthy to add that these sedentary patterns have been constructed in "stone", i.e. in durable spatial structures, which have functioned as parts of durable collective memory until the current time. But dramatic changes impacted the sedentary pattern. Towns and villages became double faced. Migration from the latter to the towns produced rural zones and districts of rural immigrants. Two faces of "being-together" emerged in villages of those who remained against those who emigrated and failed. In towns and cities the corresponding divide was that between immigrant urban villagers and the citizens. "Being-together" was impacted in both, rural as well as urban contexts. Europe's landscape was double faced. Rural villages have been down-graded, and lost vitality; in extreme cases villages died, a trend still observable today. On the urban side settlements exploded continuously, hosting the emigrating villagers.

---

7 Braudel (1990a, pp. 122 - 266) describes the creation of France as a long process of building cohesion between '*les villages, bourgs et villes*'; local and regional market places have been of eminent significance in supporting this process and it was very relevant that the sedentary patterns have been generated and supported simultaneously by mutual exchange of goods and offers completing each other, i.e. logics typical for organic beings. Braudel's capacity to describe history empirically as well as to interpret it by synthetic methods is generalised in the concept of longue durée (Braudel 1990b, pp. 476 - 487).

The development of spatial faces of Europe can be summarised as a change from chthonic, nomadic and sedentary patterns, single and double faced. But they are currently recessive, i.e. they lose power in shaping Europe's diversity since the Fifties; four faces are emerging and are becoming dominant. The innovation in traffic infrastructure radically changed the "being-here-and-there". The *neo-nomadic* pattern began to dominate and changed the other bodies of Europe's personality: "being-here" became less significant and as a consequence the "being-together" is impacted by a loss of proximity and by an increased range of possible contacts in space. New towns and agglomerations surrounded the cities and villages. Commuting became more relevant than staying and the situation comes close to ghost settlements during the day when the majority is working outside, i.e. a situation extremely visible during our visiting tour through the metropolitan encasement around Zurich.

Here we observed a further trend: neo-nomadic trends are accompanied by long distance, transnational migration attracting groups from other continents. So the old double faced patterns transform into multi faced bodies with very different ethnic and social groups bringing along distinct frames for "being-together". They remain rooted in the cultural bodies of their countries of origin even more than the rural immigrants in former times. Europe's faces are becoming more complex.

Paradoxically in metropolitan areas and in the most rural contexts the landscape bodies are looking more and more similar. The pattern of *flattened* settlements and landscapes with a similar and ubiquitous outlook has become dominant while the societal body is multi faced and heterogeneous. A further change is relevant – the electronic "being-together", the *virtual* patterns of Europe's face, have emerge and have become stronger than was expected some years ago.

The organic portrait of Rembrandt changes to the vibrating one of Rodin (Simmel, op. cit.). The basics of Europe's personality visible in landscapes, species of "being", its chthonic, nomadic and sedentary faces are overwritten by the multi ethnic, flattened and virtual faces. Under the stress of limited space resources Europe seems to lose features of its basic personality as "being" (natural landscape), "being-here" (settlements), "being-here-and-there" (traffic). But the most relevant consequence is that all these changes strongly impact the "being-together" – the societal landscape. The new paradigm of Rodin transforms the classical one of Rembrandt into a moving without anchors in the past.

What will be?

There are many signs that the dissipative trends, the nomadic and virtual developments of landscapes continue to dominate the outlooks also in European countries. Nearly all efforts of EU and national planning are concentrated on the mainstream directed to upgraded cities and expansion as metropolitan empires. Maybe there are national or regional differences of these trends and programs claiming for slow-down-strategies in order to comply with the climate agenda in the next decades, but they are not considered as realistic changes or alternatives[8] by elites and decision makers.

Let's give a voice to the current giants who have to decide on their action space in future. They generate answers about their state and preferences for the next 50 years. The first group of answers supports *Rodin's road.* These giants accept and approve the dissipative trends, the vibrations and convulsions of their bodies, its fluidity, flattening and virtualisation and the impacts on their personalities. The planning in terms of system and planimetric methods is welcomed and fostered. They are fascinated looking at the new mega-cities in the emerging economies of China (Shanghai), India (Mumbai), Brazil (Sao Paulo), Turkey (Istanbul), Russia (Moscow) or city states like Dubai or Singapore. The path to the future, symbolically represented by Rodin, attracts as mainstream, and drives for a global format of EU metropolitan centres.

In Europe's territories, however, some giants suffer under the loss of their traits as stationary, original and authentic beings. Evidently *Rembrandt's model* is endangered everywhere. The nostalgic sentiments of people express such fears. Indeed sedentary patterns shaped by the long history of earlier patterns still survived in many features of European landscapes, of nature, villages and towns or cities. Even in metropolitan areas movements of resistance are observable, expressing their wish to stay "*hic et nunc*", on the ground, defending it against economic pressures, which they try to evade. The villages encircled by the new settlements contend for their autonomy in order to preserve their faces. Several studies describe how in new settlements or districts people try to find and generate anchors motivating sedentary patterns by creating neighbourhood, associations and feelings of local attachment[9].

---

8 While scenarios of future development are led by economic fitness and performance, mega-projects are embedded into architectural imagery. Star architects and designers play the leading role in shaping visions for future development. Sociology and human sciences are often not present in these "interdisciplinary" enterprises and have failed to bring its capacities and/or complied with modern concepts close to systemic logics. The sociology of culture is overlooked or de-evaluated as conservative frame without power of describing or explaining modern societies. But sociology bears blame; it has notoriously neglected the search for personality features of societies within its body (corpus), that is its physical forms. The debate about Europe's future suffers from missing the *society* as focus of development. It is not astonishing that sociology is replaced by architects; the latter became masters to interpret the future shapes of societies on the basis of architectural design and imagination.

9 In metropolitan areas a struggle of four scenarios is evident, for instance in the case of Switzerland. The vector pushing the metropolitan mainstream is countered by the efforts to remain a village with a stable population proud of its traditional character as community; simultaneously one meets the rather defensive position to stay at place (hic et nunc) even under poor conditions (strengthened in groups of losers). But visible are also innovative

But these European giants seem to be marginalised Rembrandts in a gallery where the modern global trends dominate and evoke melancholic sentiments. It is not probable that they can be preserved or restored. A third category of responses, the *metamorphosis*, looks like an alternative; it does neither continue or adopt the dissipative trends (Rodin) nor reconstruct the past (Rembrandt) but reinvents the chthonic "being-together", the societal landscapes. Europe's personality is decisive for a turning period. More and more people, human beings, have to live together in natural landscapes, settlements or traffic areas. Because these are becoming scarce the common chthonic principles are the new challenge playing a major role since ancient history. The earth comes back as cosmic order of the actual life situations; it is the "*en kai pan*", the unity and the whole of future landscapes. This metamorphosis may trigger many forms of resistance but it also offers fascinating facilities, for example

(i) the collection and embracing of all dissipated and nomadic beings of the world body
(ii) the sustaining and reinvention of the faces of Europe's personality preserved and still vital in its sedentary patterns and
(iii) the learning from the past for the future.

The giants convinced by this change could be named "*macranthropos*", a term used by Schopenhauer (1924, pp. 605 - 611) expressing that the cosmos is more than the sum of its elements. It is a mega-giant of human and animal beings creating its body of landscapes according to the human-paradigm of *Weltanschauung* **and** planning. Europe's personality provides a very rich thesaurus of experiences, diversity and facilities in order to promote this radical change. How could this change be sustained?

Measures

Recently I admired a common buzzard circling over the construction engines and monsters over a field foreseen for a new settlement. I am not sure whether this species will be a temporary winner or a loser of metropolitan strategies. But it is helpful to take its perspective as well as that of the birds that will be abolished in the next decades. The visit through the metropolitan system emerging around our cities and villages is a passage through the EU not forgetting the fact that the EU is part of Europe's future. Evidently the EU is suffering at this time under the stress of financial problems, the instability of the currency, the gap between the feelings of citizens and Brussel's management following the Lisbon agenda. I know that my walking through landscapes or a metropolitan area is far from these debates but it is very palpable. Therefore the strategies of metropoli-

groups trying to create new forms of sedentary communities, movements which are opposing to the metropolitan mainstream.

tan areas pushed by the EU in every member state are prominent issues for anticipating the future. Human beings are living in spaces and landscapes and like birds not interested in system management, global governance and scenarios for the future in a bottomless vacuum[10]. We have noted that the EU is on the tracks of a planimetric flush. Just like in a metropolitan area it encircles Europe as a person, its diverse landscapes, and its diversity potentials in the future. The master plans of the EU seem to be drowning the basic personality of Europe.

Europe's landscapes have been the source for the best expression of its personality in poetry – according to Burckhardt (1969, pp. 69 - 70) the privileged field expressing historical eras. It is the best resource to struggle against the dominance of the planners' planimetric dreams. I guess that science is rather not able to break its overwhelming dominance. Therefore let us summarise a manifest for Europe's future body as an excellent personality in global society:

1) Avoid any equation of EU system and Europe's personality visible in its diverse spatial faces and landscapes.
2) Break down those EU decisions formed in non-spatial and abstract terms into the scope of birds and human beings living in Europe's space, i.e. metropolitan areas, towns and villages.
3) Create a dialogue between the "what-was" and "what-remained" of Europe's landscapes, of its characteristics and personality and raise the question of "what will be" instead of bottomless speculations on scenarios and models.
4) Confront the planners' mental (and real) maps, their system-paradigm, with the poetry of spaces and undertake efforts to reinvent the sciences dealing with space, i.e. the person-paradigm of landscapes[11].
5) Humanise the landscapes; populate the natural, settlement, traffic and communication ones not with users but with human beings under the condition that they have to "be-together" in the future.

---

[10] This kind of encircling is observed also on the level of institutions. Norms or institutions implanted by the EU evoke a corona of values, interpretations and practices rooted in the local context as the Hungarian scholar Kendernay-Nagydaj analysed at our symposium. On the one hand people are mixed figures overwhelmingly living in their regional variants of European values. On the other hand they perceive and adopt some of these norms mostly in a rather diffuse way. But their own values can remain more relevant than EU rules, even if they are formally accepted or institutionalised. An actual example is the case of Greece.

[11] An international project started to initiate new kinds of exchange between arts and planning "Dream of Space – Poetic Explorations of Urban Areas". See Newsletter at [http://www.swo.de/tvrstart.html].

References

Bachelard, Gaston (2003), *Poetik des Raumes*, Fischer Taschenbuch Verlag, Frankfurt a. M.

Braudel, Fernand (1990a), *Identité de la France, Les hommes et les choses*, Editions Flammarion, Paris.

Braudel, Fernand (1990b), *Identité de la France, Espace et histoire*, Editions Flammarion, Paris.

Burckhardt, Jacob (1969), *Weltgeschichtliche Betrachtungen*, Alfred Kröner Verlag, Stuttgart.

Frobenius, Leo (1933), *Kulturgeschichte Afrikas*, Phaodon-Verlag, Zürich.

Linton, Ralph (1945), *The cultural background of personality*, D. Appleton-Century Co. Inc., Meredith Corporation, New York.

Meier-Dallach, Hans-Peter (2009) Available for download at Focus papers: [http://www.cultur prospectiv.ch/de:world_observatory].

a) 'The Shaping of European Images: Past Periods (part I): The change of European images is summarised by six periods'.

b) 'The Shaping of European Images: Presence of Past (part II): The deficiency of collective memory'.

Meier-Dallach, Hans-Peter/Therese Walter (2009c), 'Walking forward – back to future? CSR in Eastern Europe – five case studies', in Savall, H. et al. (eds.), *Social Responsibility and Corporate Environment Evaluation*, Lyon: Université Jean Moulin, Vol. 2, pp. 1117 - 1135.

Meier-Dallach, Hans-Peter/Susanne Hohermuth/Therese Walter (2003), 'Aus der Agglomeration in die Berge', in H. L. Dienel/H. P. Meier-Dallach/C. Schröder (eds.), *Die neue Nähe. Raumpartnerschaften verbinden Kontrasträume*, Steiner Verlag, Stuttgart, pp. 151 - 185.

Poseidonios (2008), *Stoa und die Stoiker* (Ed. R. Nickel), Artemis & Winkler, Text 1228, p. 655.

Rothfuss, Uli (2010), 'Dream of Space – Poetic Explorations of Urban Areas', in Newsletter: [http://www.swo.de/tvrstart.html]

Szacki, Jerzy (1981), *Historia mysli socjologicznej*, Tom 1, PWN, Warszawa.

Simmel, Georg (1916), *Rembrandt – ein kunstphilosophischer Versuch*, Kurt Wolff Verlag, Leipzig.

Schopenhauer, Arthur (1924), *Die Welt als Wille und Vorstellung*, Hans Heinrich Tillgner-Verlag, Berlin/Wien.

Weber, Alfred (1950), *Kulturgeschichte als Kultursoziologie*, Büchergilde Gutenberg, Zürich.

Chapter II

Institutional Aspects

Thomas Döring – Eithne Knappitsch – Birgit Aigner

Is the European Union Doing the Right Things?

Introduction

The question of which political competences should or should not be carried out at European Union level is one that has occupied policy makers and academics alike since the initial founding of the European Union (EU) and still proves to be a contentious issue today. Inextricably linked to this question is that of European public finances and budgetary matters. Here again, there is much criticism of the allocation of funds at EU level. A number of economic commentators argue that the provision of European public goods – such as in the areas of policing or defence[1] – should be a major task of the EU. More recently, demands for a European fiscal policy[2] as well as European growth promoting policies[3] have been increasing in resonance. The latter clearly reflects the perceived need for the EU to be better equipped to cope with macroeconomic shocks like that of the current global financial and economic crisis. As regards the entire process of European integration and the advancement of the European Union *per se*, any shifting of political competences from the Member States to the European Union level clearly requires the strong backing of sound and valid economic arguments. Bearing this in mind, there seems to have been somewhat of a renaissance recently in the use of economic theories such as that of federalism in an effort to understand the European Union and the allocation of decision-making powers across different levels of government.

Against this background, we attempt to discuss relevant economic approaches regarding the sound assignment of political functions and competences between the European Union and its Member States. The contribution analyses the topic in three steps: First, the economic theory of federalism is briefly outlined by discussing two different concepts of federalism (the welfare economic and the political economic approach), both of which are used by economists to analyse federal structures and intergovernmental (fiscal) relations. This section looks at some basic theoretical principles and criteria for an efficient allocation of political functions within the EU. As a second step, a short outline of the development of the European budget as well as the budget process is given: showing the most recent budget allocation for European level policies. And finally,

---

1 See, for example, Alesina et al. (2005) or Tabellini (2003).

2 See, among others, Schmieding (2009) as well as Feld (2005); see for a critical discussion of this issue Belke/Gros (2009).

3 See, with a special focus on innovation policy as well as transport infrastructure policy, van der Horst et al. (2008) and de Borger/Proost (2008).

the contribution will critically analyse the existing structure regarding the division of political competences within the European Union, taking into account the insights offered by the economic theory of federalism. Here a brief overview and analysis of the findings of current literature are provided, offering some insight into the discussion on the optimal redistribution of competences within the EU from a normative perspective. Comparison is also drawn to the *de facto* distribution of EU competences today. Furthermore, the authors ask whether these economic considerations provide arguments for an alternative assignment of political functions between the EU and its Member States.

The economic theory of federalism

The degree of policy-making by the European Union has sharply increased over recent years. The European Union is today facing challenges in terms of the allocation of political tasks or competences between central institutions and its Member States that are typical of the kinds of challenges faced by all federal systems. Although the European Union can hardly be seen as a federal state, but rather as a union of states with federal elements[4], the theory of federalism can nonetheless be helpful in considering just this allocation of tasks. The aim of this section is to demonstrate which arguments originating from the economic theory of federalism (Oates 1972; 1999; 2005) can be used to assess the appropriate division of competences between different political levels within the European Union.[5] The economic theory of federalism is seen to provide crucial insights into the assignment of policy tasks between different levels of government. It analyses which level of government should undertake which economic tasks and seeks to find the most appropriate means of sharing responsibilities through the various jurisdictions or levels of government in order to optimise performance. It attempts to determine an optimal allocation of public finances both horizontally and vertically. Federalism, therefore, provides a useful framework for any discussion on the assignment of competences to different political levels within the EU.

The idea of federalism builds on the principle of subsidiarity. While the principle of subsidiarity is neutral about the optimal degree of centralisation (Ederveen et al. 2008, p. 20), it is seen to first and foremost assign power to the lowest effective level of government: the lowest governmental level should act, if it can do better than a higher governmental level.[6] With respect to this, the theory of

---

4 For a discussion on the extent to which the European Union is a federation see, for example, Börzl (2003). See also Benz/Zimmermann (2008).

5 See additionally for a summary of the main considerations of the economic theory of federalism Ter-Minassian (1997), Inman/Rubinfeld (1997) as well as Bailey (1999).

6 See also Döring (1996) and (1999).

federalism offers three arguments for a decentralised fulfilment of tasks. First, the heterogeneity of preferences of residents is considered. Central governments face informational problems regarding the requirements of their citizens and often also have a limited ability to differentiate policies across jurisdictions. The lower the level of government the easier it is to assess which public goods and services are demanded by local residents. In order to understand the second argument it is necessary to highlight that the economic theory of federalism stems from the so-called welfare economics approach. According to this approach it is traditionally assumed that governments act as benevolent maximizers of social welfare, meaning that a government only and exclusively tries to satisfy the preferences of the citizens.

From a political economic perspective, however, this hypothesis is considered over-simplified. If the assumption of benevolent officials is relaxed, governments may also pursue their own aims, which will not always coincide with those of society. But on a lower government level the incentive to provide market-enhancing public goods is higher, as transparency in public transactions is increased and citizens can more effectively control power. Thirdly, the existence of local and regional authorities allows for competition within the public sector. Following the considerations of Tiebout (1956), individuals vote with their feet based on in which jurisdiction service provision is best. Therefore, competition between decentralised governments produced by mobile citizens increases the efficiency of public policies and enhances political and organisational innovation, as governments have to provide for an optimal ratio of services and tax burden. According to Weingast (2009), effective competition is only possible if the subnational governments have the authority to adapt policies to their circumstances, a well functioning common market in the sense of product and factor mobility exists, the budget is constrained so that the full financial consequences of policy decisions have to be taken, and finally, if sub-national governments have institutionalised authority.

Although the arguments mentioned above clearly support a decentralised assignment of competences, a centralised provision of public services is favourable under certain circumstances, which will be outlined below. First of all it is necessary to refer again to the preference argument. In the case of largely homogeneous preferences concerning the demand for a public good, the responsibility for its provision can be centralised.[7]

Furthermore, two efficiency arguments need to be mentioned here – economies of scale and regional spillovers. A subnational government may be

---

7 This is in line with the so called principle of fiscal equivalence, which was introduced by Olson (1969) and which implies that those who consume a public good should be identical to those who pay for its provision and who decide upon its provision.

too small to effectively provide a public good for its population. If a common good exploits economies of scale, a centralised fulfilment is preferable. This is for instance true for defence policy. In the case of regional spillovers (externalities) a decentralised accomplishment of tasks may have (un)desirable consequences for neighbouring jurisdictions. This is the case, for example, for negative environmental effects due to cross-border pollution or positive external effects caused by the provision of a hospital that is also used by neighbouring regions.

Two additional circumstances under which centralisation should be considered are the existence of economic disparities and negative dynamics of competition. As regional economies differ in their income and hence their ability to offer public goods and services, redistributive justice can only be achieved by a levying of taxes of the central government and a transfer system to the subnational governments. Action by the national government is also required if the competition between the political authorities has negative effects on the economy. The competition between decentralised governments produced by mobile citizens should not lead to a 'race-to-the-bottom' in terms of taxes and hence the quality of public goods (Oates 1972).

European budget allocation – *status quo*

Before offering any further analysis of the allocation of political functions between different levels of government within the EU, it is certainly of interest to first look at the financing of the EU. Here a brief outline of developments in the budgetary situation of the EU and current trends in the European budget should provide an interesting backdrop to a subsequent analysis of how tasks are allocated or might be better allocated within the EU.

The budget of the European Union amounted to EUR 130.9 billion in 2008. This amount might at first appear quite significant, but at a second glance it becomes obvious that the figure is rather low compared to the budget of its Member States or other federations.[8] The EU budget covers approximately 1.1 per cent of the European Union GNP, which immediately indicates the small size of the budget – especially bearing in mind that federal government expenditure usually covers some 10 to 30 per cent of a nation's GNP (Ardy/El-Agraa 2004, p. 337). So in relative terms, the European budget is small and as such of marginal economic importance (Pelkmans 2006, p. 412). Another difference be-

---

8 This may explain the provocative subtitle Feld (2005) gave his paper on the level and structure of the EU budget: "Much ado about nothing?". He also states that "with such a small budget, no major EU policies in the three areas – provision of public goods, redistribution and stabilization – may be expected" (ibid., p. 259).

tween the European budget and national budgets is the fact that it is not permissible for the budget of the European Union to be in deficit: Revenues must cover the costs of all activities undertaken by the EU. The budget of the European Union is decided upon democratically. A multi-annual agreement on EU expenditures is reached by the European Parliament, the Council of Ministers, and the European Commission; whereby the latter additionally proposes annual spending plans which are negotiated by the Parliament and the Council.[9] The most recent financial framework covers the seven-year period 2007 to 2013.

Figure 1 Financial framework of the EU

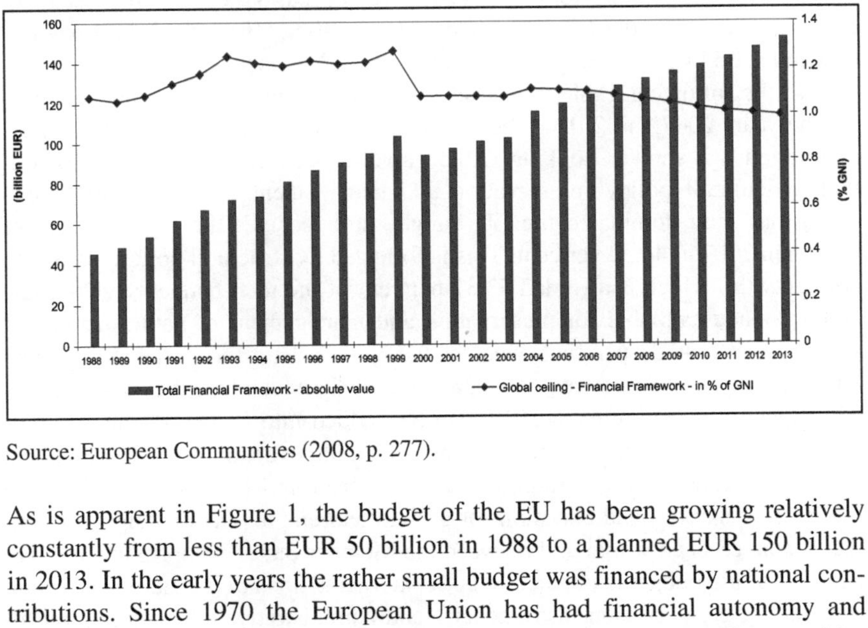

Source: European Communities (2008, p. 277).

As is apparent in Figure 1, the budget of the EU has been growing relatively constantly from less than EUR 50 billion in 1988 to a planned EUR 150 billion in 2013. In the early years the rather small budget was financed by national contributions. Since 1970 the European Union has had financial autonomy and raises a part of its revenues (14.3% in 2008 according to European Communities 2009, p. 68) by taxes that are distinct from those of the Member States (e.g. tariff revenues on imports of agricultural goods). Over the years the expenditures have grown, mainly in the field of agriculture[10] – which has been a source of dispute among the Member States. Consequently, various revisions of the budget and its arrangements have been undertaken (Delors I in 1988, Delors II

[9] For further details on the budget process see for example Zeff (2004). See also the explanation of the budget procedures in Feld (2005, 289 pp.).

[10] Agricultural spending increased from 38% of total spending in 1965 to 92% in 1970 (Feld 2005, p. 276).

in 1992). As a result, a multi-annual financial perspective and an inter-institutional[11] agreement on budgetary procedures were introduced, the agricultural policy reformed and expenditures for structural development, internal policies as well as external action increased. Further budgetary modifications were then needed due to the Eastern enlargement of the European Union (Agenda 2000).[12] Discussions over budget expenditures have been a constant ever since. The European Union is not a national state but is made up of 27 nation states. The differences between these 27 states are striking – with a variation in income levels even greater than that of the US (Ardy/El-Agraa 2004, p. 338). Hence, on the one hand aid policies for convergence are needed, but on the other hand equity is requested by the Member States. The question 'How much do I pay and how much do I get?' is the most prevalent among Member States.

In the following Table, the structure of the budget of the European Union for the years 2007 and 2013 – the beginning and end year of the current financial period – is shown. Looking at the Table, it becomes immediately obvious that agricultural policy (preservation and management of natural resources), which has long dominated the EU budget, still receives the highest share of budget in 2007 at 44.32 per cent. This is followed by structural policies (sustainable growth), which is awarded 43.37 per cent of the total budget. By 2013 the amount made available for preservation and management of natural resources will decline to 40.33 per cent, whereas the budget share for sustainable growth will increase to 45.81 per cent. Sustainable growth, which tops the table in terms of budgetary expenditure for 2013, can be divided into two components: competitiveness for growth and employment, (including expenditure on research and innovation, education and training, trans-European networks, social policy and the internal market) and cohesion for growth and employment (designed to enhance convergence within and between the Member States). Approximately five per cent of the budget is donated to both external actions of the European Union – including pre-accession instruments – and administrative expenditures for all institutions and pensions; these can be found in third and fourth position within the Table below. Finally, between 1.02 per cent and 1.56 per cent of the budget are reserved for citizenship, freedom, security and justice, including home affairs, border protection, immigration and asylum policy, public health and consumer protection, culture, youth, information and dialogue with citizens.

---

[11] European Commission, European Council and European Parliament are involved in the budget agreement procedure.

[12] See for example Baldwin/Wyplosz (2006, p. 61) for an overview on the milestones in the EU budget procedure.

Table 1 Structure of expenditure 2007 and 2013 (at current prices)

	2007		2013	
	Mio. EUR	%	Mio. EUR	%
Sustainable growth	53979	43.37	69621	45.81
Preservation and management of natural resources	55143	44.31	61289	40.33
EU as a global player	6578	5.29	9595	6.31
Administration	7039	5.66	9095	5.98
Citizenship, freedom, security, and justice	1273	1.02	2376	1.56
Compensations[13]	445	0.36	-	-
Total	**124457**	**100.00**	**151976**	**100.00**

Source: European Communities (2008, p. 253).

Table 1 provides an overview of the relative importance of policy tasks within the European Union. In the following section, the economic theory of federalism will be used to analyse whether these competences should really be carried out at European level, which of them could probably be carried out at Member States level and, last but not least, which tasks are left out in Table 1 but should be fulfilled at European level regarding economic considerations.

Are economic theory and EU practice compatible?

As described above, the theory of federalism offers a set of criteria that can be used to determine how competences can best be allocated between different levels of government. This section discusses the principles of optimal task allocation within the EU as can be read from this economic theory and provides an analysis of the current division of competences before offering suggestions on how tasks might be reallocated to the different levels of governance.

Bearing in mind the results of described above, the general guideline of economic federalism is that redistribution and stabilisation should be centralised, while the allocation of the different public goods and services should follow a decentralisation principle. Furthermore, policies should be allocated to the highest federal level in cases where economies of scale and/or spatial (supranational) externalities prevail, whereas in cases where there is a high heterogeneity of preferences relative to externalities competences should be assigned to national or sub-national levels. While it is relatively unusual for the division of competences not to be clearly defined, this is the case within the European Un-

[13] The term 'compensation' refers to temporary post-accession amounts related to the latest enlargement of the European Union (Bulgaria and Romania).

ion. The idea initially discussed as part of the European Constitution drafting process of identifying a catalogue of competences was quickly dropped as this was not considered feasible. Nonetheless, over the years the EU has acquired increased competences in a number of areas, this becomes obvious if we again consider the increasing budget described above. It goes without saying that the specificities of the European Union account for a number of differences when compared to other federal systems or federations. Hence, the conclusions of the economic theory of federalism will be analysed in terms of their applicability to the specific case of the European Union.

Generally, three major types of competence division within the EU are defined: exclusive competences of the union, shared or concurrent competences of both the union and Member States, and areas of complementary, supporting or coordinating action.[14] In a very general sense it is argued that the EU has acquired exclusive competences in market-creating policies and shares competences with the Member States in market-correcting policies. Task areas in which EU level involvement is generally considered justified are those areas in which the EU level can generate normatively higher allocative efficiency due to economies of scale realisation, internalisation of spatial (supra-national) externalities, homogeneity of preferences, or the harmonisation of (market) distorting national regulations. Bearing this in mind, the creation of a common market with a common external trade policy is probably one of the most important policy areas assigned to the EU. There is generally widespread recognition of the need for the EU to play a strong role in the implementation of the Single Market – including competition policy (because of the negative transnational spillover of uncompetitive behaviour) and the free market (see Eichenberger/Hosp 2001, Holler et al. 1996, Persson et al. 1996, Smekal 2001, Tabellini 2003 and Rischkowsky 2007). Monetary policy is widely considered to be one of the most successful policy areas of the EU. Here economies of scale are seen to be inherent in gathering supervisory information, while the possible negative transnational spillover of financial fragility is also recognised (Shah 2002, Smekal 2001 and Alesina et al. 2005).

As far as fiscal policy is concerned, policies for stabilisation purposes remain a national responsibility – while the monitoring of these policies at EU level can be seen as part of broader economic policy guidelines within the framework of the Stability and Growth Pacts (Tabellini 2003). In light of recent developments associated with the economic and financial crisis, some commentators are now calling for increased fiscal policy co-ordination at EU level. Public goods such as defence, foreign policy, internal security, border control, and immigration policy are, to a large extent, still national prerogatives; although the EU's role here is seen to be growing (as can also be seen by the increasing

[14] See Vaneecloo et al. (2006, p. 191) for a concise table outlining these EU policy divisions.

budget in the fields of 'EU as a global player' and 'Citizenship, freedom, security, and justice' in Table 1). Commentators argue that there could be increased benefits to a more centralised provision of policies in these areas. Defence and foreign affairs are considered appropriate EU competences because of the economies of scale and externalities to be exploited, assuming that geopolitical preferences are similar (see Alesina et al. 2005, Tabelini 2003, Shah 2002 and Hoeller et al. 1996). Both economies of scale and of rationalisation could enable the EU to enhance its military capabilities in relation to defence expenditures quite significantly (see Dardanelli 2005). Recent Eurobarometer results also indicate European citizens' widespread approval for increased EU involvement in these areas.[15]

In terms of the political tasks assigned to the Member States, we can identify a number of policy areas where economic experts tend to agree that responsibility should be primarily assigned to the national or sub-national government level. For example, in the case of industry, energy and agricultural policy there is general agreement that task assignment should be at national level. Agriculture is one of the oldest and perhaps most controversial EU policy areas, and it is the policy area that still receives the largest chunk of EU financial resources. EU involvement in agriculture is considered too great and calls for redistribution in this area to be scaled back are increasing in resonance. There are predominantly pragmatic arguments, such as a greater reliance on market forces, used against agriculture remaining an EU level competency (see for example Grethe 2008, Alesina et al. 2005 and Hoeller et al. 1996). At the same time proponents of centralisation base their arguments on an increase of EU-wide labour mobility through the harmonisation of academic or educational grades at EU level, or the adverse effects of sub-national activities on the stock of human capital (Ter-Minassian 1997 and Persson et al. 1996).

There are a number of tasks and competences for which it is not possible to assign responsibility to just one level. The environment is such a case. Environmental effects can be international/global or local/regional. Arguments speaking for a European Union level involvement include EU-wide externalities, economies of scale, and regulation in the case of market distortions because of disparities between national environmental standards. However, these arguments are countered in favour of Member State assignment of environmental issues based on the existence of local environmental externalities with no cross-border spillovers. The actual enforcement of environmental policies is also likely to have a strong national and sub-national component (see Alesina et al. 2005, Feld 2005, Döring 1997 and Hoeller et al. 1996). EU involvement in terms of EU-wide ex-

---

[15] Current surveys show that 79% of respondents believe that decisions on fighting terrorism should be taken jointly at European level, and 64% believe that defence and foreign affairs decisions should be a European policy. See Eurobarometer Standard 69.

ternalities certainly seems desirable. In terms of education, a number of authors make convincing arguments for the decentralisation of this competence because of heterogeneous local preferences, positive effects of inter-jurisdictional competition, or limited cross-national externalities (see Alesina et al. 2005, Smekal 2001 and Persson et al. 1996).

In the majority of cases, it can be argued that the *de facto* distribution of political tasks within the European Union corresponds to a greater or lesser extent to normative economic advice (monetary policy, environmental policy, competition policy etc.). Some discrepancies exist, as has already been pointed out, in areas such as defence and agriculture. It is widely believed that the EU role in agricultural policy should be confined largely to trade policy and not to the complete regulation of markets or the paying of direct subsidies. In defence, which is one of the public goods where supra-national externalities of decisions are strongest, centralised provision is recommended.

Conclusions

In conclusion it can be said that the current allocation of tasks within the EU is partly inconsistent with normative criteria relating to the assignment of tasks to different levels of government. A precise definition of an optimal degree of (de)centralisation is not possible because of mixed theoretical suggestions. Therefore, the appropriate degree of (de-)centralisation must be determined on a case-by-case, policy-by-policy basis. Economists focus their analysis of the assignment of competences mainly on geographical spillovers, economies of scale and the spatial structure of preferences. When comparing the *de facto* delimitation of EU competences with the normative recommendations provided by economists, discrepancies arise in particular in the fields of agriculture and defence. Additional discrepancies are detected in the fields of education (see Van der Ploeg/Veugelers 2008, Gérad 2008, Ederveen/Thissen 2008), as well as macroeconomic stabilisation and tax policy (see Keen/De Mooij 2008, Pouget/Stécle-bout-Orseau 2008). Any expansion of EU tasks in any of these areas would require significant institutional reforms – either new institutions or the reform of existing ones.

It is likely that the most important areas of federal government activity (especially budget-intensive areas such as health, social security or education) will continue to remain national. In a number of these areas, Member States and their citizens are still not prepared to transfer further responsibility to the EU; this is because the EU comprises mature national states determined to preserve a significant degree of national sovereignty. As a result, the EU does not have a budget comparable with existing federations, nor does it have significant responsibilities in relation to any of the services or political tasks that dominate central government level in mature federal systems. In keeping with its nature as a loose federation, the likelihood therefore is that the EU's role in various political areas will remain limited.

There is clearly no ideal system for the delimitation of competences. As conditions change over time, public goods experience variability in their spatial characteristics. That is, innovations, technical adjustments and/or unstable preferences change cost-functions and consequently require dynamic responses within the competence distribution scheme. Against this background it must be considered essential that both the EU and its division of competences remain flexible in order to adapt to these changing conditions. Taking the principle of subsidiarity seriously, Breuss/Eller (2003) did make some notable suggestions in order to facilitate a more flexible competence allocation within the European Union. One of their recommendations is to establish a sunset legislation (i.e. assigned competences with a limited duration) in order to prevent a permanent centralisation of various political tasks. Another suggestion is that the proponents of centralisation should bear the onus of proof in the case of intended shifts of political competences within the EU. Finally and most meaningfully, a reversibility-guaranteeing revision procedure should be developed and included in the constitutional treaty of the EU. It remains to be seen, whether such economically sound suggestions regarding procedural and institutional changes within the assignment of political competences between the EU and its Member States will be implemented in the future.

References

Alesina, Alberto/Ignazio Angeloni/Ludger Schuknecht (2005), 'What does the European Union Do?', *Public Choice*, Vol. 123, pp. 275 - 319.

Ardy, Brian/Ali El-Agraa (1982), 'The general budget', in D. K. Whynes/R. A. Bowles (eds.), *The Economic Theory of the State,* pp. 332 - 352.

Ardy, Brian/Ali El-Agraa (2004), 'The general budget', in A. El-Agraa (ed.): *The European Union*, 7th Edition, Pearson Education Limited, Essex, pp. 334 - 352.

Bailey, Stephen J. (1999), *Local Government Economics*, Palgrave Macmillan, Basingstoke.

European Communities (2008): *European Union Public Finance*, 4th Edition, Brussels.

European Communities (2009): *EU budget 2008*, Luxembourg.

Baldwin, Richard/Charles Wyplosz (2004), *The Economics of European Integration*, 2nd Edition, McGraw-Hill Education, Berkshire.

Belke, Ansgar/Daniel Gros (2009), 'On the benefits of fiscal policy coordination in a currency union-a note', in *Empirica*, Vol. 36, pp. 45 - 49.

Benz, Arthur/Christina Zimmer (2008), 'The EU's competences: The "vertical" perspective on the multilevel system', in *Living Reviews in European Governance*, Vol. 3, 30 June 2008, online article [http://european-governance.livingreviews.org/Articles/lreg-2008-3/] retrieved on 4.11.2009.

Benson, David/Andrew Jordan (2008), 'Understanding task allocation in the European Union: exploring the value of federal theory', in *Journal of European Public Policy*, Vol.15, pp.78 - 97.

Börzl, Tanja A. (2003), 'What Can Federalism Teach Us About the European Union? – The German Experience', Conference Paper, R.I. of International Affairs, Chatam House, [http://www.isn.ethz.ch/isn/Current-Affairs/Policy-Briefs/Detail/?lng=en&id=22983]

retrieved on 4.11.2009.

Breuss, Fritz/Markus Eller (2003), 'Efficiency and Federalism in the European Union – The Optimal Assignment of Policy Tasks to Different Levels of Government', *IEF Working Paper*, No. 50, Vienna.

Dardanelli, Paolo (2005), 'Conclusions: Comparative Federalism and the Constitutional Treaty', in *Regional and Federal Studies*, Vol. 15, pp. 259 - 269.

De Borger, Bruno/Stef Proost (2008), 'Subsidiarity and Transport Policy in Europe: What EU Subsidies Do We Need for the TEN', in G. Gelauff et al. (eds.), *Subsidiarity and Economic Reform in Europe,* Springer, Berlin/Heidelberg, pp. 325 - 341.

Döring, Thomas (1996), 'Das Subsidiaritätsprinzip in der Europäischen Union', in *ORDO – Jahrbuch für die Ordnung von Wirtschaft und Gesellschaft*, Vol. 47, pp. 292 - 323.

Döring, Thomas (1997), *Subsidiarität und Umweltpolitik in der Europäischen Union*, Metropolis, Marburg.

Döring, Thomas (1999), 'Marktwirtschaftliche Ordnung und föderativer Staatsaufbau – Zu den Möglichkeiten einer ökonomischen Deutung des Subsidiaritätsprinzips und seiner Anwendung in der Europäischen Union', in W. J. Mückl (ed.), *Subsidiarität – Gesellschaftsprinzip für eine freiheitliche Ordnung in Staat, Wirtschaft und Gesellschaft*, Schöningh, Paderborn, pp. 63 - 91.

Ederveen, Sjef/George Gelauff/Jacques Pelkmans (2008), 'Assessing Subsidiarity', in G. Gelauff et al. (eds.), *Subsidiartity and Economic Reform in Europe,* Springer, Berlin/ Heidelberg, pp. 19 - 40.

Ederveen, Sjef/Laura Thissen (2008), 'European Coordination of Higher Education', in G. Gelauff et al. (eds.), *Subsidiartity and Economic Reform in Europe,* Springer, Berlin/ Heidelberg, pp. 113 - 128.

Eichenberger, Reiner/Gerald Hosp (2001), 'Die institutionellen Leitplanken wirkungsvollen Förderalismus, Erfahrungen aus der Schweiz', in P. Pernthaler/P. Bußjäger (eds.), *Ökonomische Aspekte des Förderalismus*, Institut für Förderalismus, Schriftenreihe Vol. 83, Innsbruck, pp. 87 - 104.

Feld, Lars P. (2005), 'European Public Finances: Much ado about nothing?', in M. P. van der Hoek (ed.), *Handbook of Public Administration and Public Policy in the European Union*, Taylor & Francis, London, pp. 257 - 310.

Gérard, Marcel (2008), 'Higher Education, Mobility and the Subsidiarity Principle', in G. Gelauff et al. (eds.), *Subsidiartity and Economic Reform in Europe,* Springer, Berlin/ Heidelberg, pp. 97 - 112.

Grethe, Harald (2008), 'Agriculture Policy: What Roles for the EU and the Member States', in G. Gelauff et al. (eds.), *Subsidiartity and Economic Reform in Europe,* Springer, Berlin/ Heidelberg, pp. 191 - 218.

Hoeller, Peter/Marie-Odile Louppe/Patrice Vergriete (1996), 'Fiscal Relations within the Economic Union', *OECD Economic Department Working Papers 163*, Paris.

Inman, Robert P./Daniel L. Rubinfeld (1997), 'Rethinking Federalism', in *Journal of Economic Perspectives*, Vol. 11, pp. 43 - 64.

Keen, Michael/Ruud De Mooij (2008), 'Tax Policy and Subsidiarity in the European Union', in G. Gelauff et al. (eds.), *Subsidiarity and Economic Reform in Europe,* Springer, Berlin/Heidelberg, pp. 219 - 242.

Oates, Wallace E. (1972), *Fiscal Federalism*, Harcourt Brace Jovanovich, New York.

Oates, Wallace E. (1999), 'An Essay on Fiscal Federalism', in *Journal of Economic Literature*, Vol. 37, pp. 1120 - 1149.

Oates, Wallace E. (2005), 'Toward a Second-Generation Theory of Fiscal Federalism', in

International Tax and Public Finance, Vol. 12, pp. 349 - 373.

Olson, Mancur (1969), 'The Principle of Fiscal Equivalence: The Division of Responsibilities Among Different Levels of Government', in *American Economic Review*, Vol. 59, pp. 479 - 487.

Pelkmans, Jacques (2006), *European Integration Methods and Economic Analysis*, 3rd Edition, Pearson Education Limited, London.

Persson, Torsten/Gerard Roland/Guido Tabellini (1996), 'The Theory of Fiscal Federalism: What does it mean for Europe?', Paper to be prepared for the Conference *Quo Vadis Europe?*, June 1996, Kiel.

Pouget, Francios/Eloise Stéclebout-Orseau (2008), 'Corporate Income Taxation and the Subsidiarity Principle', in G. Gelauff et al. (eds.), *Subsidiarity and Economic Reform in Europe,* Springer, Berlin/Heidelberg, pp. 273 - 290.

Rischkowsky, Franziska (2007), *Europäische Verbraucherpolitik*, Metropolis, Marburg.

Shah, Anwar (2002), 'Fiscal Decentralization in Transition Economies and Developing Countries – Progress, Problems and the Promise', in *Conference Reader of the International Conference on Federalism 2002 'Federalism in a Changing World – Learning from Each Other'*, 27 - 30 August 2002, St. Gallen.

Schmieding, Holger (2009), 'The Case Against a Common Fiscal Boost in Europe', in *Intereconomics*, Vol. 44, pp. 4 - 9.

Smekal, Christian (2001), 'Zentralisation and Dezentralisation öffentlicher Aufgabenerfüllung aus finanzwissenschaftlicher Sicht', in Pernthaler, P./Bußjäger, P. (eds.), *Ökonomische Aspekte des Förderalismus*, Institut für Förderalismus, Schriftenreihe Vol. 83, Innsbruck 2001, pp. 69 - 76.

Smith, Julie/Soar Camilla (2003), 'Division of Competences in the European Union', Strategy Paper, Royal Institute of International Affairs, Chatam House, [http://www.swp-berlin.org/common/get_document.php? asset_ id=687] retrieved on 4.11.2009.

Standard Eurobarometer 69, April - May 2008, [http://ec.europa.eu/ public_ opinion/archives/eb/eb69/eb69_en.htm] retrieved on 4.11.2009.

Tabellini, Guido (2003), 'Principles of Policymaking in the European Union: An Economic Perspective', in *CESifo Economic Studies*, Vol. 49, pp. 75 - 102.

Ter-Minassian, Teresa (1997), 'Intergovernmental Fiscal Relations in a Macroeconomic Perspective: An Overview', in T. Ter-Minassian (ed.), *Fiscal Federalism in Theory and Practice*, IMF, Washington (D.C.).

Tiebout, Charles (1956), 'A pure theory of local expenditures', in *Journal of Political Economy*, Vol. 64, pp. 416 - 424.

Van der Horst, Albert/Arjan Lejour/Bas Straathof (2008), 'Why European Innovation Policy?', in G. Gelauff et al. (eds.), *Subsidiarity and Economic Reform in Europe,* Springer, Berlin/Heidelberg, pp. 143 - 156.

Van der Ploeg, Frederick/Reinhilde Veugelers (2008), 'Higher Education Reform and the Renewed Lisbon Strategy: Role of Member States and the European Commission', in G. Gelauff et al. (eds.), *Subsidiarity and Economic Reform in Europe,* Springer, Berlin/Heidelberg, pp. 65 - 96.

Vaneecloo, Clement/Augusto Badriotti/Margherita Fornasini (2006), *Fiscal Federalism in the EU and its Countries*, Peter Lang, Brussels.

Weingast, Barry R. (2009): 'Second generation fiscal federalism: The implications of fiscal incentives', in *Journal of Urban Economics*, Vol. 65, pp. 279 - 293.

Zeff, Eleanor E. (2004): 'The Budget and 'the Spending Policies', in N. Nugent (ed.), *European Union Enlargement*, Palgrave Macmillan, Basingstoke, pp. 171 - 183.

Lojze Sočan

The Role of Institutional Infrastructure in the Future of Europe

Introduction

The world today is not just in a global crisis; it's in the midst of an evolution from a globalized to a knowledge-based economy and society; a process, which is fundamentally changing the development concept, economic structure, and the governance of the majority of countries. Those, who are going to understand this process and react properly, will be facing not only a stronger global competitive position, but also safer development as well as a better life and healthier environment for their citizens. As global openness and competitiveness and the Single Market norms required the appropriate global, state and regional institutions to apply these systemic norms in practice, we are presently in a very similar position. We are even witnessing the good practices of the present global competitive and development leaders. They have been consciously and intensely building up an institutional infrastructure for promoting a knowledge-based economy and society over the past two decades. The Consensus Societies from Scandinavia, for the most part members of the EU, presently maintain an outstanding position among the global leaders, according to the International Institute for Management Development (IMD), Geneva, publishers of the World Competitiveness Yearbook (WCY), the World Economic Forum (WEF) and other relevant sources. Some EU member countries as well as some non-members are deliberately and successfully joining "this club"; these include Austria, Ireland and Switzerland in Europe, as well as Canada, Singapore, and to an increasing extent, Australia. The EU is in a good position to use the mirror of Consensus Societies with regard to its future development. However, a number of indicators suggest that the present leadership of the EU is not willing to take this opportunity.

At this most appropriate time, the Commission of the EU is launching an extremely important long-term strategic document covering its future qualitative transformation, which might also intensely influence the global development. However, in order to fulfil these expectations, profound qualitative improvements of the content and of the messages to be delivered by this document are required.

The contribution at hand first discusses the theoretical issues of the present evolution of global development systems. In this context an international comparison of the EU development concept, the structural changes, and the role of governance in the process of upgrading the globalization are put forward. In the second part the contribution goes on to elaborate selected cases of good practice from the present global development leaders during their long-term deliberate creation of modern institutional infrastructure, so as to promote the qualitative transformation of their countries into knowledge-based economy and society. The contribution strives to constantly evaluate the position as well as the behaviour of the EU in this contemporary process.

The reasons for change

Theoretical issues

Based on the theory of "economic freedom" (M. Friedman), profit-oriented capital combined with unlimited power succeeded in deregulating the global market, and created a "flat world" through an overwhelming application of ICT (T. Friedman). The openness and competitiveness of globalization brought with it unprecedented economic growth. However, this growth has been accompanied by growing ecological concerns, market consumption, and financial fundamentalism. In the name of profit the environment has been progressively ruined, the consumers have been seriously enslaved by the aggressive supply of products and services, while progressively speculative and profit-inspired financial transactions, which have reached nearly one hundred times the value of the world's GDP, have allowed capital to achieve incomparably higher rewards than a thorough investment into the complex knowledge of nations (education, R&D, upgrading, ICT), as well as into technological development. As a consequence, the global crisis was inevitable (see Diagram 1 below).

On the other hand, more than a decade ago, a smaller number of EU members, first of all the Scandinavian countries (progressively approaching are also Austria, Switzerland, Ireland, and beyond EU borders also Canada and Singapore etc.), deliberately entered a process of systemically upgrading global openness and competitiveness and the Single Market norms, respectively. The levers of such a long-term and consensus-based development vision consistently promoted complex knowledge of nations, permanent and growing investments into development and application of modern technologies (e.g. High Technology Finland, 2007), up to motivation of innovation in business, public sector, and government, covering 100 per cent of the country's GDP creation. These EU members also highly respected the Lisbon strategy targets. As a result, these efforts are not only creating a more humane form of capitalism in these countries; they have also raised their competitiveness, development efficiency and safety, and are pushing forward sustainable development. These countries, mostly called Consensus Societies, according to WCY and other leading world statistics, have recently been referred to as contemporary global development leaders.

Diagram 1 Evolution of development systems

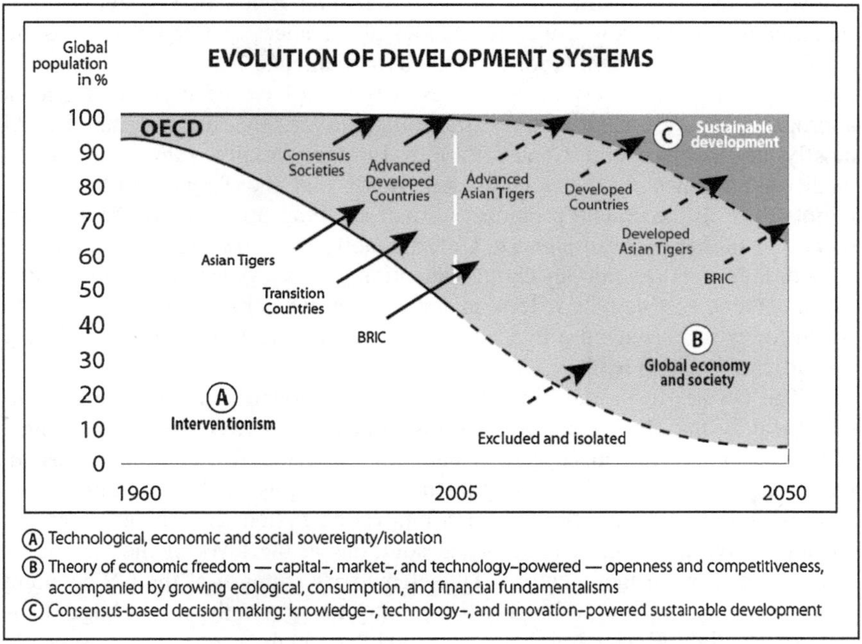

Source: L. Sočan (2006)

The most recent paper by the Commission – **EU 2020** obviously has long-term strategic aspirations; however, it seriously lacks an appropriate theoretical elaboration of the contemporary development evolution of the present world's dominant development system – **globalization** in the direction of the knowledge-based economy and society with sustainable development.

Development concept

The development concept of the EU 2020, including the proposed improvements, is obsolete, too. Over the last 50 years this integration has evolved from "The New dynamic Europe within the Old static world into the ageing of the majority of the EU (with the exception of Consensus Societies) in the New (dynamic) World" (Sočan 2008, 47 pp.).

Therefore, it calls for an upgrading of the Single Market norms by the advanced institutional infrastructure at the level of the EU, the member countries and their regions, business, labour, as well as civil society, so as to promote development on the basis of permanently growing complex knowledge (education, upgrading, R&D, ICT), constant technological advance, and comprehensive innovation. Within the EU, the Consensus Societies dispose of extremely effective innovation-oriented institutional infrastructure and innovation systems. Their functioning places knowledge, technological advance, and innovation as the number one development priority of their parliaments. Respecting this fundamental priority the governments of these countries have been carrying out the appropriate policies, measures, and financing. On the other hand, within the EU, mostly in Southern and Central-Eastern Europe, usually with insufficiently qualified administration, the belief still holds that the Single Market norms might solve all the crucial problems of their catching up with modern development and global competitiveness. Unfortunately, the most recent document of the Commission does not pay enough attention to this problem common to many EU members. Let us take a look at the reasons why the dynamic part of the world today has accepted a more advanced development concept in relation to this official one held by the EU.

The US has for a long time been the most innovative nation in the world. It's not only the Bayh-Dole act; the investments into R&D by business have been frequently co-financed, strategically enriched and also coordinated by the federal government and its leading agencies, as well as by the elite universities and institutes. The network of the US innovation system absorbs and supports the innovative ideas and technological solutions at the level of the US, of the states, as well as of their regions. This elementary strength of the US economy was largely responsible for helping the country to survive the recent huge financial crisis and the Bush administration. Notably enough, also for the present EU, as early as the Nineties, the famous economist Lester Thurow already wrote that the entire developed world would be much better off with an institutional infrastructure, similar to that of the Scandinavian countries.

To enhance development, the BRIC countries (Brazil, Russia, India and China) and the majority of Pacific countries with more than four billion inhabitants between them, have been upgrading their global openness and competitiveness with appropriate institutional levers to stimulate above average growth, regardless of the level of their economic, social and technological development:

- For more than one and a half decades Brazil has been constantly improving the Gini coefficient; mostly through offering subsidies to the poorest families when sending their kids to elementary school. In addition, the governments, the regions, and increasingly the business sector, have been organizing and co-financing hundreds of thousands of seminars and upgrading opportunities for employed and unemployed people, in order to raise their employability and, at the same time, to improve the social cohesion of this country. As a consequence, this large and rich country has been progressively creating a sufficiently capable labour force to qualify for massive investments of domestic and foreign capital into technologically undemanding sectors.

- Russia, after the collapse of the Soviet Union (SU) and its socialist economy, and having gone through very hard times in the Nineties during its rough systemic transition, succeeded in a development revival (Putin) on the basis of a well designed energy strategy. However, at the same time, this country made a serious development mistake by inviting intense FDI into low wage and low value added industrial sectors. This country disposes of sufficient general education, of a high level of technical expertise at the majority of universities and institutes, as well as of important high technology sectors, mostly in the military area. Therefore, it is now facing a process of progressive transformation of the nation's education and universities' and institutes' scientific expertise into technological advance and innovation. However, the qualitative transformation of this economy and society is not only a question of education and technological expertise; it is also a question of true democratic consensus in the process of decision-making and taking advantage of the results, from the level of the state to the level of municipalities and firms. The energy sector might be in a position to support such a process for one generation.
- Particularly during the last decade, India has invigorated the process of openness and competitiveness with a number of strategic activities. The synergy of these processes creates the ground for the above average rate of growth, and for placing this subcontinent country among the most promising and powerful economies and societies. The following strategies have to be listed: India is rapidly decreasing illiteracy, further improving its good school system and raising the quality of university education and research. The industrial North is undergoing a process of technological and innovative transformation and structural change as one of the largest industrial countries in the world. The whole country, from business to civil society is being networked by modern information and communication technologies and knowledge networks. This is the environment, which calls back to India millions of well educated and experienced professionals from all over the world, thus also helping this country with the process of cultural transformation. As a result, India is entering the club of important R&D investors, including a countless number of high tech firms in business and at the universities. The share of high technology products and services in the total exports of the country is also rising.
- China, in accordance with a long-term gradual and controlled process of openness and competitiveness, has improved the complex knowledge of its constituent nations, and is constantly raising the employability of a growing share of the total population. In addition to the extremely complex technological transformation of industry and services, including the position of the world's largest receiver of foreign direct investments, China has already become the number one exporter. What is incomparably more im-

portant, however, is that in a few years China will surpass the EU with regard to the share of GDP invested into R&D. This process has been accompanied by the deliberate repatriation, including partly working in China, of thousands of the most experienced scientists, researchers, and other experts, mostly from the US. Accompanied by an extremely high level of savings, in this country the domestic consumption has been "a must" for nearly a decade. On top of that, China has recently become by far the largest financial power of the world and the biggest financer of the US trade and budget deficit. As a result of these strategies and trends China is entering the group of main global development powers.

- The Pacific Rim, ranging from highly developed Japan to Vietnam, but not including those countries in a state of civil war and isolated dictatorships, is a huge development pool, which progressively invests into the complex knowledge of nations, including R&D. These countries are progressively accepting the technological and innovative upgrading as the core of the structural change of their economic and societal structure, regardless of their level of economic, social and technological development.

One may conclude that the majority of the EU is falling behind the development concept of Consensus Societies, US, BRIC, most of the Pacific Rim, the countries accounting for about four billion of the world's population. These countries respect the concept of global openness and competitiveness, but progressively upgrade it by the means of a stronger and stronger investment cycle into the complex knowledge of their nations, as well as into the technology- and innovation-based qualitative transformation of their economies and societies. At the same time the leadership of the EU must accept serious blame for not taking advantage of their own mirror – the Consensus Society member countries, which have been the world development leaders for nearly a decade and have reasonable dispositions to keep this position in the future as well.

Structural changes

The situation

Regarding the development concept and the level of economic, social and technological development, four major areas are characteristic within the present EU: the most advanced Consensus Societies, the large developed welfare countries, the South European members, and the newly accepted Central European and Baltic Member States – CEB.

- For the last decade, the Consensus Societies, highly developed member countries with the most advanced development concept, have been ranked within the top quarter of the most competitive global economies (the global development leaders).
- Highly developed large EU welfare states with a progressively obsolete development concept, have been ranked mostly within the second quarter of the globally most competitive economies. Germany has made the greatest progress during the recent period; a continuous approach of the largest EU economy towards the development concept of Consensus Societies might play a decisive role in the qualitative transformation process of the entire EU.
- The Southern European and the new CEB Member States with the most obsolete or even backward development concept, take a position within the third and fourth quarter of the countries analyzed, according to global competitiveness and successful development, as measured by the IMD.

Diagram 2 Qualitative transformation of the EU economies towards knowledge-based economies and societies

(Assessment for new members, Southern Europe, EU average and Consensus Societies)

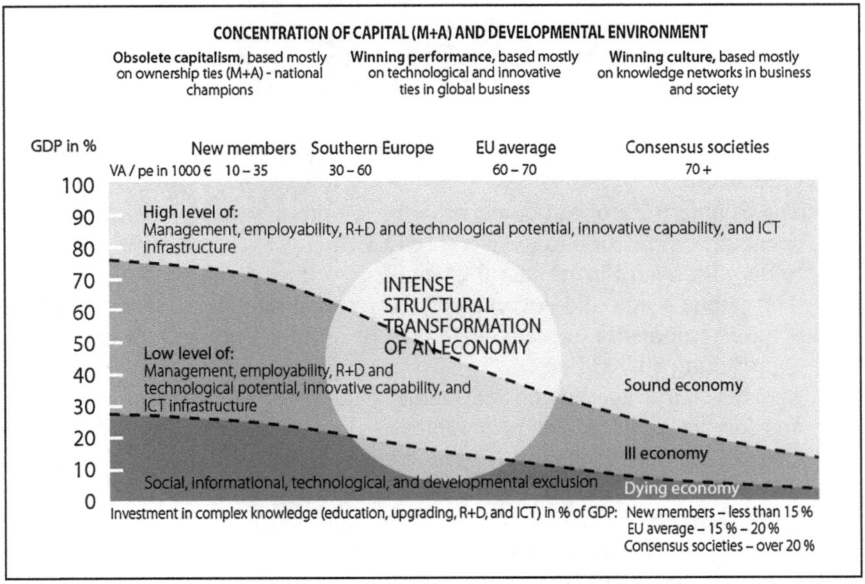

Source: Project - Simulations of sustainable development, on the basis of IMD, WEF, OECD and other data bases (Sočan, 2008)

The present economic structure corresponds to the above diverse levels of development in the four characteristic areas of the EU. According to the IMD and WEF competitiveness reports, Diagram 2 above presents the structural diversity of the EU economies across four areas. It has been assessed on the basis of the share of globally competitive economic potential of the Member States (sound economy – the upper belt) in relation to the share of economic potential with managerial, technological, financial, employment, structural, exports and other problems (ailing economy – the medium belt), and the share of dying economic potential (dying economy – the lower belt). Corresponding is also the value added per employee, where one also has to add the level of qualitative reforms in the public sector and government, progressively influencing the quality and efficiency of their services for business and citizens.

According to the four areas the results are the following:

- The least developed Member States (e.g. Bulgaria and Romania) of the CEB hardly exceed the share of one quarter of sound economy, with about half of an ailing economy, and nearly one quarter of a dying economy; the value added per employee does not reach 15,000 Euro. On the other hand, the share of sound economy in the more advanced CEB countries like Slovenia, Czech Republic, as well as Cyprus comes to about half, with a correspondingly lower share of non-competitive economy, while the value added per employee exceeds 30,000 Euro. These economies are presently in the midst of a more or less successful qualitative transformation and reforms of the public sector and government. The global crisis is spurring this process on.
- The Southern European countries have a more advanced structure in their economies in relation to the advanced CEB. However, they still have much to do with regard to structural change, as well as in the field of reforming their public sector and government. Correspondingly, their value added per employee normally exceeds 40,000 Euro (except Portugal), while Italy is approaching 60,000 Euro.
- The EU27 average has no real value, neither for the economic structure, nor for the value added per employee (around 50,000 Euro). Somehow clearer, but not sufficiently, is the average of the EU15 with over 60,000 Euro value added per employee, which is a mix of developed welfare states and Consensus Societies and Southern Europe. Still, the average of the EU15 consists of about 70 per cent of sound economy, 20 per cent of ailing economy, and about 10 per cent of dying economy.
- And finally, in the most advanced Consensus Societies (as well as in the western part of Germany) the soundness of their economies is at the highest level, and consists of close to 85 per cent of globally competitive potential, of about 10 per cent of economy with various problems, and less than 5 per

cent of dying economy. Corresponding is also the value added per employee, normally exceeding 70,000 Euro.

From this point of view, the global crisis did not "take away" ten years of growth in the EU; it took away, first of all, the globally uncompetitive part of the EU economic structure. And, what is even more dangerous, in the years to come, this process will be even fiercer, because of the present inferior development concept of the EU in relation to the countries with more than four billion population. Therefore, the present intense reforms of the public sector and the government have to continue hand in hand with the intense technology- and innovation-based structural changes of the economy, in particular in the Southern European Member States and the CEB. However, the solution to this problem, with the target to reduce the progressive loss of global competitiveness, is to improve the present development concept of the entire EU. This improvement should be directed, motivated, and even enforced in all EU member countries and their regions, in particular in the less developed ones.

The **EU 2020** also neglects the experience of the EU Member States – the Consensus Societies. These countries have achieved excellent development results through considerably higher and constant investments into the complex knowledge of their nations as a basis for growing employability and flexicurity, through the effective structural changes of their economies, as well as by thorough reforms of their public sectors and governments. These efforts have installed Consensus Societies as the contemporary global development leaders. The following Table, showing the average yearly growth of GDP and the yearly surplus or deficit in percentage of GDP during the period of "fat cows", is illustrative enough:

Table 1 Average yearly growth of the GDP in % and the budget surplus (+) or deficit (-) in percentage of GDP by some EU Member States during the period 2005 - 2008

EU member state	GDP	Budget in % of GDP	Total GDP accrual in %
Finland	3,2	4,1	7,2
Sweden	2,4	2,4	4,8
UK	2,1	- 4,4	- 2,3
Slovakia	8.0	- 2,5	5,5
Slovenia	5,0	- 1,1	3,8

Source: The Exit Strategy of Slovenia, Slovenian Government (2010)

The EU, so as to promote the qualitative transformation of the economy and society of all of its member countries, has to create the ground for a development synergy through consistent and growing investments into the complex knowledge of these nations, through comprehensive reforms of their public sectors and governments, as well as through strong and permanent technology- and innovation-based investment cycle in the economic sphere. In order to fulfil these requirements, the EU and its member countries will have to adapt or even completely transform their development concepts and governance from the present ones, which mainly support globalization, into knowledge-, technology- and innovation- supporting development concepts and governance within the open and competitive global economy and society. This task is urgent and long-term oriented. The less developed the member countries, the bigger will be their efforts, including the support of the more advanced EU member countries. The Consensus Societies can serve as a successful mirror in these efforts for all of the EU.

Evolution of governance: From governance promoting globalization to governance promoting a knowledge-based economy and society

The evolution of globalization towards knowledge-based economy and society or rather, the upgrading of globalization, has not been predominantly based on the change of policies. The process is much more profound. More than by theoreticians, this process has been consciously designed by sufficiently capable parliaments and governments of some countries or even broader regional areas like Scandinavia. The closest to this idea was the Lisbon strategy, mostly abandoned by the official leadership and the majority of the EU, except for the Consensus Societies.

The first qualitative breakthrough of this process is a new vision of development on knowledge, technological advance and innovation, which is supported by the permanent motivation of new values in an economy and society. In addition to freedom, peace, independence, democracy, openness and competitiveness, the social cohesion and tolerance, preservation of environment, the complex knowledge of nations as a basis for the growing employability of their people, technological advance and innovation, a transparency of all activities, up to long-term strategic thinking of managing the change, which progressively puts into the fore a consensus of all societal partners in the process of their decision making, carrying out the decisions, and taking advantage of qualitative changes and progress by all strategic partners (see Diagram 3 below).

Diagram 3 Contemporary evolution of governance

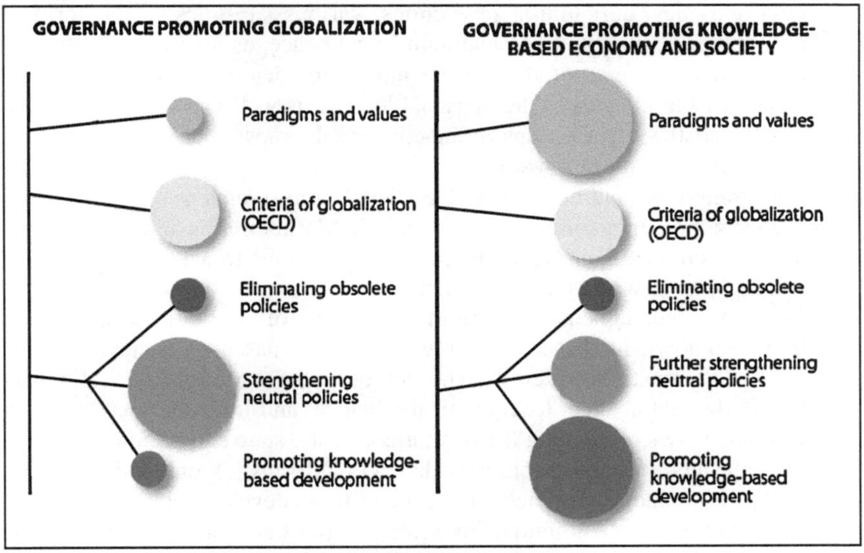

Legend:
Dimension of circles represents:
Decisive influence - the largest circles
Important influence - medium size circles
Negligible influence - the smallest circles

Source: Sočan 2007

These long-term efforts of a larger area, a country or even a region to achieve qualitative and structural changes, are accompanied by a new development concept. Its target is to upgrade the openness and competitiveness by growing investments into the complex knowledge of nations in connection with enhancing technological advance and innovation at the level of 100 per cent of GDP creation and its consumption.[1] Such efforts also encourage entrepreneurship, developmentally oriented regions, spreading information technology across knowledge networks in the economy and society, up to an integration of country-based into multinational company and civil society networks. As a result, the need for a new quality of institutional infrastructure comes to the fore.

In connection with promoting new values and a new development concept, a profound change of policies is taking place:

---

1 Finland's recent Innovation Strategy discusses the evolution from supply-push innovation to demand-pull innovation in detail.

- The elimination of obsolete policies like quantitative restrictions on business activities, agricultural protections, various subsidies in the form of cost and price distortions to maintain social peace, as well as the reduction of an excessive level of state ownership and hidden economy, brings these measures and policies to the marginal level. It is well known and approved by all statistics that Consensus Societies are the most open and competitive countries in the present world.
- The strength of neutral policies (OECD definition) remains, or even grows. It covers the alignment with the EU Single Market norms and global openness and competitiveness, up to continuing reforms to achieve a lean state and regions, as well as lean companies.
- The second fundamental change in the process of upgrading globalization into the knowledge-based economy and society has been occurring in the field of "proactive policies". The set of policies designed to stimulate knowledge abundance, technological advance, and innovation create a development synergy among the institutions of the state and regions, business (e.g. clusters, technological networks and platforms…), university and science, labour and civil society. The core of these development efforts is embedded in the efficient innovation system in most advanced countries of the present time. It consists of parliament's decision that a prosperous development should be based on knowledge, technological advance and innovation. In order to implement such a decision the governments with their agencies and other institutions design appropriate policies, measures and financial funds to hasten the creation of knowledge and technological expertise, as well as to merge the knowledge and technological expertise of companies, university and institutes, and of the institutions in civil societies in the process of promoting an uncountable number of predominantly business oriented R&D projects, an ever growing number of new high tech firms in business and at the university, as well as a growing number of technological breakthroughs within the country or within the worldwide networks.

Therefore, the qualitative changes of the concept used hitherto, economic structure and the governance of the EU require a fast and coordinated evolution of the institutional infrastructure in the entire EU, the member countries and their regions, similar to the excellently coordinated efforts in Delors' time during the process of the introduction of the Single Market norms. In this context, let us elucidate the good practices of the currently most competitive countries globally – the global development leaders.

Good practices of future oriented institutional infrastructure

Upgrading the institutional infrastructure of the EU and member countries

According to Michael Porter's development theory, the EU member countries are dispersed along the entire ladder of technological, economic and social development; from the cost competitiveness of the least developed, over the investment competitiveness of mostly industrialized countries and innovative competitiveness of developed Member States, up to the serious grounds of sustainable development, where the majority of the present global leaders are situated. The least developed Member States and most of their regions can, to a large extent, compete within the EU and globally only with their cheap labour and inexpensive state and possibly natural resources, primarily thanks to the low value added per employee. The majority of the EU member countries, particularly the new members and the Southern European states, find themselves in a phase of investment competitiveness. However, the majority of these countries have too low a level of savings, as well as foreign direct investments to enable successful qualitative transformation into innovation competitiveness over the course of one or even two generations. The developed welfare states and the majority of their regions have achieved innovation competitiveness on the basis of their technologically advanced structure of products and services, as well as the advanced material infrastructure and improving institutional infrastructure. And finally, the Consensus Societies with the most advanced institutional infrastructure, are progressively entering the phase of innovation at the level of their entire economy, public sector and government, and are thus creating the ground for the highest level of global competitiveness as well as for an extremely demanding sustainable development.

The dangerous development discrepancy between the EU and the dynamic world with more than four billion inhabitants stems mainly from the difference in concept and functioning of the institutional infrastructure, regardless of the level of development. According to the EU 2020, the hitherto common denominator of the EU development lever has been, and will also remain so in the future, the adapted Single Market norms. However, also within the EU the future target of the less developed countries and areas will be catching up with the more advanced Member States and areas within the EU and globally. On the other hand, a qualitative transformation into a higher level of development inexorably requires long-term based high level of domestic savings, including foreign direct investments, and preferably regional support, so as to be able to carry out the long-term and above average intense investment cycle. The core of these investments covers the complex knowledge of their nations and, correspondingly, the technology- and innovation-based restructuring of these economies; the synergy of these processes enables the qualitative transformation of an economy and society. In particular with regard to their domestic savings the less advanced EU member countries are seriously lagging behind the dynamic world and the Consensus Societies. For instance, the majority of the Pacific countries have been practicing an extremely high level of domestic savings (between 35% and 50% of GDP), while the Consensus Societies are progressively saving through considerably lower consumption of energy per GDP in relation to other developed countries and even many times lower in comparison to the developing world. At the same time the advanced technologies, universal innovation, as well as the implementation of new values supporting knowledge-based economy and society, result in lean and more efficient states, regions and companies, as well as in the more rational behaviour of the citizens of these most advanced countries.

The EU, according to the EU 2020 development concept, however, appears to adhere to the improved Single Market norms and regional support, which have proven to be insufficient for catching up with the more advanced members even within the EU15. This has been clearly confirmed also in the present global crisis. The positive exception has been Ireland with a very specific and advanced institutional infrastructure during the past quarter of a century.

Therefore, the present development concept of the EU does not promise a successful elimination of regional and state development discrepancies within the enlarged EU, which now exceed the US development differences among the states and regions by more than two times. As a consequence, the enlarged EU as a whole is facing a deepening loss of its developmental position in relation to the dynamic world.[2]

The case of Ireland, the Scandinavian countries and some of the other Consensus Societies increasingly proves that the above average intense investments into complex knowledge as well as into the technology- and innovation-based restructuring of the economy, public sector and government could seriously reduce the erosion of employment in the EU during the process of globalization. Such a concept could also bring higher value added per employee and reinforce the economic, technological and cultural position of the EU within the contemporary world.

Therefore, the EU urgently needs to fundamentally upgrade the hitherto deployed development concept with the common denominator – the Single Market norms, enriched by regional development policies. Changes are expected to lead in the following direction:

---

2 Several interesting points were raised by Franck Biancheri, founder of the European think tank LEAP (Laboratoire Européen d'Anticipation Politique), during his presentation entitled „The EU needs a democratic reshuffling of its institutions' geography", held at the Alpen-Adria-Universität Klagenfurt in September 2006.

- By consistent application of the values and policies (governance) to permanently promote a knowledge-based economy and society, irrespective of the level of development of the EU member countries (Diagram 3).
- By progressive investments into the complex knowledge (education, upgrading, R&D, ICT) of all the nations in the EU member countries, not only into the R&D (Diagram 4).
- The growth of the complex knowledge in the EU, member countries, and their regions should be accompanied by higher savings and the long-term technology- and innovation-based investment cycle, so as to enable the permanent qualitative transformation of economies and societies, regardless of their actual level of development (Diagram 2). As a consequence, the overall EU might expect a growing value added per employee and growing global competitiveness, as well as higher employment and a better life and environment for its citizens.

In order to keep abreast with the dynamic world of about four billion population, the basic criteria of the EU appears to be the upgrading of the present Single Market norms (i.e. openness and competitiveness and regional policies) by a development synergy of the institutional infrastructure of the EU as a whole, of the Member States and regions, as well as of business, university and science, labour, and civil society. Such an infrastructure will be the basis for the permanent promotion of knowledge creation, as well as for the constant technological advance of the economy and comprehensive innovation in the economy and society, regardless of the level of development of the member countries.

Let us review some of the present global leaders during their development period of about two decades or more. Strong evidence exists that the common levers of an above average successful development stem from an appropriate institutional infrastructure. This has been designed by the successful and consensus-oriented parliaments and governments of these countries, or even regions, or larger areas, like for instance Scandinavia. There is not much difference whether we analyze the institutional infrastructure of the US, Singapore, the group of Consensus Societies, or some countries from this group with the most advanced developmental synergy, like Sweden and Finland.

Finally, we could also find more and more elements of long-term knowledge-, technology-, and innovation-promoting institutions in the BRIC countries and in the Pacific area.

Good practice

As early as the start of the Nineties, the famous American strategist Lester Thurow already wrote that the developed countries would be much better off in global competition if they could have the Scandinavian style of institutional infrastructure at their disposal. Nevertheless, the greatest power of the US economy stems first of all from technology and innovation promoting institutions. This country for instance already started to raise sufficient amounts of risk capital throughout the states and their regions during the early Sixties. Some federal institutions and agencies, in close cooperation with the elite universities and institutions, have been inspiring and predominantly financing the majority of leading technologies – from decisive military technologies to internet. The Bayh-Dole act proclaimed knowledge as crucial development lever of the present world and gave to the universities and institutes financial independence and power on the basis of their research potential. Through various acts, passed by the parliament of the US, clear policies were designed and precise procedures for regulating the financial and business relations between the inventors, universities, research institutes and business were defined. On the other side of the world, the parliament of Singapore passed the famous act on values this country has to employ in order to become a modern state and nation as early as 1988. The act consists of five norms: the continuation of Confucianism, the motivation of individual and group efficiency, promoting the modern family, implementing consensus among the societal partners, and eliminating racial intolerance.

Ireland might formally be a controversial member of the Consensus Society group, which mostly grew on their own knowledge and innovation. However, the parliament and the governments of this country succeeded in the midst of the deepest crisis in this country during the Seventies (25% of unemployment, only about 50% level of GDP in relation to the average of the EEC) to reach a firm consensus of all societal partners on the long-term development concept. It was based on strict openness of economy and society, on permanent support to raise the quality of education, upgrading of knowledge and capability of universities, as well as on intense, but selective invitation of FDI into the country; with abundant financial support from Brussels and a high level of domestic capital formation, the groundwork for effective growth during the next generation had been laid.

For these purposes Ireland created an appropriate institutional infrastructure to carry out the designed development concept: The IIRS (Industrial Institute for Research and Standards) checked practically all Irish firms regarding their technological capability for global development and categorised them in four groups: the firms with sufficiently strong own technological capability to implement competitive programs; the firms with sufficient technological potential to follow development; the firms with very poor technological expertise, sufficient only for undemanding programs; and finally, the "peasants" with no engineers and researchers. (The majority of the present CEB states as well as the Southern European members have not yet done such homework!) At this point, the IDA (Industrial Development Agency) carried out an assessment of the financial potential of businesses and the country to launch a technology-based investment cycle. Over less than two decades the FORBAIRTH brought into the country over 150 billion US$ of FDI which, combined with the Brussels resources and important domestic capital formation, enabled one of the world's strongest economic growth leading to the qualitative transformation of the entire economy. About a decade ago, ENTERPRISE IRELAND was created in order to coordinate exports, particularly the outward direct investments of capital, technology, and knowledge from Ireland. This country offers a clear case of how a strong consensus on an advanced development concept, supported by the appropriate institutional infrastructure, brought this country from the position of the weakest economy in Western Europe to the country with the second largest value added per employee (over 75,000 Euro in 2007) in the EU, surpassed only by Luxembourg. This achievement has been reached in about one generation.

In the mid-Eighties, the Consensus Societies within the EU were still being classified as second class (this only applied to Sweden) and third class countries regarding R&D and technological capability by the OECD. However, their advanced development vision on knowledge, technological advance and innovation, consistently supported by an appropriate institutional infrastructure to promote such a development, brought them, over the course of roughly one generation, to take their place among the most technologically advanced, the most competitive economies and among development leaders. These countries are also mostly fulfilling the Lisbon strategy norms. On top of that, they are consciously eliminating ecological, consumption and financial fundamentalisms, and approaching the norms of knowledge-based economy and society with the growing role of sustainable development.

Scheme 1 below presents an assessment of the globalization policies, the structure and efficiency of the institutions promoting knowledge-based economy and society, as well as long-term structural changes in the economies and societies of Ireland and Finland in comparison with the new EU (10) members – the CEB, over the last two decades.

Ireland and Finland have been chosen deliberately because of their considerably different development approach to achieve the intense qualitative transformation of their economies and societies: Ireland through the dominant role of domestic knowledge, and the decisive role of foreign capital and technological expertise, while Finland practically did so strictly through the intense domestic creation and application of knowledge, technological advance and innovation.

The results of the comparison show that virtually all CEB new member countries had a rather obsolete development concept, as well as insufficient generation and use of domestic and foreign knowledge, technological expertise and capital. They also did not dispose of an effective institutional infrastructure to progressively create and acquire decisive levers of modern development.

Scheme 1 Influence of the innovation-based institutional infrastructure of Ireland (IE), Finland (FI) and the Central European and Baltic countries (CEB) on their qualitative change in development

Assessment for the period:		1990 – 2000 – 2010 Qualitative change	Intensity of change 1-8
Main indicators:			
1. Progress of globalization – Single Market Norms	IE		8
	FI		7
	CEB		5
2. Concentration of capital:			
2.1. Mostly ownership-based	IE		- 3
	FI		- 1
	CEB		- 4
2.2. Mostly technology- and innovation-based	IE		7
	FI		7
	CEB		3
3. Institutional infrastructure of state	IE		7
	FI		7
	CEB		3
4. Institutional infrastructure of business sector	IE		6
	FI		7
	CEB		3
5. Transformation of university and science	IE		6
	FI		8
	CEB		3
6. Innovation system	IE		6
	FI		8
	CEB		2
7. Structural changes of economy	IE		8
	FI		7
	CEB		3
8. Growth of value added per employee	IE		8
	FI		7
	CEB		3
Total:	IE	(mostly by foreign technology and innovation)	53
	FI	(mostly by own technology and innovation)	57
	CEB	(by insufficient own and foreign technology and innovation)	21

Legend:

Neutral development – 1 point for one decade

Coordinated development – 2 points for one decade

Intensely promoted development – 3 points for one decade

Very intensely promoted development – 4 points for one decade

Source: Sočan (2009)

According to the comparison the main delays of the CEB have occurred in the following areas:

Globalization: The present global leaders are the most open economies and societies worldwide. Only by high level of openness and competitiveness can they take advantage of their advanced knowledge, technology and innovation within the EU and globally. This is true for trade, as well as for the other economic, technological, environmental, social and political processes. The CEB are also rather high on the world ladder measured by this criterion. However, this achievement is only a precondition for modern development; for the real catching up with the global leaders, the CEB will also have to decisively improve their hitherto deployed development concept and institutional infrastructure.

Development levers: A number of general levers have been applied intensely in practically all economies and societies of the present global leaders. One of the fundamental efforts has been the high and ever growing investment into the complex knowledge of the whole nation. As a result, the human development index and social cohesion of these countries have reached top ranking. Connected with these efforts a high level of transparency of processes in these countries has been achieved, while, at the same time, corruption and the hidden economy have been constantly reduced. In addition to these typical general efforts some countries are characterised by some very specific levers, which have additionally raised the competitive power of these countries. For instance, a mark of distinction of Denmark has been the long-term promotion of the employability of its total population, a very flexible labour market, resulting in the process of flexicurity, while Finland is known for one of the most advanced and efficient institutional infrastructures and its innovation system. The case of Singapore mentioned earlier, with its advanced values significantly added to the very high ranking of this country in terms of global competitiveness. Similarly, Sweden as the global leader in R&D investment permanently improves its competitiveness position. In this respect the CEB countries have been very weak and even backward in relation to the Consensus Societies. The challenges for the CEB to achieve progress in these areas of activities will be long-term.

Concentration of capital: We are witnessing a constant and even accelerated process of capital concentration. Some experts even expect that in the period of one generation nearly 80 per cent of total ownership in the business sector will belong to about 100 multinationals. However, globalization is also bringing qualitative changes into this process. The elementary interest for mergers and acquisitions on a national and global level stems mostly from the concentration and faster growth of knowledge, technological expertise and innovative potential of the joined partners in order to improve their "winning performance" and global competitiveness. This evolution from "national champions" towards European and global firms has also been very clear in the EU area from the Nineteen Sixties to the present day. This process has mainly not been the case in the capital concentration of the new member countries. There was a weak environment in the new members for expanding investments into complex knowledge, and the Commission deliberately stimulated small and middle size enterprises for the sake of raising employment in the EU as a whole. There has not even been a barrier to the process of expanding taicoonization in many of new members, which has been based on existing legal norms and allowed banking credits to the newly installed owners (mostly from management) of firms and larger business networks. These banking credits to private persons have been repaid by the profits of the enterprises, at the cost of seriously weakening their R&D, technological, innovation, as well as general development potential and consequently their global competitiveness. Besides hampering modern development the negative consequences of taicoonization in the new EU members cover growing social differentiation, expelling small shareholders from business ownership, banning workers' profit sharing, as well as the negative attitude of the employees towards belonging to a firm and consensus oriented environment. The lack of attention of the EU brought to such excesses in the process of capital concentration has been to the serious detriment of the majority of the new member countries as well as to the EU as a whole.

Institutional infrastructure: The main cause for the delay of the CEB in the process of catching up with the advanced countries of the EU and globally lies in their underdeveloped institutional infrastructure. It's not only the institutions of state and regions, where the permanent growth of investments in complex knowledge of the whole population is in question. Even more important has been the deficiency of an effective merger of existing knowledge and technological expertise among the companies themselves, as well as with the universities and institutes and the knowledge networks of civil society. Lack of important institutions for promoting development on the basis of knowledge, technology and innovation, accompanied by insufficient political support for these processes by parliament and government, including the assurance of appropriate financial resources for these purposes, have seriously delayed the qualitative transformation of these economies. The following case of Finland and Sweden will clearly show that the efficient institutional infrastructure of state and regions is inevitably related with the appropriate institutions in business, like clusters, technological networks or platforms, at the university, in a way of promoting R&D and its commercialization through strategic partnership with business and society, up to the organized labour with the target to jointly stimulate the employability of a nation, and civil society with progressively growing knowledge networks. Finally, the accepted Single Market norms have not been paying sufficient attention in these countries to consistently promote a permanent investment cycle with the targets to raise the complex knowledge of the nations, as well as to promote technology- and innovation-based investments to constantly improve the structure of the economy and the efficiency of the public sector and the government. Such an investment cycle is at the same time the basis for raising value added per employee and consequently for the wellbeing of people and the revitalization of the environment. While the carelessness of the Commission of the EU to date regarding the creation of a modern institutional infrastructure might be characterized as negligence, the insufficient attention to this problem in the document EU 2020 is a huge development mistake, not only for the new Member States but for the EU as a whole.

Sweden

In Sweden, parliament and successive governments have been intensely development-oriented during the last fifty years. During the Sixties and Seventies the core of knowledge creation and research work took place at the universities (13) and industrial sector-based institutes (30). According to the EU development (Single Market norms) and the foreseen integration (1995), as well as the necessity to accept globalization and remain competitive, Sweden needed to upgrade sector-oriented targets with national strategic targets, including development-oriented regions. These efforts required intense cooperation between the state, universities, specialized institutes and enterprises in order to raise the excellence and relevance of knowledge, research and technological development, as well as to combine financial sources of the state (more than 1% of GDP) and business (more than 2% of GDP). Sweden even passed the famous "third task" act for the universities, which requires their intense research and strategic cooperation with business. As a result, the necessity appeared to give rise to a new and much more comprehensive network of agencies and institutions to promote the development of the country on the basis of knowledge, technological advance and innovation.

As a result, the main innovation agency Vinnova and a number of specialized innovative foundations with elementary own funds and additional financing from the government and business have been created in order to merge knowledge and technological expertise from the university and institutes with business and society potentials and interests. This approach created the basis for numerous joint investments of universities (with own funds), governmental agencies, foundations, regions, cities, business, and societal institutions into various institutions like science parks (about 30 Swedepark) with over 2.000 mostly high tech firms and about 50,000 employed experts. Similar was the role of regional institutions promoting the upgrading of human capital and newly established firms, as well as sector-based centres of technological competences dealing mostly with breakthrough technologies. There is no need to point out that such a method of investment in knowledge promotion and its transformation into successful businesses also creates the basis for consensus-based decision making as well as taking advantage of the results. Nevertheless, the Swedish universities always had a high level of autonomy in the field of research, commercialization of knowledge and of entrepreneurship at the university high tech firms. For instance, Stockholm University disposes of a number of its own institutions for strategic cooperation with business in the country and worldwide, like contact centres, agencies for ideas, donations and employment, innovative research, pedagogical and research contacts with firms, international cooperation etc. On the other hand, Uppsala University is the world leader or at least among the world's best in about one hundred broader sectors (e.g. renewable energy, democracy and human rights, brain research...) or smaller research groups, intensely cooperating with the business and societal institutions at home and abroad. The universities, institutes, businesses, and the institutions of civil society also create a firm knowledge basis for the development of Swedish regions.

Such an institutional infrastructure of the state and regions, university and science creates a fertile ground for the cooperation with large, medium, small and newly established micro firms. Mostly, such cooperation takes place under the auspices of large firms and universities or various development clusters, and usually under the financial umbrella of specialized governmental agencies. In Sweden, labour is not an antipode to knowledge and business. Among the crucial strategic targets of labour are the growing employability of workers and employees, their cooperation in the governing process, the profit sharing, as well as the ownership sharing. Usually this country practices a transparent growth of minimal wages, so that business and workers know in advance what kind of jobs will be endangered. Finally, the efficient public sectors and the government make permanent efforts to organize good service for the citizens, business and society. This country invests more than 20 per cent of GDP into complex knowledge and is among the world leaders regarding the use of renewable energy and preserving the environment. Energy independent new parts of cities (for instance the community of about 30,000 inhabitants in Stockholm), joint research and business activities with Finland in building similar ecological cities in China, Russia are some examples of these efforts.

Taking into account the nature of the present Swedish development system, its resistance in the face of the present global crisis (e.g. no budget deficit!), as well as the prosperity of its future-oriented activities, this country can very well serve as a mirror not only for the EU but for the world as a whole.

Finland

From the development point of view, a comparison of the position of Finland and Slovenia in the early Nineties as well as their later development is instructive. In 1990 both countries suffered the loss of more than a half of their hitherto market because of economic collapse of the former Soviet Union and Yugoslavia. Finland at that time was more advanced in the field of complex knowledge of the whole nation and in the public sector. For instance, already in the mid-

Sixties this country was the world leader in terms of the lowest mortality of new born children, while numerous public universities throughout the country guaranteed the firm ground for the subsequent qualitative transformation of the economy and society. The newly independent Slovenia was not only the most advanced republic of former Yugoslavia but during the Eighties, with nine per cent of the population and 19 per cent of GDP it was able to export to the hard currency area markets between 35 per cent and 40 per cent of the total exports of former Yugoslavia.

Finland succeeded in the first half of Nineties, before joining the EU in 1995, to adapt its system (political, legal, economic), the macroeconomic stability, public finance and the budget deficit to the existing Single Market norms of the EU. During the first half of the Nineties, Finland also laid down the core of its subsequent institutional infrastructure of state and regions, of the business sector, as well as of the universities and science, labour, and civil society, so as to carry out its advanced vision of future development on the basis of knowledge, technological development and innovation. The first democratic government of Slovenia, also inspired by the European Union's promotion of Small and Medium Enterprises (SMEs), unfortunately dismantled the leading Slovenian commercial bank, which was among the 200 largest banks in the world, creating a number of small regional banks. This process was connected with the bankruptcy of some large and leading export firms in the field of engineering activities as "remnants of socialism", regardless of their adequate export orders. The adaptation to the Single Market norms, including the acceptance of Euro, took Slovenia nearly two decades. As a consequence, Slovenia lost more than one decade of modern development compared to Finland.

Already in the first half of the Nineties the Parliament of Finland passed the act with which it proclaimed the vision of the Science and Technology Policy Council (STPC; now the Research and Innovation Council) that this country's long–term development of knowledge, permanent technological advance and innovation should be the first strategic priority of this state. On the basis of this consensual decision the governments with their ministries, agencies and other institutions created appropriate policies and measures as well as sufficient financial resources to carry out such a vision. Decisive was the fact that the proclaimed development priority was strictly respected not only by one or two responsible ministries but by the government as a whole and by the other societal partners. By these efforts Finland succeeded in permanently promoting knowledge and to merge the knowledge and technological expertise of the companies with that of universities, specialized institutes and other domestic and foreign sources in thousands of R&D business projects, in a constantly growing number of knowledge-demanding high tech firms in business and at the university (e.g. High Technology Finland, 2007), including the numerous technological breakthroughs in this country. This process appeared to be the core of the long-term technology- and innovation-based investment cycle and the basis for technological advance and innovation of Finland, for its growing productivity, value added per employee and global competitiveness, as well as for the permanent qualitative transformation of the economy and society of this country. Over a period of one and a half decades such an innovation system brought Finland among the present globally most competitive economies and among the global development leaders.

In order to bring to life the synergy of long-term development thinking and acting the governments of Finland have been establishing compatible institutions to turn the ever growing investments into complex knowledge (education, upgrading, R&D, ICT), which already at the beginning of the present decade surpassed 20 per cent of GDP and out of that more than three per cent only into R&D. As a consequence, an intense structural transformation of the Finnish economy occurred. Presently about 85 per cent of the economy is globally competitive and progressively service- and knowledge-oriented, and only about 10 per cent is facing various financial, technological, managerial, structural, and other deficiencies, while only about five per cent of economic potential of this country "is dying". The similar share for the average EU comes to about 70 per cent/20 per cent/10 per cent.

A high level of mutual targets and cooperation has always existed among the leading institutions of contemporary modern development in Finland. At various levels of the economy and society at least the following deserve to be mentioned.

The state and regional level

STPC (now RIC) plays a special strategic role within the institutional infrastructure of Finland. As a long-term thinking institution with members from politics, science, business, labour and civil society, it was the main founder of the vision, strategic development targets and policies of modern Finland. Its predominantly consensus-based views and decisions have been primarily proposed to the Parliament and the governments of Finland.

The national technological agency TEKES is the leading institution for promoting and co-financing technological development of Finland. With rather abundant funds (recently more than 0.5 billion €) this institution has continuously co-financed about one third of the total R&D expenditures of predominantly business launched projects (between 2.000 and 2.500 projects per year). The activity of TEKES has provided the groundwork for R&D cooperation among business, universities and institutes, and forms the basis of the modern technological advance of Finland.

THE ACADEMY OF FINLAND with similar amount of funds as TEKES, has predominantly co-financed fundamentally oriented research in all science disciplines; in addition, the Academy usually plays a crucial role in developing foresight and similar strategic views and studies.

VTT, as a specialized technological research institution, covers R&D in the fields of modern technological development, like electronics, information technologies, automation, chemical- and bio-technologies, food, energy, as well as various industrial technologies.

SITRA as the most responsible institution for raising risk capital is located at the Parliament and also cooperates with the Bank of Finland. Its role has been growing in the process of expanding creation of new high tech and knowledge-based firms in business and at the universities. This institution also plays an important role in considering the visionary issues of the modern global and country change.

CENTERS OF EXPERTISE have played a decisive role in the process of technological advance of Finnish regions by merging knowledge and capital from various sources to promote numerous projects of the regions.

Business

The role of business CLUSTERS was extraordinarily important in the process of structural transformation and technological consolidation of Finland's economy during the Nineties and early part of the present decade. A complex knowledge and experience of the enterprises, institutes and university sectors within the clusters enabled qualitative growth of practically all included firms in terms of management, finance, research and development, technological advance, structural changes, employability etc. Such a potential within the clusters facilitated the cooperation with TEKES and other relevant institutions in order to raise the competitiveness of all members of the clusters.

TECHNOLOGICAL PROGRAMS (networks and platforms) have been mostly focused by the financial support of TEKES. They have enabled joint R&D activities on numerous technologically demanding projects of enterprises by collaboration of the experts from enterprises, institutes and universities.

TECHNOLOGICAL CLINICS play a dominant role in transferring modern technologies from the point of origin to the users, in particularly to SMEs.

University and science

In particular, during the present decade Finland has succeeded in fundamentally changing the mission, the program of its activities, and the financing of universities and science. Universities are becoming the fundamental lever of transformation in Finland into the knowledge-based economy and society. From the hitherto main activities – to teach the students – the university has evolved into a superior R&D institution, creating numerous high tech firms and intense strategic and working ties with business and society as a priority task. As a consequence of such activities the ground for excellence and relevance of teaching at the university is being created.

One example of how the modern R&D potentials can be raised is provided by the Helsinki SCIENCE PARK, which has approximately 1,000 researchers covering the areas of biotechnology, biomedicine, environment and food. The structural share of investment into this centre of excellence was the following: government 2/7, Sitra 1/7, Helsinki University 1/7, City of Helsinki 2/7, and enterprises 1/7.

OPERATIVE INSTITUTIONS at the university, institutes, regions and companies consist of institutions promoting first of all the creation of new firms in various environments. In 10 technological parks with about 1,000 firms, close to 10,000 researchers are at work. The number of institutions for technology transfer is similar; their role is growing because of the rising importance of joint investments by different partners. In particular at the universities, since they are becoming important research institutions, the innovation centres, information centres and incubators are playing an ever greater role.

Labour

Modern Finland consistently endeavours to raise the quality of all products and services as well as their technological and knowledge input. Therefore, the state, management and the employees of this country strongly believe that the improving level of qualification and expertise go hand in hand with raising competitiveness, value added per employee, wages and profits. As a result, the employability is becoming a crucial aim of all societal partners, the government, capital and labour.

Civil society

Through the process of Finland's transformation into a knowledge-based economy and society the former differences between classical industrial work in relation to public sector and society activities are disappearing. Knowledge networks within business and society are becoming progressively compatible and serve to raise the innovativeness of the whole population. In this context, the structure of the economy is changing, too. Finland, as well as the other Scandinavian countries, has been progressively evolving into a knowledge- and innovation-based and service-oriented economy and society (The Nordic model, 2009; Finland's national innovation strategy, 2009).

Taking into account the hitherto development of modern Finland, as well as its institutional basis for a consistent qualitative transformation of its economy and society, Finland deserves to be accepted among the contemporary global development leaders. A careful study of its development might be very fruitful, not only within the EU, but worldwide.

A remark on China

While Brussels appears not to want to see and understand the good practices of the Consensus Societies, contemporary China does. Some years ago this country established the "Scandinavian Center" in Shanghai. This centre was designed as location for meetings with experts from Scandinavian countries – professors, business people, politicians, students and other professionals. One of the high officials of the Chinese government was asked (before the global crisis!) about the purpose of this centre. He replied in the following way: China is rejecting the American type of capitalism. This country also does not have much to learn from the large developed countries of the EU. But, he said, the Scandinavian countries have the best socialism in the world.

Summary

The evolution of European integration might be defined as follows: Most of the second half of the former century, up to the Single Market norms, and even the Lisbon strategy and the introduction of the Euro, was a period of creation of a new, dynamic Europe within an old, static world; recently, we are witnessing the progressive ageing of the EU, with the exception of Consensus Societies, within the new and progressively dynamic world.

During the late Forties the institutions, enabling the basic norms of a democratic society, safety, economic cooperation and development were created, mostly under the influence of the US. As a consequence, during the Fifties, the ground for European integration was laid down and the EEC was created. The appropriate institutional infrastructure was implemented to eliminate internal trade restrictions and the customs union appeared during the Sixties. Unrestricted investments within an important economic area hastened the evolution of enterprises from national champions toward European and global corporations. The promotion of small and middle enterprises and supportive regional policies were a compatible process. Then, within the period of Delors, the most comprehensive and efficient institutional infrastructure – the "Single Market norms" – were implemented. The EU consisting of 12 and later 15 members, was firmly on the track of globalization. In the year 2000, the EU launched the most far reaching vision of this integration – the knowledge-based economy and society with deepening and enlarging aspirations. However, this vision of the development of affluent knowledge, abundant development and use of modern technologies, as well as overwhelming innovation at all levels of GDP creation, had no real basis in appropriate institutions to promote such a process, with the exception of the so called Consensus Societies, consisting mostly of the Scandinavian member countries. As a result, during the past decade, the Consensus Societies achieved a position of global leadership regarding competitiveness and developmental safety, while the majority of the EU has been gradually relinquishing its position as global technological, economic and even trade superpower. And finally, this year (2010), the EU is launching the document "EU 2020", which is based predominantly on the slightly advanced Single Market norms of 1990. As a consequence, the countries of more than four billion of population (Consensus Societies, the US, BRIC, and the majority of Pacific countries) have a more advanced development concept and institutional support than the EU. They are consciously upgrading globalization efforts by an intense promotion of complex knowledge (education, upgrading, R&D, ICT) of their population, as well as by launching an immense technology- and innovation-based investment cycle to constantly accelerate the qualitative transformation of their economies and societies.

In this context the above contribution discussed two main issues: The first covers the basis of modern change, elaborating theoretical issues, development concepts, structural changes and the evolution of modern governance, while the second part presents examples of contemporary good practice from the future-oriented institutional infrastructure of typical states and broader areas.

References

Competitiveness Council (2007), 'Nonpaper by the Commission on Research', Brussels.

EBRD (2002), *Transition Report 2002 (10 years of transition)*, EBRD, London.

ERT, Various Reports; European Round Table of Industrialists.

ETLA (The Research Institute of Finish Economy) (2007), *The Nordic Model (Embracing globalization and sharing risks)*, Helsinki.

European Commission, COM (2010), *2020: A strategy for smart, sustainable and inclusive growth.*

EU (2001), *A Sustainable Europe For A Better World: A European Union Strategy for Sustainable Development*, Commission of the European Communities, Brussels, [http://europa.eu.int/eur-lex/en/com/cnc/2001/com2001_ 0264en01.pdf] 29. 04.2003.

Faos, S. K. Anders/M. Mailand (2005), *The Danish Flexicurity Model*, University of Copenhagen.

Finnish Ministry of Labor and Industry (2009), *Finland's Innovation Strategy*, Helsinki.

Friedman, Thomas L. (2005, 2006), *The World is Flat*, Penguin Books, London.

IMD (2004; 2005; 2007; 2009), *IMD World Competitiveness Yearbook*, Institute for Management Development, Lausanne.

Muukkonen, Martti (2008), 'The Power of Belief in European Welfare-Thinking', in J. Langer (ed.), *Forces Shaping the EU*, Peter Lang, Frankfurt a. M./New York, pp. 153 - 173.

OECD (2001), *Governance in the 21st Century*, OECD, Paris.

Radermacher, F. J. (2003), *Balance or Destruction (Eco-Social Market Economy as a Key to Global Sustainable Development)*, Ökosoziales Forum Europa, Vienna.

Rowen, Henry S. (2007), *Making IT, The Rise of Asia in High Tech*, Stanford University Press, Stanford.

Sočan, Lojze (2008), 'EU in the Global Context – a Developmental Approach', in J. Langer (ed.) *Forces Shaping the EU*, Peter Lang, Frankfurt a. M./New York, pp. 47 - 70.

Sočan, Lojze (2009), *University and the Transformation of Slovenia into a Knowledge-based Economy and Society*, UL, Ljubljana.

Stiglitz, Joseph E. (1997), 'The Role of Government in Economic Development', in M. Bruno/B. Pleskovic (eds.), *Annual World Bank Conference on Development Economics*, World Bank, Washington.

The European House (2004), *Creating Value for Europe, European Companies and Institutions*, (confidential document).

Tekes Newsletter (2010), available at [http://www.tekes.fi/en/community/Home/351/Home/473] retrieved on 10.1.2011.

The Scientist (2007), 'The Best Places to Work in Academia', Philadelphia.

The University of Helsinki (2006), *The University of Helsinki Strategic Plan 2007 - 2009*, UH, Helsinki.

The Finnish Academies of Technology (2007), *High Technology Finland*, Helsinki.

The Academy of Finland (2006), *Finnsight 2015*, Helsinki.

Tschirky, Hugo (2004), *Technology and Innovation Management on the Move*, Verlag für Industrielle Organisation, Zürich.

University of Uppsala (2007), *Strategy for Research and Education 2009 - 2012*, Uppsala.

University of Ljubljana (2007), *EUA Evaluation Report*, UL, Ljubljana.

World Economic Forum (2006), *World Competitiveness Report*, Macmillan Publishers Limited, Basingstoke.

Vittorio Olgiati

On the Women Lawyers' Voice in Europe: Scenarios for a Legal Education Agenda

Introductory remarks

According to a well-established legal tradition, lawyers in Europe are constitutionally provided with an absolutely unique *status activae civitatis*, i.e. are legally authorised to act as key-actor in the political-institutional arenas due to their formal-official role as boundary-agents between law and society. In its turn, such a qualification is grounded on their disciplinary expertise as regards the functioning of basic power structures concerned with public order and social justice (Olgiati 1987, 1996; Larson 1989).

Within this general normative frame, legal education constitutes the essential pre-condition of lawyers' expertise. On the one hand, it specifies the potentials of their *status activae civitatis* – not to be confused with lay-people's "active citizenship" that merely enables them to take part, or be involved, in the so-called "deliberative democracy" –; on the other hand, it provides evidence of the quality – meaning and agency – of the *habitus* (Bourdieu/Wacquant 1990) – not to be confused with a mere professional attribute or credential – that these professionals embody. Altogether therefore legal education allows, and reflects, the degree of "*authority to speak*" (Foucault 1981) about the basic "principles of truth" – i.e. the "*doxa*" (Bourdieu 1990) – of the professional realm, within, but also outside, the province of law.

The aim here is to take the above topics seriously by looking at them from an unusual, but increasingly significant, point of view: that of the women lawyers' *voice*. More precisely, an attempt will be made here to sketch a cognitive grid useful for a prospective gender-oriented professional agenda enabling the European women lawyers' "voice" to be significantly heard, and adequately considered, at any European decision-making level. For this purpose the focus will be put on major epochal legal changes concerned with, or related to, legal education demand-supply in Europe.

In this respect, three main interrelated questions cannot be avoided:
(1) What about the current professional standing of European women lawyers within the European legal domain, especially in the light of the EU general principles of "equal opportunities" and "non- discrimination"? (2) How far are the epochal socio-legal mainstreams occurring within and outside EU legal space affecting European lawyers' knowledge and know-how in general, and European women lawyers' expertise in particular? (3) What has to be done in the field of legal education to provide the European women lawyers' voice with more specific legal provisions and allow it to be significantly heard by a wider audience?

These questions have not been selected by chance. As we will see, they imply a detailed analysis of the changing patterns of the professional model, and of women lawyers' agency within it, in relation to the ongoing fragmentation of the overall province of law. In turn they call for an evaluation about socio-institutional and political-ideological implications of the rising competition between public and private legal systems, either at professional or at educational level. Last, but not least, they are entangled with the most serious challenge that EU processes and policy have to face at present as regards the whole realm of expert systems and professionalism in Europe: i.e. the urge to re-set higher education, in general, and higher legal education in particular, in order to re-produce EU *organic intellectuals* in tune with the general principles of the EU constitutional process (Olgiati 2008, 2009).

As far as European women lawyers are specifically concerned, therefore, the above questions can be reframed in this way: given potentials – and limits – of EU "equal opportunities" (fair competition) and "non-discrimination" (just recognition) principles and directives (Morondo Taramundi 2004), what sort of legal education guidelines can provide the kind of power-knowledge that they – as professional women equal to men – are entitled to embody within and outside the EU socio-institutional *Strukturbildung*?

Theoretical framework: a socio-legal "scenario" approach

As European society at large is the historically determined, but quite unsettled, context that qualifies the topic of this contribution in the final instance, it is apparent that a congruent theoretical grid is required. For the purpose, a *scenario* approach to major socio-professional issues currently shaping the European legal domain seems an appropriate entry-point to set up a prospective gender-oriented agenda enabling women lawyers to authoritatively speak within and outside the fieldwork.

By suggesting such an approach I am not referring here to the European legal domain as a superstructural variable, as the ancient notion of the Law as *Theatrum Mundi* might suggest. Even less I am referring here to the EU *acquis* as a "scenario" structure in Jeremy Bentham's sense, i.e. as an artificial device in which lawyers act as "impresarios" of a particular type of governance system (Bentham 1787/1843).

Rather, I am suggesting a constructivistic frame of reference enabling us to envisage at a theoretical level something that does not yet exist, but it is likely to occur in Europe. In other words I am referring to the notion and the theory of "*Futuribles*" – in English "Futures" – as suggested by a French intellectual: Bertrand De Jouvenel.

According to De Jouvenel "futures" are a constitutive, irrepressible, part of any social action, just like past experiences are. In this respect, the theoretical utility of a *scenario* approach stems from the fact that it can be used as a preliminary cognitive and interpretative grid to depict, perceive, sketch, embryonic patterns or potential conditions that are reasonably considered useful to enhance a project, to promote a strategy, to sort out possible trajectories, to deepen the understanding of emerging trends, etc.

Needless to say, the social-scientific validity of a constructivist approach of this sort matters. For this very reason, therefore, it requires a serious reflection and a cautious evaluation about given context-based experiences as well as a refined perception about certain path-dependence variables, each and all supported by the widest range of historical records and scientific knowledge. If these methodical guidelines are fulfilled a "scenario construction" helps to handle – possibly in strategic terms – either knowledge's uncertainty or indeterminacy due not only to "scientific doubt" or "Socratic ignorance", but also to something felt as not (yet) fully defined or clearly perceived, i.e. that kind of "uncontrolled" cognition and understanding that is traditionally conceived by some schools of thought as "not knowledge" in proper academic/disciplinary terms (De Jouvenel 1964).

Well. It is not the case here to further enlighten the features of this theoretical model. Let me just add that we owe the notion of "uncertain knowledge" to Milton Keynes who first made clear the importance of "futures" as "scenario technique" in socio-economic studies. In fact, Keynes distinguished foreseeable from unforeseeable, but equally useful, forms of contingency in the field of political economy. Interestingly, he did so in order to manage social complexity and reduce the risks that economic action – as any social action oriented to the future – always entails (Beck 2006).

Limits and potential of current women lawyers' standing in the professional arena: empirical evidences

Having made clear the theoretical framework, let us discuss the underlying precondition and prospective issues of the three questions mentioned above. In this respect, the general theme "Being Heard in the Future Europe" of the 8th Congress of the European Women Lawyers Association (in association with the Women Lawyers' Forum) held on July 4th - 5th 2008 in London, offers us an enlightening entry point. In fact, as with any possible variable implied by this general theme, one can but wonder: Why do European women lawyers raise, here and now, the claim to be *heard* in the future Europe? And what sort of past and present socio-legal experiences suggest to them to look *ahead*, to envisage and/or promote an additional and/or a different gender-oriented professional scenario in which their "voice" could be significantly perceived and valued?

As we know, for more than a century, women have claimed to be entitled to enter and to have an equal standing with men within the "unpromised land" of legal professionalism (Olgiati 2003; 2006a). Today the rising feminization of legal professions, i.e. the rising proportion of women amongst law student, public officials and private practitioners, is an unquestionable matter of fact. The historical mainstream along which women openly claim access, inclusion and recognition as fully educated and qualified legal professionals has been successful. They are in. Even more: They are likely to become the majority group within the field, if their current entry in Law Schools and Professional Associations continues at the current rate (Schultz/Shaw 2003).

However, what is highly remarkable as regards this historical progression is that, in the meanwhile, women lawyers experienced another, rather *unexpected* because *substantial*, type of "professional closure": having gained the *formal* access, their professional *status activae civitatis* has been and still is limited and /or downgraded by a number of, manifest-latent, social, cultural and structural constraints *within* the professional jurisdiction. In short, they now suffer from what scientific literature calls "*glass ceiling*", i.e. an invisible closure preventing a generalised upward professional mobility (Davis 1996).

As a matter of fact, evidence shows that, their increasing number notwithstanding, their qualitative potentials are not fully recognised yet. Not only is their entry into those professional councils, boards, directorates, etc. in which basic decisions about law-policy making are taken, or important organizational tasks about the functioning of the justice system are at stake, not yet proportionally comparable with that of their fellow men, but, in the case of election, selection, cooptation or recruitment, their presence implies, by rule, mere suppletive functions and low decisional autonomy.

This does not mean to say that the overall gender "state-of-the-art" still is as it was in the past. Even though the rising quantity did not transubstantiate into a fully generalised qualitative upward mobility process, the whole province of law has been deeply influenced anyway by the rising presence and daily work of women lawyers in the legal system. If one leafs through the number of gender studies specifically devoted to women lawyers' professional performances, one cannot but notice, in particular, three remarkable cultural achievements: (i) the successful effort to promote a more generalised use of interdisciplinary approaches in the treatment of any sort of legal cases; (ii) the successful effort to promote a "responsive", rather than mere "formal", cognition/interpretation/enforcement of the same formal-official law, thus (iii) providing it with a wider socio-legal, context-based, legitimacy and efficacy.

Beside the above, significant evolutionary gender-specific developments in legal practice are clearly recognizable both at behavioural and theoretical level. I am referring here to gendered ways of knowing and communicating, reasoning and interacting, evaluating and judging. In turn, the above items decisively contributed – among other things – to speeding up and/or deepening the surmounting of up-dated legal viewpoints and concepts within both legal doctrine and law-policy making, as demonstrated by current critical standing as regards (i) formalistic conceptions of the law as a self-referential system *vis-à-vis* society;

(ii) traditional one-dimensional male-dominated construction of legal structures and discourses; (iii) stereotyped ideological and social attitudes as regards gender legal professionalisation.

Yet a question is still open: Does all the above mean that European women lawyers, having achieved an uncontested numerical presence in the legal system and having "marked" it with their performances up to the point of driving its evolution towards some substantial achievements, have also improved or empowered their "voice" up to the point of being significantly heard?

Women lawyers' answer to this question – and my personal response, too – is: *not enough yet*. And this is true, in my view, far beyond the level of what is now defined as either "interprofessional communication" or "public relations".

Women lawyers' "voice" in actual practice: a critical glance at professional performativity, socialization and self-consciousness

To state that European women lawyers have not broken the whole structure of the so-called "glass ceiling" yet, and therefore that their "voice" can still not be significantly "heard" in Europe, is quite easy. Much harder, by contrast, is it to identify a way to overcome the problem. For this purpose, a better understanding of how women lawyers' "voice" is perceived and conceived at present is absolutely necessary.

Let us look at the studies by two renowned scholars, both specifically devoted to deciphering women lawyers' "voice" in the legal domain: Sherry's "Civic virtue and the feminine voice" (Sherry 1986) and Menkel-Meadow's "Portia on a different voice" (Menkel-Meadow 1997). According to these studies, evidence shows that women lawyers' "voice" in Court is more concerned with a (social) "ethic of care" than with a (legal) "ethic of justice". With this finding being interpreted as a typical gender attitude, these scholars maintain therefore that such an "ethic of care" will increasingly mark the conceptual evolution of the legal system to the extent that the number of women lawyers acting in Court will grow.

If this forecast were true, the problem of improving women lawyers' "voice" would be easily solved quite soon without any particular exterior intervention. In other words: there would no need to promote any specific legal education or whatsoever law-policy reform, for gender specificity, as such – i.e., as a "natural" and irrepressible (bio-psychological) pattern – will lead the evolutionary trend anyway.

In actual fact, things are not as simple as the above "computational" perspective suggests. The problem is much more complex and calls for a change relating to basic socio-cultural and political-institutional conditions.

I am not suggesting here to go back in space and time and to update the coupling of "care" and "justice" as it occurred in that kind of ancient law that Bachofen, in his extraordinarily refined analysis, called "*Mutterrecht*"

(Bachofen 1861/1943). Even though Bachofen's insights cannot be undervalued or ignore, it is clear that in contemporary society "legal justice" is quite detached from "justice-as-care" either as ideal value or as an opèrational task. In turn, I am not denying either that women, in general, and so women lawyers too, might perform "in a different voice" as compared to men, as the title of Gilligan's path-breaking study suggested (Gilligan 1982). Rather, it seems to me that, at least, a more plausible analytical frame is required, for (i) numerical "quantity" cannot be transubstantiated into a valuable "quality" unless, and to the extent only, the issues at stake are consciously taken on, and strategically pursued, by subjects acting as *leading* agents, and (ii) an inclination towards an "ethic of care", as such, cannot be conceived as a sort of women's "feminine essentialism" (Petersen 1996), especially if and when women are practicing law in Court as qualified professional lawyers.

Let us look therefore at women lawyers' "voice" from a different perspective: for example, let us focus on how they evaluate their own legal discourses and statements.

According to an interview study carried out by Beatriz Kohen on women judges in Argentina – but the study is certainly valid for women judges in Europe also – evidence shows that they tend to deny any gender differences that might affect their cognitive activity as judges, even though they recognize that they might have a greater sensitivity for the (socio-psychological) complexity of certain matters, especially if these matters stem from particular law-and-society interplays and raise a specific concern for interpersonal interactions. In any case – Kohen says – a systematic review of the scientific literature available so far shows that women judges' "moral orientation in law" is not a conclusive pattern as to what they really are, say or do in their daily work (Kohen 2009).

In principle, I personally agree with Beatriz Kohen's last statement, i.e. that, gender "moral orientation in law" is a significant but not conclusive issue. However, I would add this: that the denial of any gender difference in legal performances on the part of women judges sounds to a large extent to be a sort of reflexive quest and/or psychological confirmation about the effective existence of an equalitarian legitimacy within both the legal system and the professional arena: a quest that recalls a still widespread traditional conception of either legal expertise or professional status-role as inspired by, and devoted to, personal "independence" and "autonomy". Indeed, the (hidden) point at stake here is that a typical educational "de-formation" might have occurred, often related to the difficulty of the same women lawyers to culturally surmount still persistent organizational constraints of the justice system as a male-structured institution, as well as still persistent stereotyped legal education and doctrine about the "law's empire" as a "neutral" social domain (Hunter 2002).

Having said this, however, it is worth adding something else: As we know, we owe to John Austin one of the most remarkable attempts to carefully disentangled interpretative variables in legal discourses from the surrounding socio-legal contexts. Yet, we also know that, by contrast, Wittgenstein maintains that given contexts include the rules of their language game. Besides, we cannot ignore that within the "law's empire" in particular, legal rules are contained within the same legal discourse's game – for legal disputation about different normative orientations is the basic rule of the law's theoretical and practical reproduction as a meaningful social system (Mohr 2000). This being so, it is apparent that a basic pre-condition to raise women lawyers' "voice" is that they must become directly and manifestly aware of such too often covered, underestimated or ignored "constitutional framework" .

In this respect, it is interesting to note that, without abandoning or repressing their own bio-socio-psychological "moral orientations in law", women lawyers are now qualifying their gender specificity not only from the "interior", but also from the "exterior" legal viewpoint in order to question to what extent legal education and professional structures – as organizational settings – are "dependent variables" as regards their individual and collective expectations. In other words and in a nutshell, they are now engaged in critically discussing the "construction" of their professional setting from either a cultural or a structural perspective, in order to promote – to fully embody – what might be called the "gender-oriented added-value" of the professional power-knowledge nexus. And this is done well beyond the above mentioned bio-socio-psychological "ethic-of-care" attitude.

Proof of the above is offered by a wider debate such as that which occurred at the 5th European Conference on Gender Equality in Higher Education held in Berlin 28th - 31st August 2007. During this conference women claimed: (i) the necessity to reframe current quality standard grids about higher education's contents and credentials, given the increasing diverse demand/supply options of/about knowledge, science and education in different countries: this, on the socio-political premise that the more women enter into higher education, the more their gender potentials have to be recognised as a qualitative matter; (ii) the necessity to take into account the intersection of different – asynchronous and asymmetrical – space-time inequality constraints not only between men and women, but also among women, either at EU level or within each country-specific legal fieldworks, i.e. to openly recognize the "non-simultaneity" of opportunities to gain comparable excellence, positions, voices, etc. in both the European higher knowledge area and the European legal space; (iii) the necessity to devote studies to achieving a better understanding of the overall social impact of the rising "feminization" in higher education and gendered division of labour in academic and professional systems, to consequently set up appropriate provisions in each EU country and in each disciplinary fieldwork; (iv) the necessity to decouple either teaching from research or teaching/research from management, in order to make apparent and/or emphasize gender potentials (creativity, ability, commitment, etc.) in each legal field; (v) the necessity to promote theoretical definitions of a general model of "feminization" at institutional level in order to overcome, once for all, traditional conceptions of knowledge and know-how as a "neutral" social constructions (Blattel-Mink 2008).

As one can see, altogether, the above claims deal with a number of gender issues that are pivotal for contemporary European society in general, and EU governance policy in particular. Looking at each and all of them from the gender "voice" perspective, therefore, it is noteworthy that they put into question the whole EU "equal opportunity" and "non discrimination" law-policy making as a way "to make Europe the most advanced knowledge society in the world within the next decade" (just to recall the well-known 2001 Lisbon Programme official statement). In fact, (i) the quest for "equal opportunity" and "non discrimination" is not referred, as it was in the past, to male *versus* female unbalances, but directly to intra-professional cleavages among the same would-be women lawyers; in turn (ii) the quest to get rid of the "non-neutrality" of knowledge and know-how as a social construction is not referred to an undetermined fieldwork, but to a significant part of the Bologna Process, that is "suffering the consequences" of the EU eastward enlargement in particular.

In any case, however, what is striking is that in the course of the Conference a major emphasis has been put on variables concerned with a general re-definition of professional status-roles and credentials, rather than on developing a deeper introspection about the changing patterns of both the professional *habitus* and the professional *doxa*. In other words, what has been left aside – and therefore what is still lacking – is a serious concern for the core topic of any education, i.e. the *rationale* of professional status-roles and credentials in relation to the broader *epistemic* conditions of the institutional system as a whole.

This being so, it seems useful to move now towards this so far rather unexplored context and offer some insights suitable for a prospective gender-oriented professional agenda. For this purpose, let me sketch four socio-legal scenarios concerning the European province of law.

First scenario: The impact of legal polycentricity on European lawyers' "cognitive maps" and "nomic function"

The need to focus on current and prospective trends within the whole province of law in Europe is quite self-evident: Without a comprehensive understanding of the general state of the legal domain in Europe it is impossible for any European lawyer to have anything significant to say about the professional realm. This holds even more true for European women lawyers', for such an understanding can not only significantly mark the "not neutral" specificity of their socio-cultural standing, but can also significantly improve their "authority to speak" within the professional arena.

As we know, the province of law in Europe – as in many other parts of the world – is no longer as it was even in the most recent past: Not only do we live in an era of "legal polycentricity" (Petersen/Zahle 1995), but the same plurality of legal systems changed in the last decades. Legal pluralism today does not imply a mere (relatively independent) "co-existence" only, but also a veritable interactive "co-evolution" between an increasing variety of different legal sources. These sources perform, in their turn, different forms of legal cognition, production and enforcement. In other words, as current processes of legal collisions and collusions, transplantations and rejections, convergence and fragmentations, interpenetration and decoupling, indicate, we are witnessing a veritable erosion of vested legal arrangements, while we are also involved in a radical complexification of new legal mainstreams (Olgiati 2006b).

At a theoretical level, some scholars give a phenomenological definition of the above worldwide legal dynamic as "interlegality" (Sousa Santos 1987). By contrast, other scholars, see it as a conflictual legal playground and warn about "the vain search for legal unity in the fragmentation of global law" (Teubner 2004). In turn, serious doubts are cast about the fact that a "global law" – as William Twining put it – ever existed or exists today at all (Twining 2001).

Needless to say, such a disquieting state of affairs has a devastating impact on the so-called *"knowledge mandate"* of any legal professions: in particular, on lawyers' everlasting mission "to reduce socio-legal complexity" (Luhmann 1972; Friedman 1989). In fact, to the extent that this mission becomes problematic and less effective, any attempt to construct a coherent legal discourse and a coherent professional setting loses a great deal of its core "rationale". Empirical evidence of this trend is clearly provided at present by a variety of processes deconstructing traditional "cognitive maps" of lawyers trained according to the theory and practice of State-nation's positive legal system. Not only can the kind of "power-knowledge" that they embodied so far hardly be operationally assessed as an undisputed hegemonic legal discourse anymore, but it is routinely challenged by other, basically different (if not entirely incompatible), legal cultures, structures and techniques. The rising "colonising" performativity of an extra-territorial legal field such as *lex mercatoria*, or the increasing legal autonomy (self-determination), autarchy (self-organization) and autocriny (self-jurisdiction) of most powerful transnational economic corporations acting as veritable sources of legal cognition and production, are just two cases in point (Olgiati 2005).

Needless to say, compared to other continental contexts, the current state of legal polycentricity takes on an even greater relevance in Europe, due to the fact that the promotion of the EU constitutional process couples with the exhaustion of the century-old State-Nation building project: a fact that aggravates the already advanced epochal decline of the, once hegemonic, role of State-produced formal-official positive law. Besides, the same EU constitutional process fosters the EU quest for new EU-oriented "organic" legal expertises, i.e. for a general "professional reconversion" of legal practitioners towards EU issues, and accordingly a new set of EU-specific qualification grids. Altogether, therefore, traditional European lawyers' technical *speciality*, cultural *identity* and socio-political *loyalty*, i.e. their pivotal professional "commitments" towards both national legal settings and national interests and values, are also seriously challenged. In short, and in a nutshell, not only are European lawyers witnessing the erosion of their century-old State-centred professional model, but they are also perceiving that the professional "power-knowledge nexus" that they embodied no longer exists, and will not be in the future, coherently shaped as it previously was either at the interior, or at the exterior institutional level (Olgiati 1996; 2006c).

Why it is important to recall these issues? Because (i) law – any law – cannot be reduced to a matter of mere legal education and, even less to mere legal doctrine, it being neither a true science, nor a mere cultural domain, for (ii) it is specifically tailored to *mediate* in actual practice – in terms of "defence", "stabilisation" and "promotion" – the variety of issues stemming from both vested constituencies (the claim for political order) and the broader social dynamic (the claim about new arrangements). Consequently (iii) lawyers can steadily assess the utility and necessity of their expertise in society, if – and only if – they are able to perform a veritable "*nomic*" function, i.e. are able to act as proper "*(b)ordering*" (gate-keeping) agents between public order and social justice (Olgiati 1998).

But: What sort of *nomic* function can a European lawyer perform in an age of horizontal and vertical legal polycentrism? What sort of legal expertise will a European lawyer need in order to manage in a technically coherent and socially trustworthy way the kind of legal complexity that the asynchronous, asystematic and asymmetrical co-variation of the existing variety of legal systems produces in Europe at present? These are the pivotal questions that European lawyers, European women lawyers included, cannot avoid. And these are the items that European women lawyers should put at the top of their professional agenda if they wish to be authoritatively "heard" within and outside the future EU legal domain. Otherwise they might be trapped into additional difficulties. After all: How can one exclude that the kind of legal polycentrism that is running in present day society does not reproduce, at another level, a new sort of "glass ceiling", i.e. the spreading of unequal opportunities and discriminations as constitutive patterns of the selfsame polycentric legal dynamics?

Second scenario: Lawyers' "(b)ordering" function, the new "struggle for the law" and the EU's "defensive modernization" law-policy making

Unfortunately, it is not possible to discuss how effective the "*nomic*" function of lawyers acting as "boundary agents" between political power and social dynamics can be, if such a function is coherently supported by an equally coherent set of legal methods and contents. A discussion of this sort would imply going through the whole history of both legal education and legal professionalism.

However, to make clearer the kind of problems that current legal polycentricity raises as regards the (b)ordering function of lawyers, let me just open a window and deal with the impact on legal professions of the veritable "struggle for the law" between public and private legal systems that characterizes at present, and will characterize even more in the future, the European law-and-society dynamic, and EU governance in particular.

As we know, the legal professions' power-knowledge knot in Europe began to be seriously questioned from the beginning of last century onwards. Since then, the rising impact of social and legal pluralism compelled European lawyers to reorient their "cognitive maps" from legal positivism and idealistic formalism (Kelsen) to legal realism (Hagestrom). At the educational level, such a move was an explicit reaction to the coupling of two diverging socio-cultural trends: the rise of a veritable "*Kampf um's Recht*" (Jhering 1872), as well as a "*Kampf um die Rechtswissenschaft*" (Kantorowicz 1906) within State-oriented law-policy, and the rise of the so-called "living/unofficial law" at societal level (Ehrlich 1912). More recently, however, it is apparent that European lawyers are inclined to abandon both legal positivism and realism, and to take on a more pragmatic and eclectic legal viewpoint. Some of them, morally and culturally "disenchanted" by the declining validity and efficacy of positive State law are even attracted by new theoretical models, as studies devoted to legal surrealism (Warat 1988) and legal nihilism (Irti 2004) indicate. Other lawyers, having perceived the growing relevance of transnational economic corporations' "legal activism" worldwide, are simply "escaping" from State law-oriented legal practice to gain a new status and a new expertise as agents of market-oriented values and interests. In the meanwhile, evidence shows that a variety of new legal professionals are now directly trained, and are practicing, as "organic" agents of transnational corporations' legal systems.

As a matter of fact, transnational corporations' legal systems and legal professions have grown geometrically in the past decades at both cultural and operational level, thanks to their strategic policy to set up their own, self-referential, legal training and research centres. Given the above, it is hardly surprising to note that their own qualified lawyers are now acting as economic corporation-oriented legislators, counsellors and constables, running their own legal court systems and are able to disseminate their own values and interests according to their own legal press and scientific studies also. As if this is not enough, thanks to their financial resources, they are not only increasingly acting as sponsors of traditional public higher legal education institutions, but are now pursuing an "aggressive merger" policy in this respect.

The fact that as early as 2006 one could read in the English newspaper *The Independent* an article titled "Oxford dons have rejected plans to hand over control of the 900-year-old university to business and political leaders" (The Independent, January 10th, 2006) should not be undervalued: It is just one of the most remarkable signs that epitomize the fact that transnational economic corporations are now oriented to overcome the kind of "competition" that they have been carrying out so far *vis-à-vis* the whole field of State-oriented legal theory and practice. They are now trying to officially establish a visible "cultural supremacy" at the most prestigious institutional level. In other words, they are now trying to assess their own "organizational dominance" over the entire legal domain. If this statement is correct, legal education, therefore, is going to become a veritable battlefield from now on, as the undisputed supremacy of any "professional projects" can only stem from an undisputed control of the most refined legal tradition also. In fact, is it not true that, by its very nature, "organizational dominance" (Olson 1986) can neither be achieved nor steadily kept by virtue of mere economic or political power, but requires the assessment of a hegemonic position at symbolic level? And is it not true that, sooner or later, such an assessment requires an explicit socio-institutional legitimation?

Well: If one now considers that full legal legitimacy is precisely what economic corporations are now claiming in order to be officially recognised as veritable social and legal "institutions" concerned with social values and higher culture (Cameron/Taylor-Sand 2007), one can even say that the news that has been quoted *supra* signals indeed an epochal turning-point: By historical analogy – and, of course, *mutatis mutandis* – it reminds us of what occurred in Europe during the Middle Ages – an age of widespread social and legal pluralism –, i.e. either the well-known political, cultural and institutional consequences of the challenge epitomised by the claim "*Silete Theologi in munere alieno*" made by Alberico Gentili, law lecturer at Oxford, against the traditional legal education of his time, or the equally well-known "*fight for investiture*" started by Philip the Handsome – as a prototype of a new political-patrimonial force acting as *pouvoirs constituants* (the emerging national Monarchies) – against the religiously vested *pouvoir constituèe* of the time (the Holy Roman Empire). In short, what is seriously at stake at present is who will culturally define and politically rule from now on the prerogatives of those legal agents who officially "make apparent" who is entitled to hold the highest normative power (Olgiati 2007).

Given all that has just been said, it is not by chance that, as early as 1988, Rectors of the most prestigious European Universities signed in Bologna – on the occasion of the celebrations of the Ninth Centenary of the *Alma Mater Studiorum* – the *Magna Charta Universitatum* to interlock and protect the century-old University system. Equally, it is not by chance that, since then, the EU, as such, is pursuing a systematic preventative "defensive modernization" policy as regards higher knowledge reproduction (as the EU Directive on Mutual Recognition of Diplomas, the Bologna Declaration, the Nice Treaty, the Lisbon Declaration, etc., demonstrate).

Elsewhere I have dealt with the evolutionary steps of this kind of EU "defensive modernization" law-policy making in detail (Olgiati 2001; 2006c; 2007). Here it is worth stressing only that a major political result of the EU attempt to defend and promote the European centuries-old *trésor caché* – to quote a well-known Jacques Delors' definition (Delors 1996) – has been the official assessment of an absolutely new *joint* conceptualisation of "European science" and "European governance": In fact, "European science" is now officially conceived by the EU as a "policy-related science"; in turn "European governance" is now conceived by the EU as the "institutional/political synthesis between European science and European society" (CEC 2000; 2001). Needless to say, the importance of this new EU conceptualisation is an issue that no one in Europe should underestimate: To the extent that it makes explicit the kind of threat that is encroaching on a number of age-old European civilisational patterns, it also compels to reframe the theory and practice of educational systems and professional knowledge and know-how as institutionalised fieldworks provided by a margin of "relative autonomy" *vis-à-vis* their broader socio-political context. It is clear therefore that if European lawyers – women lawyers included – wish to keep alive the core issues of a thousand-years-old professional experience such as that of the *nomic* agency between political and social dynamics, they have to theoretically "interpret" and practically "handle" such EU provisions accordingly.

As far as European women lawyers are concerned, the above might even offer the opportunity to reflexively react to the new EU framework not only by "giving voice" to a *specific* gender perspective, but also by "calling" their fellow-men to take full advantage of the so-called "creative freedom", i.e. that kind of ability stemming from those change-oriented learning processes that – as Bauman, following Bateson, put it – help to "release the brain" from up-to-date cognitive standards (Bateson 1976; Bauman 2002).

Third scenario: The assessment of the "*ratio juris*" as a core issue of any legal education supply

The sketchy picture of the above scenarios provides us with a sort of "understanding net" to widen the discussion and focus on an additional item that is usually left aside and ignored: the selective choice of a given *ratio juris* as core issue of current legal education supply. To deal with the topic let us take as exemplary models recent experiences about the so-called "formation while on duty", otherwise labelled "Continuing Legal Education" for active practitioners.

On this kind of formation – sometimes also qualified as "refresher courses" – a rising amount of literature is now available (Saitta 2007). Unfortunately, however, studies and research carried out on the topic emphasize, as a rule, the novelty and specialism of given educational methods and contents as major qualifying and appealing items of the courses on supply. By contrast, it is now increasingly apparent that what is much more culturally relevant are either their manifest/latent underlying structural/functional pre-conditions – i.e. the competing variety of current legal systems – or their manifest/latent socio-institutional and political-ideological implications, i.e. the dissemination of *certain* legal values and interests.

The rising importance of such too often neglected variables, can be outlined by looking at two radically different, but exemplary, experiences, both regarding the role and function of *public* supply: those condensed respectively into (i) the comparative analysis on "Lawyers' Continuing Legal Education" Law School Courses in various countries, carried out at the European Law Faculties Association Conference held in Hamburg, February 28th - March 1st 2008 (Griffith-Baker 2007); and (ii) the general guidelines of a highly selective EU education and training programme for European judges carried out in recent years under the aegis of the EU Council (Piana 2007).

As far as the 2008 ELFA Conference comparative analysis is concerned, two opposite views have been stressed. Some speakers maintained that the persistence of national differences in providing Continuing Legal Education Courses on the part of Law Schools should be considered positively, due to the fact that, in spite of their local organizational patterns, such differences could turn into a veritable systemic "added value" for Europe. Consequently they also stressed the opportunity to allow Law Schools – once adequately re-organized for the purpose – to further enlarge their CLE supply, by officially allowing them not only to run such courses, but to supervise quality standards and provide *ad hoc* academic credentials. This, on the assumption that CLE courses run by private agents – basically law firms – are considered not able to produce an adequate systematic apprenticeship and a cumulative learning experience, given the harsh competition among the same private agents and their rush to cover "just in time" the occasional variety of new items raised by the broader socio-economic change. Other speakers – by contrast – maintained that University Law Schools "should think long and hard about whether CLE fits in with their mission statements", as "CLE does not require the disinterested academic analysis to which Law Schools are accustomed" (Griffith-Baker 2007, pp. 128 - 129).

As one can see, during the Conference the real issue at stake was the kind of *ratio juris* that CLE courses can provide at present in Europe and/or are meant to promote and disseminate in the future. In this respect it is significant indeed the extent to which the distinction between public (State)-oriented and private (market)-oriented CLE courses has been assessed not so much in terms of demand rates, but in terms of the suppliers' educational mission. In other words, the Conference's debate ran around the cultural and political implications of current legal polycentrism and the way in which its impact could vary at European level in the future.

Let us look now at the experience of the EU education and training programme for national judges carried out in recent years under the aegis of the EU Council. The peculiarity of this sort of CLE programme is that it (i) concerned a small, pre-selected, group of judges already active in their national jurisdictions, and (ii) aimed at assessing the degree of their "judicial capacity" as agents of EU judicial *Strukturbildung* according to the provisions and principles of the Schengen and Copenhagen EU Treaties. Given such a refined framework, five items were selected as basic programmatic guidelines: to establish highly selective, elitarian, judicial networking groups; to develop trans-national judicial cooperation; to promote specialised administrative/managerial "twinnings"; to elaborate common visions about given legal issues; to strengthen processes of socialisation. In summing up: to establish either convergent or shared socio-professional standards in order to improve the coupling of judicial activities at EU level in spite of persistent differences at national legal systems' level. What is remarkable about this programme, therefore, is the emphasis put on the joint construction of a common legal consciousness and a personal acquaintance: a process that can be carried out, so far, at elitarian level only. Equally striking, in turn, is the fact that – albeit at elitarian level – EU, as such, took on the leadership in the field of experimental courses on EU legal education and training, by assuming directly, at that time, the demand as well as the supply role-function: a mission that perfectly matches with the original task of the well-known EU Venice Commission, i.e. the first EU arena specifically set up not only to provide socio-cultural exchanges, but also, and above all, to elaborate common judicial ideologies and disseminate common doctrinarian EU-oriented legal recommendations based on common judicial experiences. It goes without saying that in this EU Council programme, the core issue at stake has been the assessment of the EU *ratio juris*, not as such, but in relation to a wider, hierarchically subordinated, polycentric legal field: i.e. by means of a "consensual" superimposition, rather than an "open" competition.

Why have I put to the fore two radically opposite experiences? Because they make apparent to what extent the legal education demand-supply models that are running in Europe cannot be – because they are not – immediately related, in the first and last instance, to mere market issues only. Of course, no one denies or underestimates either the number and quality or the social, legal and political impact of private, market-oriented CLE courses in Europe. But, even at a superficial level of insight, it is clearly apparent that what really matters – even in this case – is precisely the kind of *ratio juris* that these market-oriented CLE courses "embody" and promote.

As the experience of Continuing Legal Education supply provided by public institutions such as University Law Schools shows, any course has, and will have, to take into account the existence of market-oriented legal stuffs and therefore offer a type of education and training enabling (mainly private) lawyers to practice law in a general context of legal polycentricity and interprofessional competition. However, their main task is still, and will be, that to handle these variables in terms of contents and methods in accordance with their unique institutional mission as well as their compliance with their reference legal system. In other words – *because* of current state of legal polycentricity – the main problem of CLE Law School courses, is, and will be, to assess the *ratio juris* that qualifies their legal fieldwork and legal practitioners respectively, as their own, specific, cultural "added values" and professional "competitive advantages".

In turn, the experience of the EU education and training programmes for judges offers us another side of the same coin. In this case the problem is not interprofessional competition, but the opposite, i.e. professional operational convergence, in order to come to terms as soon as possible with the theoretical and practical cleavages still existing between the EU *acquis communautaire* and national legal systems. As has been noticed *supra*, this task implies the recognition of a state of "vertical" legal polycentricity. Surely such recognition does exclude a concern for private, market-oriented legal arrangements. But, if so, the core meaning of those programmes – i.e. the assessment of EU *ratio juris* – becomes even more self-evident.

Well: Having considered the *rationale* of the above CLE experiences, one wonders: what about gender variables, i.e., in our case, what about the European women lawyers' "voice"?

As we know, as regards private market-oriented agencies providing CLE courses, women lawyers' "voice" does not play a significant role, the increasing number of women attending notwithstanding. Surely certain courses on certain legal matters – e.g. family law – can be particularly attractive for women lawyers' legal practice. But, due to the fact that the *ratio juris* of private legal orders is basically oriented towards economic and interprofessional competition, the enforcement of "equal opportunity" and "non-discrimination" principles does not matter, for gender, as such, merely constitutes an individual, personal, social variable.

As far as public Law School CLE courses are concerned, by contrast, women lawyers' "voice" is taken into account in so far as it is perceived as a relevant variable for the democratic asset and constitutional implications of national legal systems. However, in spite of the rising attendance of women, it is clear that their major concern is not "gender difference" in law, but the attempt to recruit attendants to keep steady their credentialing system, while complying with EU law-policy making.

Rather different, in turn, is the case of EU training programmes for judges on duty at the national level. In this case the "gender" is explicitly and increasingly heralded as an issue of fundamental importance. Evidence of such a political-ideological tendency is provided by the EU sponsored international comparative Research Project promoted in 2004 by the Italian "Consiglio Superiore della Magistratura" (with the participation of the French Ministry of Justice, the Spanish General Council of the Judicial Power, the Italian Ministry of Justice and the Office of Public Prosecutors of the Romanian Supreme Court) on "*La partecipazione equilibrata degli uomini e delle donne al processo decisionale*" (*Partecipation équilibrée des hommes at des femmes dans la prise de décision*) in order to identify and remove the obstacles to women judges' equal opportunities and non-discrimination in any matter related to the Judiciary system (Quaderni del CSM 2004): a Research Project nurtured by early works carried out in the course of a decade by the "*Comitato per le Pari Opportunità nella Magistratura*" set up at national level by the same Italian CSM. (Quaderni del CSM 2002).

Having said this, however, one cannot hide or ignore that the above Research Project started at the time of the "Kalanke Ruling", made by the European Court of Justice in 1995, and involving the threat that the same EJC, supporting a traditional interpretation of the concept of "equality", outlawed national measures of "positive action" on behalf of women, on the premise that such actions were incompatible with EC law (Liebert 1999). Equally, one cannot undervalue that, even though the assessment of "fair competition" and "just recognition" principles is now clearly established in EU decision-making, the above Research Project was aimed, firstly and foremost, at addressing a much wider political issue: to reduce the ongoing "EU democratic deficit", i.e. to contribute to the assessment of what might be called a prospective "the EU doctrine of EU governance interests".

Given all the above, it is clear that a sharp professional agenda able to provide European women lawyers with an authoritative "voice" on any variables concerning legal education demand and supply cannot fail to illuminate the extent to which a gender perspective could be relevant to supporting and refining (or not) not so much "the law", as such, but the kind of *ratio juris* that better fits with human needs and values.

Fourth scenario: The rise of a post-national question of European intellectuals – democratising professional expertise and reducing the EU "democratic deficit"

All that has been said so far could not be omitted: It leads us straight to what might be considered the most relevant scenario about the same themes that have been discussed so far: the rise of a post-national question of European intellectuals at EU level and within European society as a whole.

Elsewhere I had the chance to deal with this topic in detail (Olgiati 2006c; 2008; 2009). Here, it is worth stressing just one major item: the coupling of this epochal question with the ongoing EU "democratic deficit". The problem raised by such a coupling is clear: the urge to sketch a politically plausible and socially adequate theoretical framework able to enlighten the way in which the EU is going to pursue the material and symbolic *re-conversion* of a polycentric system of professional bodies and jurisdictions that for more than two centuries have been organically entangled with – and are still normatively connected to – the civilisational paths of a variety of State-nation's forms.

Needless to say, the problem does not stem from the "burden" of still living legacies of the past only. It stems, also and above all, from paradigmatic changes in current global-local mainstreams: changes that now compel – and will compel even more in the future – EU institutions to carry out a systematic "re-engineering" strategy in order to re-produce "EU-organic European intellectuals" according to a EU specific cultural guidelines and educational structures. In fact, given the nature and space-time impact of said global-local mainstreams, EU institutions increasingly need not mere higher expertise, but trustworthy learned professionals, enabling them to come to terms with the increasing complexity and variability of overall EU decision-making. And here the other side of the same coin becomes apparent: whether (or not) the broadening entry of learned professionals within the EU policy-making systems allows a process of "democratization of their expertise", which in turn provides an increment in the degree of "democratic intelligence" – or "wise democracy" – useful for the whole EU governance. Some fear, in fact, that this broadening could lead, by contrast, to a veritable "comitology", i.e. unaccountable clanic groups of experts able to establish, by virtue of their undisputed superior knowledge and know-how, secretive lobbyist arenas, thus impeding, rather than favouring the kind of public debates and civic participation that are required to reduce the existing EU "democratic deficit" (Liberatore/Functowicz 2003).

As one can see, the epistemic scenario that has just been described is remarkable indeed: Political pressure for "expertising" and "democratising" EU decision-making raises – for the first time – the institutional problem of assessing the existence (or not), of a *genuine* commitment of European learned professionals to a *full* – i.e. vertical and horizontal, *ex ante* and *ex post* – accountability and a *fair* – i.e. democratically-inspired – involvement within the wider process of EU "organizational learning" aimed at stabilizing the same EU by constitutional project by means of a wider "communitarian convergence" at the social and cultural level.

Well: If the above is correct, it follows that any European professional group is, and will be even more in the future, called to provide and share their expertise at EU level according to a *new EU-oriented* professional "*doxa*": a *doxa* – it is worth stressing – that, in the case of European lawyers cannot but be assessed according to a *new official qualification* of their unique "*status activae civitatis*", otherwise they will be entitled to act – as Habermas would put it – as a mere "medium" only, rather than as a proper "institution", or – to put it otherwise – as mere "law merchant" lacking any democratic "virtue", rather than as a proper "law-and-society builder" reminiscent of the symbolic and material legacy of a legal tradition spanning from ancient Roman jurists to Rudolf von Gneist's professional ideal-type.

Having said this, *il va de soi* that if European women lawyers were able to commit themselves and develop a gender-oriented theoretical contribution on the two issues mentioned above, they would gain the most extraordinary prize that they are still dreaming of: to let their "voice" mark substantially the future history of European legal professionalism.

(*) This contribution is the revised and expanded product of an occasional speech on "Legal Education" that I had the opportunity to give at the 8th EWLA Congress "Being Heard in the Future Europe", organized by the European Women Lawyers Association (in association with the Women Lawyers' Forum) at the BPB Law School, London, UK, in July 2008.

References

Bachofen, Johann Jakob (1861), 'Mutterrecht', in K. Meuli (ed.) (1943), *J. J. Bachofens Gesammelte Werke*, Basel.

Bateson, Gregory (1976), *Verso una ecologia della mente*, Adelphi, Milano.

Bauman, Zygmunt (2002), *L' istruzione post-moderna*, Il Mulino, Bologna.

Beck, Ulrich (2006), 'Living in a World Risk Society', *Lectio Doctoralis, Laurea Honoris Causa*, Facoltà di Giurisprudenza, Università degli Studi di Macerata, lecture held on 12.10.2006.

Bentham, Jeremy (1787), 'Panopticon, or the Inspection House', in J. Bowring (1843) (ed.), *The Works of Jeremy Bentham*, Vol. IV, William Tait, Edinburgh.

Blättel-Mink, Birgit (2008), 'Reinventing Gender in Higher Education. Conference Report: 5th European Conference on Gender Equality in Legal Education, Berlin, Germany 28th - 31th August 2007', in *Equal Opportunities International*, Vol. 27, No. 1, pp. 107 - 111.

Bourdieu, Pierre (1990), *The Logic of Practice*, Polity Press, Cambridge.

Bourdieu, Pierre/L. D. Wacquant (1992), *An Invitation to Reflexive Sociology*, Polity Press, Cambridge.

Cameron, Camille/Michelle Taylor-Sands (2007), 'Corporate Government as Model Litigants', in *Legal Ethics*, Vol. 10, 2, pp. 154 - 175.

CEC, Commission of the European Communities (2000), *Governance and Expertise*, [htpp://governance.Jrc.it/] retrieved on 10.1.2011.

CEC, Commission of the European Communities (2001), *European Governance. A White Paper*, [http://ec.europa.eu/governance/white_paper/index_en.htm] retrieved on 10.1.2011.

Davies, Celia (1996), 'The Sociology of Professions and the Profession of Gender', in *Sociology*, 30/4, pp. 661 - 678.
Delors, Jacques (1996), 'Learning: The Treasure Within', *Report* to UNESCO of the International Commission on Education for the Twenty-first Century.
De Jouvenel, Bertrand (1964), *L'art de la conjecture. Futuribles*, Editions du Rocher, Monaco.
Ehrlich, Eugen (1912), *Grundlegung der Soziologie des Rechts*, Duncker & Humblot, München/Leipzig.
Foucault, Michel (1981), *L'Ordre du Discours*, Gallimard, Paris.
Friedman, Lawrence M. (1989), 'Lawyers in Cross-Cultural Perspective', in R. Abel/P.S.C. Lewis (eds.), *Lawyers in Society. Comparative Theories*, Vol. 3, University of California Press, Berkeley, pp. 1 - 26.
Gilligan, Carol (1982), *In a Different Voice*, Harvard University Press, Cambridge/ Massachussets.
Griffith-Baker, Janine E. (2007), 'Report from 2008 Conference of the European Faculties Association', *Legal Ethics*, Vol . 10, part 2, pp. 124 - 130.
Hunter R.(2002), 'Talking on Equality: Women Barristers and the Denial of Discrimination', in *Feminist Legal Studies*, Vol. 10, No. 2, pp. 113 - 120.
Jhering, (von) Rudolf (1872), *Der Kampf um's Recht*, Manz'sche Buchandlung, Wien.
Kantorowicz, Hermann (1906), *Der Kampf um die Rechtswissenschaft*, C. Winter Universitätsbuchhandlung, Heidelberg.
Kohen, Beatriz (2009), "The Family Law Judges of the City of Buenos Aires. A View from Within", in *International Journal of the Legal Profession*, Special Issue on Gender Judging, (in print).
Kuhlman, Ellen (2008),"Gender, Law and Professionalism: Intersecting Areas of Changing Governance Practices in Europe", in V. Olgiati (ed.), *Higher Legal Culture and Postgraduate Legal Education in Europe*, ESI, Napoli, pp. 67 - 81.
Irti, Natalino (2004), *Nichilismo giuridico*, Laterza, Roma/Bari.
Le Feuvre, Nicky (1998), 'Feminisation of Professional Groups in Comparative Perspective: Some Theoretical Considerations', in V. Olgiati/L. Orzak/M. Saks (eds.), *Identity and Order in Comparative Perspective*, IISL Onati Papers, 4/5, pp. 233 - 253.
Liebert, Ulrike (1999), 'Gender Politics in the European Union: the Return to the Public', in *European Societies*, Vol. 1, No. 2, pp. 197 - 239.
Liberatore, Angela/Silvio Functowicz (2003), 'Democratising Expertise, Expertising Democracy', in *Social Science and Public Policy*, Special Issue 3, No. 30, pp. 146 - 150.
Luhmann, Niklas (1972), *Rechtssoziologie*, Rowohlt Taschenbuch Verlag, Hamburg.
Menkel-Meadow, Carrie (1996), 'Women's Ways of "Knowing" Law: Feminist Legal Epistemology, Pedagogy and Jurisprudence', in N. Goldberg/J. Tarule/B. Clichy/M. Belenky (eds.), *Knowledge: Difference and Power. Essays Inspired in Women's Ways of Knowing*, Basic Books, New York, pp. 57 - 84.
Menkel-Meadow, Carrie (1997), 'Portia on a Different Voice: Speculations on a Woman's Lawyering Process', in H. Barnett (ed.), *Sourcebook on Feminist Jurisprudence*, Cavendish Publ., U.K., pp. 196 - 2003.
Mohr, Richard (2000), 'Authorised Performances: the Procedural Sources of Judicial Authority', in *Flinders Journal of Law Reforms*, Vol. 4, No.1, pp. 63 - 79.
Morondo Taramundi, Dolores (2004), 'Parità e Pari Opportunità nel pensiero femminile', in L. Califano (ed.), *Donne, politica e processi decisionali*, Giappichelli, Torino, pp. 131 - 144.

Olgiati, Vittorio (1987), 'Avvocati e notai tra professionalismo e mutamento sociale', in W. Tousjin (ed.), *Le libere professioni in Italia*, Il Mulino, Bologna, pp. 83 - 102.

Olgiati, Vittorio (1995), 'Process and Policy of Legal Professionalisation in Europe. The Deconstruction of a Normative Order', in Y. Dezalay/D. Sugarman (eds.), *Professional Competition and Professional Power*, Routledge, London, pp. 170 - 204.

Olgiati, Vittorio (1996), *Le professioni giuridiche in Europa. Politiche del diritto e dinamica sociale*, Quattroventi, Urbino.

Olgiati, Vittorio (1998), 'Can Legal Ethics Become a Matter of Academic Teaching ? Critical Observations from a Late Modern Perspective', in K. Economides (ed.), *Ethical Challenges to Legal Education and Conduct*, Hart Publ., Oxford, pp. 85 - 104.

Olgiati, Vittorio (1999), 'The Policy of Legal Higher Education in Europe', in F. Cownie (ed.), *The Law School: Global Issues, Local Problems*, Ashgate, Aldershot, pp. 163 - 194.

Olgiati, Vittorio (2001), 'Vers une refonte des communautés épistemiques en Europe', in L. Parini (ed.), *Etats et Mondialisation: strategies et roles*, L'Harmattan, Paris, pp. 191 - 223.

Olgiati, Vittorio (2002), 'The EU Charter of Fundamental Rights. Text and Context to the Rise of a "Public Interests" EU-oriented European Lawyers', in *International Journal of the Legal Profession*, Vol. 9, No. 3, pp. 253 - 250.

Olgiati, Vittorio (2003), 'Professional Body and Gender Difference in Court: The Case of the First (Failed) Women Lawyer in Modern Italy', in U. Schultz/G. Shaw (eds.), *Women in the World's Legal Profession*, Vol. II, Hart Publ., Oxford, pp. 419 - 435.

Olgiati, Vittorio (2005), 'Lex Mercatoria e Communitas Mercatorum nell'esperienza giuridica contemporanea', in *Sociologia del diritto*, No. 2/3, pp. 351 - 378.

Olgiati, Vittorio (2006 a), *Donne & Lavoro. L'inclusione della differenza di genere nelle attività economiche e professionali*, I quaderni dell'Istituto di Sociologia, Università degli Studi di Urbino 'Carlo Bo', No. 3, Ed. Goliardiche, Trieste.

Olgiati, Vittorio (2006 b), 'Il nuovo pluralismo socale, il nuovo pluralismo giuridico e la nuova identità del giurista', in A. Poggi/O. Roselli (eds.), *Trasformazioni sociali e trasformazioni giuridiche*, ESI, Napoli, pp. 59 - 91.

Olgiati, Vittorio (2006 c), 'Le trasformazioni costituzionali del professionalismo giuridico europeo', in O. Roselli (ed.), *Osservatorio sulla formazione giuridica 2006*, ESI, Napoli, pp. 61 - 88.

Olgiati, Vittorio (2007), 'Legal Polycentrism and the "Struggle for the Law" in Contemporary Legal Education in Europe', in V. Olgiati (ed.), *Higher Legal Culture and Postgraduate Legal Education in Europe*, ESI, Napoli, pp. 21 - 65.

Olgiati, Vittorio (2008), 'The European Learned Professions and the EU Higher Education Project', in *European Societies*, Vol. 10, No. 4, pp. 545 - 564.

Olgiati, Vittorio (2009), 'Potentials and Obstacles in the Promotion of Higher Knowledge in the European Area. The Post-National Question of European Intellectuals', in J. Langer (ed.), *Knowledge Region: The Alps-Adriatic Challenges,* Peter Lang, Frankfurt a. M./New York, pp. 35 - 57.

Olson, Mancur (1986), *The Logic of Collective Action,* Harvard University Press, Chicago.

Petersen, Hanne/Henrik Zahle (1995), *Legal Polycentricity. Consequences of legal Pluralism in Law*, Dartmouth, Aldershot.

Petersen, Henrik (1996), *Home Knitted Law. Norms and Values in Gendered Rule-Making*, Dartmouth, Aldershot.

Piana, Daniela (2007), '"Judicial" Education in the European Legal Space: The French Model of Ecole Nationale de la Magistrature as a Policy Enterpreneur', in V. Olgiati (ed.), *Higher Legal Culture and Postgraduate Legal Education in Europe*, ESI, Napoli, pp. 151 - 171.

Quaderni del Consiglio Superiore della Magistratura (2002), *Le Pari Opportunità in Magistratura. Dieci anni di attività del Comitato per le pari opportunità in magistratura*, Pubblicazione interna per l'Ordine giudiziario, No. 126.

Quaderni del Consiglio Superiore della Magistratura (2005), *La partecipazione equilibrata delle donne e degli uomini al processo decisionale*, Pubblicazione interna per Ordine giudiziario, No. 145.

Saitta, Pietro (2008), 'Between Promises and Reality. Supply and Demand of Masters and Refreshment Courses in Legal Matters in Four European Countries', in V. Olgiati (ed.), *Higher Legal Culture and Postgraduate Legal Education in Europe*, ESI, Napoli, pp. 189 - 202.

Larson, Magali Sarfatti (1989), 'The Changing Functions of Lawyers in the Liberal State: Reflections for Comparative Analysis', in R. Abel/P.S.C. Lewis (eds.), *Lawyers in Society. Comparative Theories*, Vol. 3, University of California Press, Berkeley, pp. 427 - 477.

Larson, Magali Sarfatti (1990), 'In the Matter of Expert and Professionals, or How Impossible it is to Leave Nothing Unsaid', in R. Torstendhal/M. Burrage (eds.), *The Formation of Professions: Knowledge, State and Strategy*, Sage, London, pp. 24 - 50.

Larson, Magali Sarfatti (2000), 'The Professions' Nomic Functions and the End of Modernity', in A. Febbrajo/D. Nelken/V. Olgiati (eds.), *Social Processes and Patterns of Social Control*, Yearbook on Sociology of Law, Giuffré, Milano, pp. 145 - 172.

Sherry, Suzanna (1986), 'Civic Virtue and the Feminine Voice of Constitutional Adjudication', in *Virginia Law Review*, Vol. 72:493, No. 3, pp. 543 - 616.

Schultz, Ulrike/Gisela Shaw (eds.) (2003), *Women in the World's Legal Professions*, The Onati International Series in Law and Society, Hart Publ., Oxford.

Sousa Santos, Boaventura (1987), 'A Map of Misreading: Towards a Post-Modern Concept of Law', in *Journal of Law and Society*, No. 20, pp. 274 - 302.

Tega, Diletta (2008), *Rappresentanza politica e riequilibrio di genere*, Il Mulino, No. 3, pp. 469 - 478.

Teubner, Gunther (2004), 'Regime-Collision: the Vain Search for Legal Unity in the Fragmentation of Global Law', in *Michigan Journal of International Law*, Vol. 25, pp. 999 - 1046.

Twining, William (2001), 'A Cosmopolitan discipline?', in *International Journal of the Legal Profession*, No. 8, pp. 26 - 36.

Warat, Luis Alberto (1988), *Manifesto do Surrealismo Juridico*, Ed. Academia, Sao Paulo.

Chapter III

Knowledge Europe

Franc Mali

The European Research Space

Introduction

In this contribution, I shall seek to show that for small scientific communities the increased processes of globalization are not only a source of challenges, but also of opportunities. For new, small EU Member States such as Slovenia increasing the level of international R&D cooperation is an essential concern. Isolated and parochial scientific communities can no longer be viewed as favourable environments for scientific excellence. In fact, this has never been the case in the history of science: In the past, various forms of cooperation between scientists had already become an important element in the internationalisation of science. Indeed, historical investigations show that right from its beginnings science has been internationalised, deterritorialised and depersonalised. For example, the first promoters of the idea of transnational scientific integration in Europe were the universities of the Middle Ages. They were able to create a truly European science at a time when the continent was interwoven with hundreds of political entities. One of the main features of the beginning of modern science in the mid-Seventeenth century was the rapid diffusion of new scientific discoveries and theories across Europe. At that time, the first scientific journals, such as the *Philosophical Transactions* of the Royal Society in London and the *Comptes Rendues* of the *Académie des Sciences* in Paris, were published nationally, but they circulated freely and were cited indiscriminately throughout the European scientific world. Nevertheless, the historical records on mediaeval universities or the first scientific journals are far away from the position of science in the recent processes of globalization. The recent changes in the processes of globalization of science, as we are experiencing them, are totally new and revolutionary. Compared to the past, the present-day situation is more complex, wider in influence and deeper in its invasiveness in the global arena. To use the words of John Ziman, through the new forms of the internationalisation of science "[…] the traditional cosmopolitan individualism of science is rapidly being transformed in what might be described as transnational collectivism." (Ziman 1994, p. 218).

In the recent processes of globalization scientific activities have become increasingly collaborative and many new organisational forms have emerged to form cross-border links among scientists. The EU is becoming a respectable political entity, situated between the national and global levels, which undertakes practical leadership in relation to the global governance of science and technology. The starting point for this contribution is that although the position of the

EU as a trans-national entity is ambiguous in many ways[1], for new, small EU Member States it is very important to accept its R&D philosophy formed in the context of the new European Research Area (ERA). Namely, in its Communication to the Council, the European Parliament, the Economic and Social Committee and the Committee of the Regions "Towards a European research area" the Commission proposed in January 2000 the creation of a European Research Area with a view to consolidating and structuring the European research landscape (cf. COM 2000). The establishment of the new ERA as a key means of achieving the strategic goals of the Lisbon strategy has lead to the establishment of various Research and Development (R&D) policy instruments that are intended to help to overcome the fragmentation of R&D activities and R&D policies across Europe and to increase various forms of R&D collaborations, which cross national borders (cf. COM 2007). The new ERA is open not only to the world, but also to cooperation with partner countries. Of course, R&D policy cannot simply be 'translated' from one country to another, since each national R&D system is shaped by historical and cultural contingencies. Nevertheless, a recent EU R&D policy approach towards more international cooperation among scientists has assisted in building bridges between national scientific communities.

For new EU Member States from Central and Eastern Europe it is strongly expected that they will open up and integrate their national R&D efforts into the larger European R&D space. In this regard, the concern of national R&D policy actors around the ERA wouldn't be oriented so much towards the politics of a 'fair return' ('*juste retour*') – actions leading to common EU R&D programmes and policies would become much more important. EU Research Framework Programmes are primarily oriented to support the joining of national R&D efforts at the EU level. They reduce differences among EU Member States and thus lead to their convergence. The Open Method of Coordination (OMC), which is coupled with the stronger guiding and co-ordinating role of the European Commission and the use of voluntary guidelines and recommendations in the context of the ERA also stimulate the processes of convergence. Although the question arises as to how far such processes of convergence have an effect on the structural aspects of national R&D systems, there is no doubt (especially for Slovenia as a small country, which joined the European Union in 2004) that it is very important to follow the processes of cross-border co-operations in science. The recent processes of globalization are leading to the unprecedented integration of nations and localities in a new global order. Even nations with very large R&D human resources are being forced to join their R&D efforts within

1 Josef Langer warns that in the era of national budget shortages for R&D, the common EU research programmes offer opportunities for public research institutions. On the other hand, with 'agenda setting' the EU is defining what it considers as important, not only in science, but in society in general (cf. Langer 2008, p. 14).

supranational entities. Of course, it would be naive to expect that in Slovenia radical changes in the internationalisation of science can be made over night. Notwithstanding this, due to the fact that Slovenia is somewhat regarded as still suffering from the heritage of the past communist times when the scientific system was strongly ideologically controlled and closed, more effort must be made to make all parts of the scientific system more internationalized. The basic assumption in this contribution is that although a reorganisation of the national R&D system had already begun in Slovenia by 1990 (including a restructuring of R&D policy as well as the implementation of a R&D system) there is still a need to make greater efforts to internationalize science.

It is not possible in this short essay to analyse comprehensively all the issues of scientific internationalisation, which have been put before Slovenia in the recent processes of globalization. For this reason the goal is not to give a detailed description of every single case, but rather to explain only the key issues, which I believe address the openness of science to the international arena.

Some requirements for increasing the links of scientists in Slovenia with the European research landscape

The reorientation of Slovenian researchers to the common EU research landscape is important for various reasons.

1. The first and perhaps the most important reason is that in a small scientific community, for many specialised research fields the relevant professional colleagues can only be found abroad. To this regard, the argument that scientists who focus entirely on taking part in the international community are running the risk of their work being of limited national relevance is not acceptable. Quite the contrary: increasing scientific specialisation produces the need and opportunities for international scientific collaboration. "Scientists who come from scientifically small countries are likely to find few, if any, colleagues in their own country. In order to avoid isolation, they have to look for partners from other countries." (cf. Lukkonen et al. 1992, p. 5). The rational organisation of science at the national level requires integration of national R&D efforts with world science. Scientific cosmopolitanism counteracts parochialism and enhances participation in transnational research networks spanning the globe.

2. The second reason is that in the context of common EU research projects, the centre-periphery model in scientific communications is less emphasised. The hierarchy between centre and periphery known from the past (cf. Scott 1993) is reduced, although not entirely abolished.[2] A broad set of actors

---

[2] Some analysis shows that universities and other research institutions from the Western and Northern part of Europe, and particularly in a limited number of regions, have the highest involvement in integrated networks. (cf. Key Figures Report 2009/2010).

(partners from EU Member States) has the chance to come to more equitable relations and positions in the common EU research networks. From this light, it is important to look at R&D activity as something that is carried out not only in centres from which knowledge spreads like waves on water, but rather as an activity going on in many places at the same time – creating a far more complex interplay.

3. The third reason is the possibility of scientists from the peripheries having higher visibility and a greater impact on the European scientific community. Sciences on the "periphery" are often put in this position not so much because of their lesser societal relevance or lack of scientific quality, but mostly because of their lack of visibility within the wider European scientific community. One of the reasons for this diminished visibility arises from the fact that in some scientific fields the results are often disseminated mostly through local scholarly publications. We must be aware that the part a small-sized country like Slovenia plays in creating basic scientific knowledge in the world will always be negligible, but access to global scientific and technological resources must show regard for a well developed domestic scientific base as well. Scientists should know how to make use of the global scientific and technological information system, how to adapt it to local needs and how to pass the knowledge on to others.

4. Last but not least, the additional (important) reason is the need for new, small EU Member countries, which have suffered from the heritage of the past communist regime to develop new R&D intermediary structures and democratic forms of decision in science. If R&D collaboration and integration occur across national borders, it also means that at the same time these processes of internationalisation increasingly foster the links between science and politics, science and the economy, and last but not least, science and society at large. The recent phenomenon of globalization is a complex set of processes in which the various social systems, which previously have been functionally differentiated tend to become integrated at various levels of structure. In the former communist regime situations of small EU Member States from Central and Eastern Europe it was just the opposite. In contrast to the proclaimed political ideology of social integration, the reality was a separation between the different social spheres. For example, academic researchers often entered into contracts with industry merely to demonstrate that the socialist intelligentsia was acting to support the working class. In reality, science was strongly controlled by a political party, which pressed researchers into isolationism on both the international and the domestic economy levels (cf. Mali 1998). There was no room left for the self-dynamism and self-organisation of science. There was an absence of any policy concept, defined by Karl Popper as "piecemeal social engineering" (cf. Popper 1997, p. 16).

Political democratisation in 1990 brought with it the requirement to promote political culture, which put forward the idea of hybrid communities in society. "Hybrid communities consist of people who have been socialised in different subsystems, disciplines or working environments, but who subsequently adopt different styles of thought, modes of behaviour, knowledge and social competence" (cf. Gibbons et al. 1994, p. 37). In the context of the hybridisation between science and politics, it was very important that various types of intermediary structures were formed. Namely, the intermediary bodies in a parliamentary democracy have a relative autonomy from the state, which is especially important in the negotiation processes between the interests of different parts of society (cf. Braun 1997). At the same time, it is expected that these intermediary bodies will try to find the balance between the autonomy and the heteronomy of the science system. Namely, the traditional definition of autonomy (being self-governing or self-ruling, not being responsible for the social environment) is no longer adequate today. The creation of new research councils could be treated as an important step in the establishment of modern intermediary scientific structures.[3]

Today systemic concepts such as interpenetration, networks etc., which appear in the writings of the modern systemic authors are heuristic, and very useful in helping to analyse intermediary scientific structures. Interpenetration occurs when two systems overlap in some manner (share certain elements or have closely coupled elements) without however losing their autonomy and identity. The interactions between interpenetrating systems are different from those which occur between supersystems and their subsystems or between independent systems with sharply defined boundaries. They are much more subtle and difficult to measure. Some of the links are deeply hidden from an external observer, others are weak but have important cumulative effects over longer periods of time, and so on.

It is interesting that in Slovenia, during the first phase of transition in the 1990s, no intermediary structures such as research councils were created. The Slovenian Agency for Scientific Research was not established until 2000. It has constructed its own system of peer review panels to evaluate research proposals and make recommendations regarding funding, etc..

With the creation of the Agency for Scientific Research, scientists gained a more important role in R&D policy regulation. The R&D policy discourse depended more on expert decision-making, not only on voluntary political actions. However, as observed by many analysts, modern social regulation of science

---

[3] In the context of the principal-agent theory, which fundamentally deals with delegation as a particular kind of social relationship, research funding agencies and councils have been regarded as an intermediary between the principal (policy-makers) and the agents (the researchers). The intermediary is in a situation in which "the needs and interests it formulates towards the agent are actually someone else's interests, and, likewise, the performances it shows towards the principal are also performances of others" (cf. Van der Meulen 2003, p. 328).

cannot be left only in the hands of scientists and politicians (cf. Felt/Fochler 2008; Jasanoff 2005). There is also a need for engagement of civil society in the social governance of science. The need to embrace the new role of citizens in R&D matters resonates with the debate around upstream public engagement and the call to move away from a mode of governance, which focuses on issues of risk and safety to a governance of innovation, which addresses the way innovations develop, and how they are co-produced with the imagination of the society in which they are supposed to be embedded.

What is still missing in Slovenia, is merely the engagement of civil society in a more open and honest bi-directional dialogue with scientists and policy decision makers about science and technology and their products, including not only their benefits but also their risks and pitfalls.

Although the processes of S&T globalizations have a strong tendency to make the world homogeneous, these processes are interwoven with different cultural, economic, historical traditions, institutional designs and legal arrangements. Local differences, local values and local knowledge matter. For this reason, weight is being added to the argument for greater local participation of citizens in R&D matters. In many Western European countries the representatives of civil society are in a closer dialogue with government bodies and scientists on the appropriate directions and means for steering modern scientific and technological development. Through dialogue and other practices of commitment, non-governmental organisations endeavour to augment traditional communication models so that discourse and learning can flow not only from policy-makers and scientists to the public, but also in the reverse direction. Such efforts aim at more broadly orchestrated societal inputs than those used in the past. In some Western European countries various forms of participation of citizens in R&D policy decision-making processes have already been realized. In practice, different types of citizen participation have been formed: lay people's panels, focus groups and science shops to name just a few. Of course, consensus conferences can be seen as one of the more elaborate deliberative instruments for allowing the 'public' to take part in scientific decision-making (cf. Jamison/Lassen 2004).

Unfortunately, in Slovenia there has not been, as yet, an engagement of the lay public in R&D policy decision-making processes. The inflexible forms of communication between the different stakeholders involved in R&D policy decision-making hinder a more active role on the part of civil society. For this reason it is necessary to shift R&D policy discourse away from the authority of scientists, who for the most part advocate the classical 'deficit' model of communication[4], and from politicians, who still lack knowledge about the new type of

---

4 The classical 'deficit' model of communication is based on the assumption that only the 'rational' discourse of science is important (cf. Bucchi 2004). Today there is a need for a shift away from the deficit model towards a dialogue between citizens and experts.

'governance' of science and technology.[5] The role of civil society groups is still under-developed. There is especially a lack of civil society groups that are able to cope with the global risks of scientific and technological progress. Namely, the newly emerging sciences represent an expanding source of new risks and vulnerability in society. This risk has all the characteristics of long-term risk. In the case of the newly emerging sciences such as 'bio-', 'nano-' and the info-sciences we are facing new risks whose features are manifold: (1) the magnitude of potential damage might be unprecedented; (2) damage from the new risks might take many years to become evident and its effects could last for generations; and (3) the new risks might be vexingly uncertain for various reasons (sometimes a technology is so novel that there has simply not been enough time to test its effects within the wide range of applications in which it will be used), etc. (cf. Mali 2009).

In these new circumstances, scientists' expectations that they would be able to comprehensively and credibly identify, control, compare and evaluate the scientific risk cannot be realised. Namely, their judgments are based too strongly on formal analysis and, where possible, on a quantitative estimation of the risks. There is need to create a modern agora as the new public space where science and society co-mingle. "The modern agora is a space in which different perspectives are brought together, ultimately creating different visions, values and options" (cf. Nowotny et al. 2001, p. 209).

The need to overcome some obstacles in Slovenia to make science more internationally oriented

International scientific collaborations have many desirable outcomes, but it is also clear that collaborations that cross borders can be difficult, expensive in both time and money, and entail non-trivial problems of coordination and communication among sometimes diverse scientists that can undermine even the best of intentions. In view of this fact, international scientific collaboration is very much a 'double-edged sword'. But, in the case of small scientific systems, there is no doubt: the internationalisation of science has to be a priority of national R&D policy efforts.

The new ERA strategy initiated by the European Commission stimulates researchers to increase cooperation in Europe and to establish a 'critical mass' of researchers at the European level.[6] To achieve this broad strategic goal of mobilis-

5 The concept of 'governance' reflects the currently changing modes of political action. By talking about governance, political actors are not referring to top-down decision-making. Instead, they are talking about interdependence, networks, partnerships (cf. Kjaer 2004).

6 As stated in the Green Paper, "closer coordination is necessary between the EU and Member States, for mutual benefit, as well as between S&T cooperation policy and other areas of external relations." (cf. COM 2007, p. 29).

ing and activating the cooperation of researchers across national borders, various instruments have been launched. Some of the most important instruments are the EU Framework Programmes. After the launch of the EU Framework Programmes it could be said that scientists no longer appear as individual members of the transnational scientific community, but as members of a well organized and structured European R&D network. The Sixth and Seventh EU Framework Programmes in particular introduced many new actions important for adapting the members of national scientific communities to this new European research network. (cf. Siune/Schmidt/Aagaard 2005; Lukkonen/Nedeva/ Barre 2006)

Inclusion in common EU research programmes provides members of small scientific communities access to world-class knowledge and raises the quality and visibility of their R&D activity in the international arena. For Slovenia, as a new EU Member State, the inclusion of scientists in EU Framework Programmes is not only important for processes of integration, but also as a reorientation to interdisciplinary and practically relevant types of research. Namely, researchers participating in the EU Framework Programmes have the best opportunity to learn how to co-operate with the business-enterprise sector. Although Slovenia had one of the highest levels of economic development of the new EU Member States during the whole transitional period, society here still faces substantial lags in implementing new R&D and innovation policy. There remains a lack of adequate mechanisms to implement the new paradigm of cooperation between academic science and industry (cf. Mali 2006).

In comparison with some other small EU Member States, Slovenia is still less exposed to the processes of R&D internationalisation, as can be observed via the international mobility of researchers, the number of publications in international journals and other types of publications, and co-authorship publications with professional colleagues from other countries. According to some bibliometric studies the publication strategies in some new EU Member States (for example Hungary) have significantly changed, from publication in national to publication in international journals. In comparison with some small EU Member States, Slovenian researchers in some fields of science still prefer to publish too much in national journals instead of highly reputable international journals. (cf. Glaenzel/Schlemmer 2007; Must 2006)

It seems that the positive exemption in the recent processes of internationalisation of science in Slovenia is represented by the high level of participation of researchers in the 6th EU Framework Programme. Although the possibility for researchers to be included in some EU research programmes had already been given before Slovenia's entry into the EU, radical change has been made within the 6th EU Framework Programme[7]. In this period, Slovenian scientists

[7] Slovenian scientists had the possibility of formally joining the EU Framework Programmes in 1999. They became a full member after Slovenia's entry into EU.

have increasingly entered into EU research networks. For example, in the 6th EU Framework Programme Slovenia has obtained the highest number of participations per thousand researchers among all EU Member States: 159 participations per thousand researchers (cf. Key Figures 2009/2010). In this regard, Slovenia has followed the practice of other small EU Member States who also have a high number of participations per thousand researchers. Namely, the propensity to participate in the 6th EU FP, as well as in other major funding instruments co-ordinated at the EU level (COST, EUREKA, etc.), is usually the highest in the relatively smaller EU countries. Scientists from Slovenia prepared 1.2 per cent of all submitted R&D proposals in the context of the 6th EU FP. The big EU Member States (Germany, Great Britain, and France) lagged far behind Slovenia. For Slovenia, as a small EU country, it is very good result.

However, the real problem seems to be that the Slovenian scientists participating in the EU Framework Programmes mostly hold positions as partners and do not take coordinating roles. It suggests that they are not especially successful in gathering their particularized and fragmentized efforts at home to be more competitive at the European level. One of the reasons for this situation is the national R&D policy discourse, which does not sufficiently encourage the big research groups to be more internationally oriented. In Slovenia, research activity is carried out in the context of research programmes and research projects.[8] The main aim of research programmes is to ensure the long term stability of research groups across all main scientific disciplines. The Slovenian Agency for Scientific Research is currently providing financial support for about 250 research programmes in all scientific fields. In the financing of these research programs (which enable the long range stability of the big research groups), there is a lack of mechanisms to reorient scientists to compete at the international level. The R&D activity of research programmes is still strongly dependent on state financial support. For this reason, the State is in the position of key stakeholder, defining 'the rules of the game' in science. It depends mainly on these R&D policy mechanisms – if it comes to the orientation of scientists in directions towards or directions away from international excellence and cosmopolitanism.

It seems that R&D policy actors in Slovenia are still not successful enough at reorienting researchers in Slovenia to the international arena. Let us look at the results of the newest bibliometric analysis dealing with the trends in international co-authorship patterns in Slovenian science (cf. Mali et al. 2010; Kronegger et al. 2010). In our bibliometric analysis we studied complete longitudinal co-authorship networks of selected scientific disciplines in Slovenia: physics,

[8] In the structure of the whole budget of Slovenian Research Agency, the funding of research programmes and projects represents the main instrument for promoting scientific research at universities and non-university public research establishments, and accounts for 48% of all budget funding. Another 19% goes to funding young researchers, 12% is for funding research infrastructures, and 20% is for other funding.

mathematics, biotechnology, and sociology. The basis for our study was Newman's (2004) analysis and a comparison of co-authorship networks constructed from three bibliographic databases in biology, physics, and mathematics. Our examination of the patterns in the collaboration networks of Slovenian scientists draws on his study and adds two substantial components. We include the collaboration networks of sociologists in order to extend the comparisons of strictly natural and technical sciences to include a representation of the so-called soft sciences. Also, we have studied the changes in the structure of collaboration networks over time (1980 - 2005). Our data sets were obtained from the Current Research Information System (SICRIS), which includes information about all active researchers registered with the Slovenian Research Agency and the Co-operative Online Bibliographic System & Services (COBISS), which includes a complete bibliography for each researcher included in the SICRIS database.

The results of our bibliometric analysis showed that scientific co-authorship collaboration in all selected disciplines consolidated into a typical core-periphery structure over time. There exists a group of well-known, highly visible researchers in Slovenia, i.e. scientific 'stars', who mostly publish their results together with their professional colleagues abroad. However, this group of scientific 'stars' mostly does not work in the very cohesive and long-range stable research groups financed by the Slovenian Agency for Scientific Research. In contrast to the 'freelance' scientific 'stars', the members of the programme groups are more oriented towards domestic publications. This suggests that in the case of Slovenia, R&D collaboration in the compact 'small world'[9] clusters is oriented towards publications, which are more often written for a local audience. Actually, the scientists in the programme groups tend to produce quantitatively more publications than the scientists working on the periphery. But, these publications are locally 'coloured'.

I do not claim that our bibliometric study offered conclusive evidence that the scientific community in Slovenia is parochial *in strictu senso*. However, in light of our analysis we saw that the R&D evaluation system in Slovenia still does not adequately stimulate big research groups to be more outwardly oriented

[9] In the social studies of science, there has always been great interest in linking scientific production to network structures of the scientific community. The various models for large-scale scientific networks correspond theoretically to expectations about scientific production. The local and global characteristics of scientific networks help to define network topologies such as 'free-scale network', 'small-world network' etc. In the case of the small-world network structures, the level of local clustering (one's collaborators are also collaborators with each other) is high, but the average number of steps between clusters is small (cf. Berg 2004). The results of our analysis argue that 'closed' and dense co-authorship networks in science have a negative effect on international orientation of scientists in small scientific communities. It does mean that in regard to scientific performance and scientific excellence, there are many more important 'open', or brokered networks, rich in structural holes.

– in spite of the fact that having an international publishing orientation (publications in highly reputable journals with an impact factor, international co-authorized publications, etc.) is important, and even necessary, for a small scientific community such as is the case in Slovenia (cf. Kramberger/Mali 2010). Visibility, one of the preconditions for the 'attractiveness' of science, can only be created by publishing internationally. The most internationally open scientific communities, even in so-called 'book-publishing disciplines' such as the humanities and social sciences, are characterized by increased publication activity in the international arena (cf. Aalotojarvi et al. 2008; Hornbostel 1997).

One of the reasons that the programme groups, which form a core structure of the Slovenian R&D landscape, are still too locally oriented in their publication behaviour is the overly high influence of informal lobby groups on the R&D evaluation system of the Slovenian Agency for Scientific Research. The excessive power of these informal groups (the principal investigators of research programmes, the directors of research institutions, etc.) leads to situations, which favour parochialism instead of internationalism. Namely, Slovenia is not only a small country, but – if we may use Thorsteinsdóttir's term – a 'mini-country' (Thorsteinsdóttir 2000, p. 434). The small size of the country does not necessarily lead to a high degree of transparency in R&D decision-making processes. With the limited formal mechanisms for co-ordination and control there is the ever present risk that R&D policy is too poorly equipped to assure more transparency and flexibility. Here, we can talk about the limits of the still overly closed scientific community and about the negative effects stemming from the excessive influence of day-to-day politics on R&D policy decision-making processes.

The indicated deficiencies of R&D policy discourse in Slovenia have negative consequences for the quite ambitious goal of increasing the size of the national core of excellent young researchers. Namely, Slovenia like all other EU Member States needs more young, highly educated experts who are employable in various sectors of society. Only in this way will it be possible to gain a leading position in the current global socio-economic competition. In fact, for more than 20 years there has been a highly organised governmental R&D policy action to recruit and educate young researchers in Slovenia. It is called The Young Researcher Programme. Due to the great diversity of national R&D systems among EU countries, it is difficult to compare the mechanism of recruitment and education of young researchers in Slovenia with similar R&D policy actions in other EU Member States. Notwithstanding this, it seems that during the whole transitional period Slovenia was heading in the right direction with its Young Researcher Programme. Last but not least, the success of this action is reflected in the fact that the age structure of scientists in Slovenia decreased in this period. It is even better than in some highly scientifically and technologically developed countries in the EU. The action has contributed to a lowering of the average age of researchers in Slovenia by more than five years in the last two decades. For example, Slovenia has 37 per cent of its highly qualified S&T workers in the 45 - 64 age group, compared to around 42 per cent in the 25 - 34 age group (cf. Statistics in Focus 2008).

From the outset the main goal of The Young Researcher Programme has been to provide new research and research-teaching staff in research organisations and to increase the research capacity of groups carrying out programmes as well as basic, applied and research development projects. Since the beginning, the action has attracted significant interest among graduates. In fact, more than 300 graduates per year were engaged in the first years of the governmental programme of financial support for young researchers. In total, 6,268 young researchers have been included in the programme over a period of about 20 years.

Let us list, at the end of our discussion, some advantages and disadvantages of the Young Researcher Programme in Slovenia. The advantages include the following successes:

1. Throughout the whole transitional period the policy action created good incentives for young people to take up a research career. At the time of the transition, it was important for young people to have a chance to acquire stable forms of financing during their doctoral studies and thereafter to have better chances of finding employment in their profession.

2. As a small transitional country with a small scientific community Slovenia was able to maintain the core of its human resources in science and technology. Under the programme Slovenia had a constant flow of young research potential, even in times of uncertainty for the science system and the brain-drain phenomenon seen at the beginning of the 1990s. Slovenia's brain drain in the transitional period can be estimated as negligible (cf. Mali 2003).

3. PhD candidates in the framework of the Young Researcher Programme do not hold the status of a fellowship. They are included in research groups within the mentor's institutions. This probably provides an explanation as to why the failure rate of PhDs is quite low.

4. More standardised procedures were established for the selection of senior researchers who can take on the role of mentors or supervisors of PhDs. More standardised criteria are also used in the selection of PhD candidates. Scientific inbreeding in the selection process is thereby reduced. At the same time, information and reputation in the labour market of researchers have improved. But, women as mentors are still underrepresented. Only about a quarter of all PhDs' mentors in the last five years have been women. One of the reasons is a general lack of female scientists with the required position detailed in the call for applications for a PhD mentor. This is a crucial aspect of 'vertical functional segregation', wherein the proportion of women with high academic titles decreases (cf. Mali/Groboljsek/Skafar 2010).

The chief disadvantage of the Young Researcher Programme is that the goal of enhancing the inter-sectoral mobility of young researchers has not been realised. From the beginning, one of the main goals of the programme was to increase the mobility of scientists (after finishing their PhDs) from academic institutions to industry. This goal has largely remained unrealised. Only a few of those with a PhD degree have entered industrial R&D departments. In total, about 60 per cent have remained in academic research institutions (75% of all PhDs), about 20 per cent have joined the business sector (10% of all PhDs) and a similar number have continued their career in public administration (15% of all PhDs). Researchers who have finished a PhD in Slovenia are still more highly concentrated in the public sector.

This lies in contrast to all the basic strategic goals of the ERA. As previously stated, from the time the ERA strategy was accepted there has been a big policy challenge for the EU on how to achieve adequate mobility amongst competent young researchers between different sectors at the national and European level. It is thus little wonder that in the context of the ERA it has exposed as a mantra the need in The European Research Area's Vision for a full opening of academic research positions and national research programmes across Europe, with a strong drive to recruit researchers internationally, and easy movement between disciplines and between the public and private sectors.

Conclusions

As a new, small EU Member State the main challenge for Slovenia is to raise the international quality and visibility of researchers. Because of the legacy of the past it is a much more urgent need. Namely, in the old communist regimes all areas of science in this part of the world were for decades (after World War II) relatively closed in their national borders, and therefore parochial and locally 'coloured'. Of course, the political democratisation at the beginning of the Nineties opened the national borders for science as well. Notwithstanding this, even at a time when Slovenia is already a six-year full member of the EU, there is a need to lead R&D policy discourse that will strongly encourage researchers to open up to the international arena. In the present short essay, a modest attempt has been made to point out the main reasons why the process of internationalisation (better said: Europeanisation) of science in Slovenia is so important and what the main obstacles still preventing this process of internationalisation are. As mentioned earlier, Slovenia has one of the smallest scientific communities in Europe. Therefore it is obligatory for this scientific community to open up and integrate into the larger space. The new ERA strategy initiated by the European Commission has established a new political context in which the opening up and integration of scientists from Slovenia in new forms of transnational scientific networks is possible. Unfortunately, these possibilities have still not been entirely realized.

References

Aaltojaervi, Inari/Ilkka Arminen/Otto Auranen/Hanna-Mari Pasanen (2008), 'Scientific productivity, web visibility and citation patterns in sixteen Nordic sociology departments', in *Acta Sociologica,* 51(1), pp. 5 - 22.

Berg, Christian (2004), *Vernetzung als Syndrom. Risiken und Chancen von Vernetzungsprozessen fuer eine nachhaltige Entwicklung,* Campus Verlag, Frankfurt a. M./New York.

Braun, Dietmar (1997), *Die politische Steuerung der Wissenschaft,* Campus Verlag, Frankfurt a. M./New York.

Bucchi, Massimiano (2004), *Science in Society,* Routledge, London/New York.

COM (2007), *Green Paper. The European Research Area: New Perspectives,* Brussels, 04.04.2007, p. 161 final.

COM (2000), *Towards a European research area. Communication from the Commission to the Council, the European Parliament, the Economic and Social Committee and the Committee of the Regions,* Brussels, 18.01.2000.

Felt, Ulrike/Maximilian Fochler (2008), 'The bottom-up meanings of the concept of public participation in science and technology', in *Science and Public Policy*, 35(7), pp. 489 - 499.

Gibbons, Michael/Helga Nowotny/Peter Scott (1994), *The New Production of Knowledge. The Dynamics of Science and Research in Contemporary Societies,* Sage Publications, London.

Glaenzel, Wolgang/Balazs Schlemmer (2007), 'National research profiles in a changing Europe (1983 - 2003). An exploratory study of sectoral characteristics in The Triple Helix', in *Scientometrics*, 70 (2), pp. 267 - 275.

Hornbostel, Stefan (1997), *Wissenschaftsindikatoren. Bewertungen in der Wissenschaft,* Westdeutscher Verlag GmbH., Opladen.

Jamison, Andrew/Jesper Lassen (2004), 'Assessing Genetic Technologies in Denmark', in M. Haeyrinen-Alestalo/E. Kallerud (eds.), *Mediating Public Concern in Biotechnology,* Norwegian Institute for Studies in Research and Higher Education, Oslo, pp. 23 - 48.

Jasanoff, Sheila (2005), *Designs on Nature: Science and Democracy in Europe and United States*, Princeton University Press, Princeton.

Key Figures Report (2009/2010), *Science, Technology and Competitiveness. A more research-intensive and integrated European Research Area,* Luxembourg: Office for Official Publications of the European Communities.

Kjaer, Anne Mette (2004), *Governance,* Polity Press, Cambridge.

Kramberger, Anton/Franc Mali (2010), 'An evaluation system of the science and international orientation of social scientists: The case of Slovenia', in I. Palne Kovàcs et al. (eds.), *Internationalisation of Social Sciences in Central and Eastern Europe. The catching up – a myth or a strategy?,* Routledge, London/New York, pp. 192 - 215.

Kronegger, Luka/Anuška Ferligoj/Patrick Doreian (2010), 'Collaboration Structures in Slovenian Scientific Communities', in *Quality and Quantity,* in print.

Langer, Josef (2008), 'Where does the European Union go? Social Science Questions and Answers', in J. Langer (ed.), *Forces Shaping the EU. Social Science Approaches to Understanding the European Union,* Peter Lang, Frankfurt a. M./New York, pp. 11 - 25.

Luukkonen, Terttu/Maria Nedeva/Rémi Barré (2006), 'Understanding the dynamics of networks of excellence', in *Science and Public Policy*, 33 (4), pp. 239 - 252.

Lukkonen, Terttu/Olle Persson/Gunnar Siversten (1992), 'Understanding Patterns of International Scientific Collaboration', in *Science, Technology & Human Values,* 17(1) pp. 101 - 126.

Mali, Franc/Luka Kronegger/Anuška Ferligoj (2010), 'Co-authorship trends and collaboration patterns in the Slovenian sociological community', in *Corvinus Journal of Sociology and Social Policy*, in print.

Mali, Franc/Blanka Jelnikar/Maja Skafar (2010), 'The recruitment of young people for R&D activity and the issue of gender equality – the case of Slovenia', in *Sociología y tecnociencia*, 2 (1), pp. 1 - 33.

Mali, Franc (2009), 'Bringing converging technologies closer to civil society: the role of the precautionary principle', in *Innovation - The European Journal of Social Science Research*, 22 (1), pp. 53 - 75.

Mali, Franc (2006), 'Second academic revolution: new ways of creating, transferring and exploiting knowledge at universities and institutes', in M. Rebernik et al. (eds.), *Cooperation between the economic, academic and governmental spheres - mechanisms and levers : proceedings of the 26th Conference on Entrepreneurship and Innovation Maribor, 30th - 31st March 2006,* Faculty of Economics and Business, Institute for Entrepreneurship and Small Business Management, Maribor, pp. 153 - 166.

Mali, Franc (2003), 'Socio-economic transition and new challenges for the science and technology policy in Slovenia', in P. Biegelbauer/S. Borras (eds.), *Innovation policies in Europe and the US: The new agenda,* Ashgate, Aldershot/Burlington, pp. 211 - 321.

Mali, Franc (1998), 'The Eastern European transition: barriers to cooperation between university and industry in post-communist countries', in *Industry & Higher Education. The leading international journal on business-academic collaboration,* Vol. 12, No. 6, pp. 347 - 356.

Must, Uelle (2006), '"New" countries in Europe – Research, development and innovation strategies vs bibliometric data', in *Scientometrics*, 66 (2), pp. 241 - 248.

Newman, M.E.J. (2004), 'Coauthorship networks and patterns of scientific collaboration', in *Proceedings of the National Academy of Science of the United States of America,* 101, (Suppl. 1), 6, pp. 5200 - 5205.

Nowotny, Helga/Peter Scott/Michael Gibbons (2001), *Re-Thinking Science. Knowledge and the Public in an Age of Uncertainty,* Blackwell Publishers Ltd., Oxford.

Popper, Karl Raimund (1997), *The Poverty of Historicism,* Routledge & Kegan Paul, London/New York.

Schott, Thomas (1993), 'World Science: Globalization of Institutions and Participation', in *Science, Technology & Human Values*, 18(2), pp. 196 - 208.

Siune, Karen/Kalpazidou Evanthia Schmidt/Kaare Aagaard (2005), 'Implementation of European Research Policy', in *Science and Public Policy*, 32 (5), pp. 375 - 384.

Statistic in Focus (2008), *Human Resources employed in Science and Technology Occupations.* Available at: [http://epp.eurostat.ec.europa.eu/cache/ITY_OFFPUB/KS-SF-08-077/EN/KS-SF-08-077-EN.PDF].

Thorsteinsdóttir, Halla (2000), 'Public-sector research in small countries: does size matter?', in *Science and Public Policy*, 27(6), pp. 433 - 442.

Van der Meulen, Barend (2003), 'New roles and strategies of a research council: intermediation of the principal-agent relationship', in *Science and Public Policy*, 30(5), pp. 323 - 336.

Ziman, John (1994), *Prometheus Bound. Science in a dynamic steady state,* University Press, Cambridge.

Vlado Sušac – Tomislav Krpan

European Language Policy Between Theory and Practice

What is (a) language?

Since the primary aim of this article is to present the language policy of the most relevant European political organizations and to discuss its further developments, it is indispensable to define the very notion of language, frequently used in everyday communication, but no less frequently misunderstood. In other words, without a clear definition of language, it is impossible to set the firm criteria of language policy.

However, there is no unanimous agreement about the definition of language, since the expression itself can be used in various contexts, referring to different meanings. The etymology of the word leads us to Latin *lingua,* lingua or tongue, which is a metaphor based on the use of the physical organ of speech. Although the origin of the word restricts its usage to primarily human and verbal communication, modern theories of communication recognise other forms of languages, which can be studied as a part of a much wider domain of enquiry: *semiology* or *semiotics*. Since it investigates the structure of all possible sign systems, it can include linguistic and non-linguistic forms of communication belonging to all kinds and species. But even if we remain within the strict domain of linguistics, it will hardly restrict our choice of possible definitions. Crystal (1997, p. 400) quotes a number of scholars on this subject, offering definitions like: "Language is a purely human and non-instinctive method of communicating ideas, emotions and desires by means of voluntary produced symbols" (E. Sapir); "A language is a set of arbitrary vocal symbols by means of which the members of society interact in terms of their culture" (G. Trager), etc. The author also offers a number of Webster's Dictionary definitions, but none of them would satisfy our need to explain the language in the context of explaining European language policy, having primarily in mind the European Union and the Council of Europe. This implies the question whether the idea of language can be observed from an exclusively linguistic point of view or if it should include other criteria, political ones in the first place.

Modern structural linguistics is based on the de Saussurean dichotomy of *langue* and *parole,* marking the distinction between the abstract system of language and its concrete actualization known as speech or the language used by individual speakers (Saussure 1990, p. 14). This dichotomy is important as it focuses on the language as a synchronic system and a structure shared by all its users, but without interest in their external manifestation of it, which can vary from one speaker to another even if they belong to the same social group.

The second necessary dichotomy lies in the ideas of *language* and *dialect*. This particular opposition cannot be understood by taking into account exclusively linguistic standpoints without any reference to a certain number of relevant political factors. The difference between the two terms is not clear-cut since there are different ways of using and understanding them in various languages and cultures. Originally in Greek, and according to Haugen (1966), the dialect referred to a number of distinct *written* varieties in use in Classical Greece, each associated with a different area and used for a different kind of literature. The word is used in a similar context in French as, unlike *dialecte*, the word *patois* refers to regional varieties, which are not written. In English, on the other hand, the term *dialect* loses its original meaning, but is attributed to the varieties, which are not used in formal writing. The varieties, of course, imply that there should be a wider notion they belong to. This leads us to the term of *language*, which can be taken as a matter of *size*, being a sum of written or unwritten dialects, or even a matter of *prestige*, which in the British tradition would deprive a dialect of any wider 'language identity' if it is not written and in such a way codified (Hudson 1996, p. 32). Obviously, the fact that dialects can be seen both as written and unwritten does not help us answer the question how a dialect becomes a language. In order to answer the question it is important to make a clear distinction about which part of the answer lies within the domain of linguistics and which part belongs to politics.

The delimitation of languages

A strictly linguistic point of view in dealing with the demarcation of languages has to apply another criterion, that of *mutual intelligibility*. It is frequently said that dialects of one language should be mutually intelligible in order to be part of that particular language. The problem with this criterion is that dialects belonging to one language are not necessarily mutually intelligible in their spoken form. Moreover, it is hard to find a single language, which would apply to such a criterion. On the other hand, it also frequently happens that dialects of two different languages are mutually intelligible, which complicates the matter even further. In addition, modern linguistics recognizes a phenomenon called a geographical *dialect continuum* (Crystal 1997, p. 25). The idea is that there is a chain of dialects without definable inner boundaries in a particular wider area, where the speakers of one dialect can always understand the speakers of the neighbouring dialect. But it is most likely that the speakers of the dialects spoken in the extreme parts of the continuum or at the two ends of the chain will not be able to understand each other. Nevertheless, they are linked by the chain of mutual intelligibility. The linguistic map of Europe shown in Figure 1 recognizes a number of such dialect continua, e.g. West Romance, West Germanic, Scandinavian, North Slavic and South Slavic. These, of course, include an even larger number of individual or national languages. So the theoretical problem is rather obvious – at what part of the chain does one language end and the next begin?

Figure 1 Five basic dialect continua in Europe

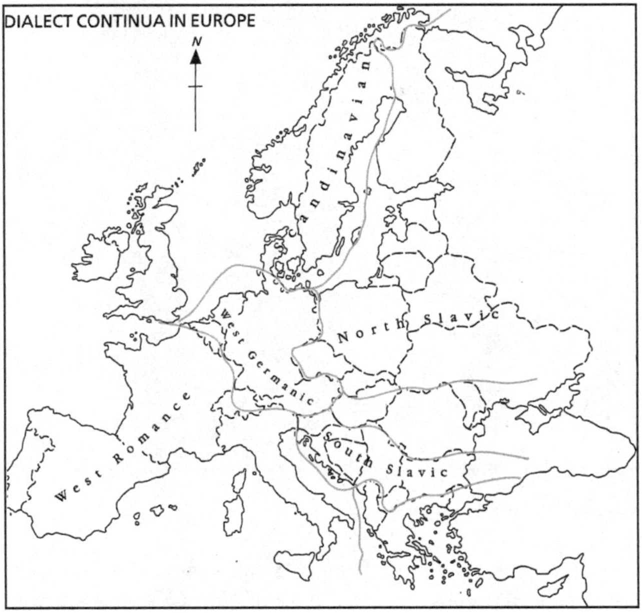

Source: Crystal (1997, p. 25)

Within the mentioned *dialect continua*, and by using much stricter intelligibility criteria, one can further identify an additional number of inner dialect chains, where basically the speakers at the ends of the chain can or are more likely to understand each other, which is not the result in the previous case. So, if we choose this 'purely linguistic' approach, we might recognize e.g. only two Scandinavian 'languages' (Continental and Insular) and only three South Slavic ones (West, Central, Eastern). In the former case, it is widely accepted that Continental Scandinavian languages can be divided into Swedish, two standards of Norwegian and Danish, while the insular part consists of Icelandic and Faroese. However, the latter case of South Slavic languages is usually disputed, especially considering the central part previously known as the territory of the 'Serbo-Croatian' language, although the two standards possess a larger number of distinctive features than most of the Scandinavian languages (Kovačić 2005, p. 195). The Slovenian language in the west, the Macedonian and the Bulgarian language in the east are less disputed although the latter two offer the basis for the same kind of argument as is the case with 'Serbo-Croatian'.

Figure 2 Languages in Europe

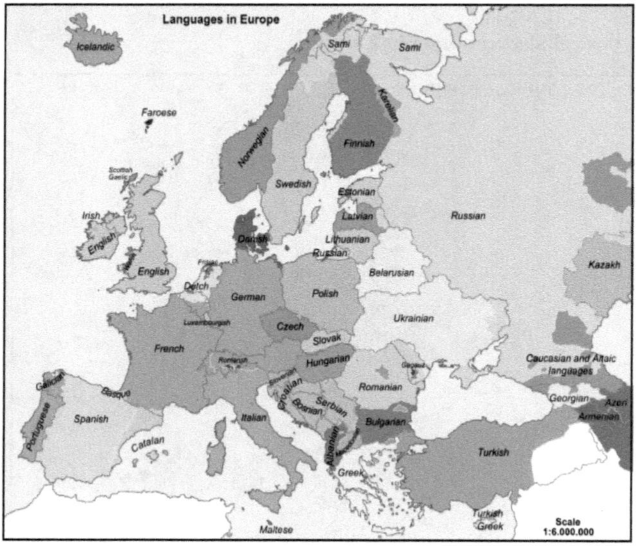

Source: Comrie/Matthews/Polinsky (2003, p. 41)

The reality of widely recognized Scandinavian languages and beside them a large number of other languages on the map of Europe still does not answer the initial question on which basis they were recognized and accepted as individual languages, especially in view of the fact that intelligibility as a linguistic criterion is not sufficient. It leads us to another criterion, generally known as *standardisation.* Hudson (1996, p. 33) offers four processes needed for a variety or a dialect to become a *standard language.* These include (1) *selection* from the repository of relevant spoken dialects or from a variety with no native speakers at all, e.g. Hebrew; (2) *codification* in dictionaries and grammar books; (3) *elaboration in function*, which makes it possible for the selected variety to be used in all kinds of functions; (4) *acceptance* by the population as a national language. But still, if we compare the above mentioned criteria with the present and recent situation on the language map of Europe, we can find some discrepancies among various standardized languages. There have been cases where the process of standardization did not result in an immediate recognition of one's language identity, but for various reasons certain languages used to be either denied as separate language units (Macedonian vs. Bulgarian) or were considered as standardized varieties of larger language combinations (e.g. Serbo-Croatian). Eventually, in order to find an explanation for such discrepancies, we should abandon the field of 'pure' linguistic criteria and definitely include non-linguistic ones.

These include *political*, *ethnic*, *religious* or other identities (Crystal 1997, p. 286). In other words, we should accept the reality that linguistic and political identities merge, but a wider and international recognition of such a reality usually coincides with the process of gaining national sovereignty and independence (Hindi vs. Urdu, Bengali vs. Assamese, Serbian vs. Croatian, etc.). Consequently, the saying that *"a language is a dialect with an army and navy"* is one of the most frequently used aphorisms in the discussion between a dialect and language. It does not necessarily mean that every single nation will have its own language as is the case with English used in the UK and Ireland or German used in Germany, Austria or Switzerland, but it still remains as an option for every single nation if it finds it appropriate to codify possible differences in a standard language with its own name. The outcome in such a way will never be 'less linguistic' as modern linguistics accepts the idea of language identity as a combination of both political and linguistic criteria. On the other hand, the opposition to such a process, although claiming to be exclusively linguistically motivated, will hardly be 'less political'.

The case of the 'BCS'

The dissolution of former Yugoslavia created not only a new political reality, but also a new language situation. Namely, the Central South Slavic diasystem, mostly known as Serbo-Croatian and used as an umbrella term for all the dialects spoken in what is nowadays Croatia, Bosnia and Herzegovina, Serbia and Montenegro, followed the political destiny of its constituent parts. Croatian, Bosnian and Serbian became recognized as separate languages and the term Serbo-Croatian gradually declined in use, from official documents to linguistic literature. Significantly, the separate names for all Central South Slavic languages (Croatian, Bosnian, Serbian, and Montenegrin) appeared in the recent EU language publications (European Commission 2009). In the meantime, an alternative combined name emerged abroad – Bosnian/Croatian/Serbian or BCS. It has been particularly fostered at the International Criminal Tribunal for former Yugoslavia as the *"Bosnian-Croatian-Serbian language"*. The singular noun expresses the official standpoint of the Tribunal that it is to be considered a single language. Moreover, an official Tribunal document of 2004 supports this view, when upon a specific request of one of the defendants to "disclose materials in written form and in Serbian", and not in the "hybrid BCS language", was decided as follows:

"[...] the Accused's insistence on the existence of a separate language known as 'Serbian' is divorced from reality. Linguistically, the Serbo-Croatian language cannot be split into two or more languages. While nationalists like the Accused may insist on referring to the 'Serbian' or 'Croat' or 'Bosnian' languages, these are just different labels attached to the same member of the South Slavonic sub branch of the Indo-European family of languages. The difference in spelling, syntax and pronunciation are not significant enough to warrant treating 'Serbian' and 'Croatian' and 'Bosnian' as separate languages. Any autonomy that does exist between these so called 'different languages' stems from ideological and political values, which, from a scientific, linguistic perspective, are worthless." (ICTY 2004, p. 3)

It is obvious that the response of the Prosecution exceeds the main requirement of the Statute of the Tribunal stipulated in Article 21 considering the rights of the accused "to be informed promptly and in detail in a language which he understands of the nature and cause of the charge against him." (ICTY 1993, p. 8) Namely, the idea of intelligibility within the Central South Slavic diasystem is undisputable, as explained in the previous paragraphs, but it was also clearly shown that modern linguistics does not take it as an eliminating factor in the process of language identification while distinguishing it from the rest of the diasystem (e.g. Scandinavian languages). However, the Prosecution's response is involved in providing 'a verdict' regarding the linguistic status of the three respective languages and offering a rather doubtful explanation to support the claim. It completely neglects the fact of a long and separate process of codification and standardization within two separate literature traditions of both the Croatian and the Serbian people and that the idea of Serbo-Croatian is a political construct created in the Nineteenth century as an expression of the ideology of pan-Slavism. Moreover, the linguistic arguments provided in the claim seem to be deliberately defective in order to fit in the initial assumption about one language. It mentions the differences in spelling, syntax and pronunciation, which are not significant, although existing, but it completely omits the lexical differences as the most distinctive feature between the two languages, which was verified in a number of publications and dictionaries both in Croatia and Serbia. (cf. Brodnjak 1991 and Ćirilov 1989) The Prosecutor's response also makes reference to the Serbian linguist R. Bugarski (1994, p. 58) with a rather bold and biased statement naming him "the most respected linguist in former Yugoslavia", who, of course, supports the idea of one language:

"Serbo-Croatian is not exclusively the possession of either Croats or Serbs. This language is used in four of our republics by the members of four of our nations, with almost all those who declared themselves as Yugoslavs. [...] It would be absurd to carve out a separate language for each national identity within the former Yugoslavia." (Bugarski 1994, p. 58)

Having in mind the previous Prosecutor's statement about "ideological and political values" being the guidance for the proponents of separate languages, one cannot but remark that the above mentioned statement with all its argumentation, is not less politically and ideologically loaded and can potentially be viewed as an expression of Yugoslav nationalism that even after the collapse of former Yugoslavia speaks about *our* republics. The linguistic arguments (especially if partially used) that speak in favour of both confronted concepts cannot be understood any differently than as a red herring, meant to disguise political and ideological motives. As already explained, they can both be 'right' in different political realities, and therefore, one should take into account that the political reality in South-East Europe has changed and the language policy towards that part of Europe should act accordingly – unless one has no intention to recognize it.

The option for the BCS can also be motivated by merely pragmatic and financial reasons. There have been a number of formal and informal occasions when some EU officials brought up this matter. For example, in May 2008, it was reported by the Deutsche Welle that during a two-day conference in Brussels about the EU perspective for southeast European countries, the president of the EU Parliament Pöttering suggested a smaller number of interpreting booths for the following gathering since he realized that most of the participants did not use earphones while listening to their colleagues from the same region. This provoked a reaction not only by some delegations, but also by some MEPs, e.g. H. Swoboda and D. Pack. They pointed at the practice of interpreting within the EU Parliament even in the cases when the two languages were mutually intelligible, while reminding that language is also an issue of national identity (Deutsche Welle 2008). The described event implies the question whether similar financial reasons in the future will collide with the advocated language policy and the respective EU legislation in force.[1]

The EU language policy – legal basis

The European Union has nurtured language equality since it was founded as European Economic Community. This approach has been verified in a number of documents and formal decisions and their crucial statements will be mentioned in chronological order:

---

1 The same financial concerns where expressed on 13th January 2010, when two representatives of the Green Party in the European Parliament, Franziska Brantner and Marije Cornelissen, proposed an amendment (No. 18) within the discussion on Croatia's progress report 2009 (PE430.300v02-00): "The European Parliament draws attention to the fact that the original Serbo-Croatian language is now divided into various official languages in some countries which are potential candidates, observes that the costs of translation and interpretation significantly affect the budget of the EU institutions and invites the Commission together with the Croatian authorities before accession to make an exemplary arrangement on the Croatian language, which will prevent later concluding a comprehensive agreement on language with Bosnia and Herzegovina, Montenegro and Serbia, when these countries become EU members". After reactions from Croatia supported by the explanations expressed in this article, the authors withdrew their amendment. The following interview appeared in the Croatian daily newspaper "Slobodna Dalmacija" on the 30th of January 2010, [http://www.slobodnadalmacija.hr/Spektar/tabid/94/articleType/ArticleView/articleId/89807/Default.aspx] (retrieved on 6.11.2010).

- Treaty Establishing the European Community (Art. 21): "[...] Every citizen of the Union may write to any of the institutions or bodies referred to in this Article or in Article 7 in one of the languages mentioned in Article 314 and have an answer in the same language."
- Treaty Establishing the European Community (Art. 314): "[...] This Treaty, drawn up in a single original in the Dutch, French, German, and Italian languages, all four texts being equally authentic, shall be deposited in the archives of the Government of the Italian Republic, which shall transmit a certified copy to each of the Governments of the other signatory States. Pursuant to the Accession Treaties, the Danish, English, Finnish, Greek, Irish, Portuguese, Spanish and Swedish versions of this Treaty shall also be authentic."[2]
- The EEC Council Regulation (Art.4): "Regulations and other documents of general application shall be drafted in the four official languages." (EEC Council 1958)
- The Charter of Fundamental rights of the Union (Art. 21): "Any discrimination based on any ground such as sex, race, colour, ethnic or social origin, genetic features, language, religion or belief, political or any other opinion, membership of a national minority, property, birth, disability, age or sexual orientation shall be prohibited."
- The Charter of Fundamental rights of the Union (Art. 22): "The Union shall respect cultural, religious and linguistic diversity." (European Parliament 2000)
- "Linguistic diversity is a value in itself and its preservation a sign of respect for the cultural identities of the EU's citizens. It is also a democratic right. The EU adopts legislation which is directly binding on its citizens, who cannot be expected to comply with laws which they do not understand. Therefore these laws must be promulgated in their languages." (European Commission 2004)
- "Each country, before it joined, stipulated which language it wanted to have used as an official language for EU purposes. The agreement on this matter is then recorded in the Act of Accession." (European Union 2005)

The above-mentioned statement leaves no doubt that the official language of a member state will *automatically* become an official language of the European Union. The result is that at present there are 23 official EU languages: Bulgarian, Czech, Danish, Dutch, English, Estonian, Finnish, French, German, Greek,

2 Previously Art. 8d and Art. 248 of the "Treaty of Rome" (1957), which was later renamed "Treaty Establishing European Community" after being amended and consolidated by the "Treaty of Amsterdam" (1997). Articles 21 and 314 cited above are from the amended version, which refers to the EU instead of the E(E)C.

Hungarian, Italian, Irish, Latvian, Lithuanian, Maltese, Polish, Portuguese, Romanian, Slovak, Slovene, Spanish and Swedish.

The recent developments and strategies also speak in favour of fostering language diversity. Namely, the year 2001 was generally proclaimed by the EU institutions as The European Year of Languages and the central idea of all the initiatives was formulated as "*unity in diversity*" and the European Parliament in its Resolution of 13th December 2001 called for measures to promote language learning and linguistic diversity (European Parliament 2001). The Education Council invited Member States to take concrete steps and invited the European Commission to draw up proposals in these fields, which responded with an Action plan with a number of objectives, but the central one is reflected in the idea for European citizens of mastering two other languages beside their mother tongue (European Commission 2003 and 2004a, p. 17). It was followed by the Commission's Framework strategy for multilingualism, which further elaborated the central objectives for "[...] promoting multilingualism in European society, in the economy and in the Commission itself. The aim is to build up citizens' linguistic skills until each citizen has acquired practical skills in at least two languages other than his or her mother tongue." (European Commission 2005)[3] Eventually, the Lisbon Treaty, as the fundamental document of the European Union, clearly stated in Article 2 that the EU "[...] shall respect its rich cultural and linguistic diversity, and shall ensure that Europe's cultural heritage is safeguarded and enhanced." (European Union 2007)

It is quite clear from the excerpts that the legislative heritage of the European Union strongly supports the idea of language equality and diversity and that it has embedded such a policy in its future action strategies and that any attempt to implement double standards in language policy would be strongly at odds with the EU fundamental documents and decisions.

Financial concerns

The proclaimed language strategies require, naturally, a huge machinery of interpretation and translation staff and services and, as explained earlier, the most frequent objection is directed against excessive financial costs. At present,

---

[3] It is worth mentioning that the expression *multilingualism* is somewhat confusing since the Council of Europe clearly distinguishes it from *plurilingualism*. The former is defined as "the presence in a geographical area, large or small, of more than one 'variety of language': i.e. the mode of speaking of a social group whether it is formally recognised as a language or not; in such an area individuals may be monolingual, speaking only their own variety." The latter is described as "the repertoire of varieties of language which many individuals use, and is therefore the opposite of monolingualism; it includes the language variety referred to as 'mother tongue' or 'first language' and any number of other languages or varieties. Thus in some multilingual areas some individuals are monolingual and some are plurilingual." (Council of Europe 1997)

namely, the EU is the only entity in the world with 23 official languages. The process of translation and interpreting produces 506 language combinations and with 33 languages the number of combinations would increase to 1056. The total EU staff involved in translation and interpretation reaches a number of more than 7000 people, with a total expenditure of 1.1 billion Euro per year. Although the figures may seem excessive, the analysis shows that the given amount is distributed to 2.5 Euro per EU citizen yearly, which represents only one per cent of the EU's annual budget (Lönnroth 2008). Cost-benefit analysis and respective conclusions should definitely allow for the primary goal of translation and interpreting services, i.e. a guarantee for every EU citizen to be able to communicate with the EU institutions and to read their legal documents in their own language. Especially in view of the fact that more than 50 per cent of the EU population can communicate in their mother tongue only (European Commission 2006). With that in mind, the price cannot be too high.

The data presented above also show that financial argumentation can hardly be valid in the context of the previous discourse concerning the doubtful official status of Central South Slavic languages in the process of future accession into the EU. Moreover, if it is worth defending the principle of multilingualism and unity in diversity in the case of Irish or Maltese, the disproportion of costs and the number of speakers can be even less valid as an argument.

Financial concerns are, of course, legitimate. But the reductions of costs, without regard for how high or low they are, cannot be made by means of double standards concerning the present regulations. It would jeopardize the basic principles of the EU and they are worth defending and investing in. Significant retrenchment measures, if necessary, can only be implemented by changing or abandoning the present EU legislature and by introducing an official *lingua franca* in the EU or, in the worst case scenario, the first and second rate languages and cultures.

Unity in uniformity?

The idea of a common European language is not new and ranges from recognizing the unofficial role and worldwide dominance of English to introducing a dead language like Latin or an artificial language like Esperanto. The proponents of such ideas are guided by various motives. They mostly include a desire for easier communication or an ideological and romantic assumption that a single common language would lead to a stronger cohesion within the EU and to the further development of a 'European identity'. Such views are sometimes strongly challenged.

One of the most thorough analyses of the language policy issues in Europe is offered by Robert Phillipson (2003). Firstly, the author expresses the risks of *laissez faire* language policies as they often lead to discrimination, which can be prevented only by proactive and explicit language strategies. In the analysis of

European languages and cultures he points out that privileging one language such as Serbocroat in ex-Yugoslavia does not guarantee political harmony. It can be added that it did not contribute to the idea of a new (supra)national identity either as only a minor number of ex-Yugoslavian inhabitants officially declared themselves as Yugoslavs. This implies the question whether a majority of Europeans would ever want the kind of identity based on a common language. The author also leaves open the idea of Esperanto as a way of introducing more justice in international affairs. Since it is a non-national language, it would not privilege any particular nation as is the case with English and its native speakers. Whether it would make communication easier in comparison with English or any other dominant non-artificial language is rather doubtful because of very poor corpus repository and lack of literature tradition. It would take a lot of time and education to avoid the jeopardy of any artificial or dead language remaining a vernacular of a narrow political elite. However, this dilemma brings us back to the initial chapters of this article, whether language is merely a means of communication that should primarily serve the idea of intelligibility or is it the expression of one's culture and identity. By favouring the former stance, the role of English is unquestionable in the ongoing language reality, while fostering the latter would eliminate the threat of one's cultural hegemony (English or American) to the cost of communication by a risky investment into a new (European) language identity. The present theory and practice in the EU ensures a balanced approach. The existing identities are protected by the policy of language diversity and the unity is preserved by equal treatment of all the EU member countries and their citizens. Disturbing the balance by neglecting or favouring any of the two language components in the future EU geography might cause a domino effect that might put into question the basic principles of its existence as a union.

References

Brodnjak, Vladimir (1991), *Razlikovni rječnik srpskog i hrvatskog jezika*, Matica Hrvatska, Zagreb.

Bugarski, Ranko (1994), *Language from Peace to War*, Beogradski Krug, Belgrade.

Ćirilov, Jovan (1989) Hrvatsko-srpski rječnik inačica. Srpsko-hrvatski rečnik varijanti, Stilos, Belgrade.

Comrie, Bernard/Stephen Matthews/Maria Polinsky (2003), *The Atlas of Languages*, Bloomsbury, London.

Council of Europe (1997) Language education policy, [http://www.coe.int/t/dg4/linguistic/Division_EN.asp] retrieved on 3.1.2010.

Crystal, David (1997), *The Cambridge Encyclopaedia of Language*, Cambridge University Press, New York/Melbourne.

Deutsche Welle (2008), 'Borba za hrvatski jezik u Europskoj komisiji', [http://www.dw3d.de/dw/article/0,,3373888,00.html] retrieved on 3.1.2010.

EEC (1957), 'Treaty Establishing the European Economic Community', [http://eur-lex.europa .eu/en/treaties/dat/11997E/htm/11997E.html#0173010078] retrieved on 6.11.2010.

EEC Council (1958), 'Regulation No 1 determining the languages to be used by the EEC' [http://eur-lex.europa.eu/LexUriServ/LexUriServ.do?uri=CELEX:31958R0001:EN:NOT] retrieved on 3.1.2010.

European Commission (2003), 'Action plan 2004 - 2006 on language learning and linguistic diversity', http://europa.eu/legislation_summaries/education_training_youth/lifelong_learning /c11068_en.htm] retrieved on 3.1.2010.

European Commission (2004), 'Commission steps up its translation capacity to meet demands of enlargement', [http://europa.eu/rapid/pressReleasesAction.do?reference=MEMO/04/ 34&format=HTML&aged=0&language=EN&guiLanguage=en] retrieved on 3.1.2010.

European Commission (2004a), 'Many tongues, one family. Languages in the European Union', [http://ec.europa.eu/publications/booklets/move/45/en.pdf] retrieved on 3.1.2010.

European Commission (2005), 'A new framework strategy for multilingualism', [http://europa.eu/legislation_summaries/education_training_youth/lifelong_learning/c110 84_en.htm] retrieved on 3.1.2010.

European Commission (February 2006), 'Eurobarometer: Europeans and their Languages', [http://ec.europa.eu/public_opinion/archives/ebs/ebs_243_en.pdf] retrieved on 3.1.2010.

European Commission (2009) 'A field guide to the main languages of Europe', [http://ec.europa.eu/dgs/translation/publications/brochures/field_guide_languages_en.pdf] retrieved on 3.1.2010.

European Parliament (2000), 'NON-DISCRIMINATION – Charter of Fundamental Rights', [http://www.europarl.europa.eu/comparl/libe/elsj/charter/art21/default_en.htm] retrieved on 3.1.2010.

European Parliament (2001), 'Resolution on regional and lesser-used European languages', [http://www.europarl.europa.eu/sides/getDoc.do?pubRef=-//EP//TEXT+TA+P5-TA-2001-0719+0+DOC+XML+V0//EN] retrieved on 3.1.2010.

European Union (2007), 'The Lisbon Treaty', [http://bookshop.europa.eu/eubookshop/ download.action] retrieved on 3.1.2010.

Haugen, Einar (1966), 'Dialect, Language, Nation', in *American Anthropologist,* Vol. 68, Malden, MA, pp. 922 - 35.

Hudson, Richard A. (1996), *Sociolinguistics,* Cambridge University Press, New York/Melbourne.

ICTY (International Criminal Tribunal for the former Yugoslavia), Case No. IT-03-67-PT, 'Prosecution's Response to Accused's Request for Disclosure of Materials in Written Form and in Serbian', 23.11.2004, The Hague.

ICTY (1993), 'Statute of the International Tribunal for the Former Yugoslavia', The Hague. [http://www.icls.de/dokumente/icty_statut.pdf] retrieved on 3.1.2010.

Kovačić, Marko (2005), 'Serbian and Croatian: "One Language or Languages?"', in *Jezikoslovlje'* 6.2, Zagreb, pp. 195 - 204. [http://hrcak.srce.hr/file/48911] retrieved on 3.1.2010.

Lönnroth, Karl-Johan (2008), 'CEPS, Why is the Language Policy in EU Political Dynamite?', [http://ec.europa.eu/dgs/translation/publications/presentations/speeches/ 20080222_ceps_eu_language] retrieved on 3.1.2010.

Phillipson, Robert (2003) *English-Only Europe; Challenging Language Policy*, Routledge, London/New York.

Saussure, Ferdinand de (1990), *Course in General Linguistics*, Duckworth, London.

Chapter IV

Enlargement and Borders

Reis Mulita

Europe: Between Diminishing Political Borders and New Social Borders

The human inclination towards power over nature and the society is altering the borders in the area between the Atlantic in the West and the Urals in the East. The wish to expand is not only a historical trend, but also very natural and has travelled with society throughout time and generations, particularly in Europe. That is how we find it in our midst in the present day, as a trend that appears to be very modern, and though it is so in some aspects that I shall discuss further, such inclination is deeply rooted in our nature and history and so it shall be in the future.

In modern communication this is reflected in the tendencies towards social and economic integration, where it has found a more primitive expression through conquest, occupation, colonialism, the Crusades. Independently from the expression and the type of expansion, be it modern or primitive, we must recognize that the inclination of every society is enlargement, expansion and the exploitation of natural and human resources.

Is there a qualitative difference in terms of time, between the historical and modern inclination for prevalence upon nature and society of the European civilization? What is the difference between the contemporary inclinations of the European society, in comparison with the same, though in different historical periods of time?

By answering such questions, I wish to asses and discuss the mobile or static future of the political and social map of the EU through the presentation of sound argumentation. I assume that the European Union will be a space that will support the natural and social prevalence of the European society within its natural borders, as an expression of the strength, the will and the concrete action of the peoples of Europe, in order to develop society and nature within the standards of sustainable development.

It will become a society that is oriented towards economic and social models of the Anglo-Saxon, the Scandinavian and the Romano-Latin Europe. A society that will carry the power of partnership and of the natural map that will include all the environmental resources as well as the knowledge, experiences, information and innovation that flows in the Romano-Latin, Anglo-Saxon, Slavic, Turkish, Balkan and Baltic indigenous peoples, etc. These groups will outline the social and economic profile of Europe in the future.

How will communication take place between local “host” societies and the “migrated” or “guest” parts of it, in reference to the initial map of the EU? If we examine the communication of the European society before the Twentieth century, we notice that the social conflict and the relations established as a result are the ones that dominated and shaped the map of Europe. It is different now and it will be different in the future of an enlarged Europe. There may be differences in terms of behavioural standards between the social groups within the Union and those that are awaiting such integration, however such differences might not be very significant, or rather, the contrasts might not be significant enough as to generate conflict.

This argument is supported by the governance as well as the political realities of Member States and non EU states. They enhance social integration, cohesion and cooperation among social groups with different ethnic, social and cultural backgrounds. Communication within the united society in the expanding Europe will generate social diffusion, based on the values of a society with emphasis on integration and social and economic cohesion.

The relations of communication effects "social diffusion", will see a "hosting" community with higher living standards that will face the waves of enlargement, however, the greatest benefits of such phenomenon in the view of the larger Union, stand at the openness towards this process and therefore the control over it. By confirming themselves as "hosting" communities and therefore legitimating their position to controlling the process, such societies will, in the future, dictate the pace and the trends of power in the future of the enlarged European Union. With reference to the population count between the Atlantic and the Urals, numeric prevalence stands not on the side of the "nucleus" states of Europe. However, considering that the Union states dictate the ways of life in the societies willing to integrate as well as their political representation, the Union will naturally control every step of the integrating societies. This will lead to the control of eventual votes of the future members in the decision-making process regarding community matters.

Considering the issue under these indicators, an estimated value may be drawn on the efficiency of representation of a hundreds of million-strong population such as that of the actual Union and that of the societies that are to be integrated in the future (Russia, Turkey, Ukraine, etc.)

This process will be carried out through some indicators that I wish to discuss in the following.

The enlargement of the Union and the EU integration are now two well explored practices. The integration between states will not be immediate, rather by degrees. Consequently the states to join the EU will not have the power of the *whole* but of the parts. At the same time, as the integration process undergoes several stages of controlled membership, consequently the integrating states enter the community while preserving the cultural identity and their social profile.

Why will the enlargement of the EU political map continue?

Returning to the concept of power and the wish to attain it, we must admit that such thing exists also within the Union. However, in modern times, power over nature and the resources does not have the meaning of mere exploitation. The novelty stands in the exploitation and protection as well as regeneration of the resources. Viewed under such a light, the joining of the societies in a large European Union will become a joining of wishes, wills and capabilities, aiming not only at mere exploitation, but at a better use, development and protection of the resources.

This group of joined societies will protect nature efficiently from the destructive effects of global warming, climate hazards; it will better preserve the environment, the natural and cultural biodiversity and will be more attentive to the needs of the vulnerable categories of nature and society. Moreover it will generate more resources and opportunities of a global dimension for the society within its borders. A small and divided Europe cannot protect and preserve nature alone, with borders that are not secure and are continuously subject to change. Such a Europe would not be able to generate contemporary leadership in the interest of its own society as well as the interest of the global society.

That is why the boundaries of social Europe are changing into the *Natural European* boundaries. At this point, however, the limits of its social and cultural values will exceedingly surpass its natural boundaries for a united Europe will prevail internationally with its unique set of values.

The modern and contemporary trend of humanity is the desire for more power over nature, and nature in the interest of the human society for the present and future of humankind and a sustainable development. There are many arguments that speak in favour of enlargement, though the most important lies in the necessity of a sustainable development of the society and nature of Europe. It is not possible to achieve a sustainable development if the society is divided in its standards.

With regard to environmental issues for instance, may there be effective results in environmental protection measures if they are fragmented and separate? May there be built a barrier to the masses of polluted air to prevent their movement from one country to another?

May there be built a barrier to stop contaminated underground water, that moves under layers of the earth from one country to another? Certainly this is not possible. What is possible, is the joint effort to achieve joint objectives with competitive standards. This is the reason why the union is inevitable. Joint actions for risk and threat prevention however, are not the only reason. First and foremost the EU will unite to enrich itself through the exchange of social and cultural values as well as creativities in relation with the societies involved and the geographical environment where these are developed.

Social and economic mobility

A quick examination of the relation between states shows that many successful steps have been taken by the EU institutions, such as the expansion of the territory, the unification under the Euro, the removal of economic barriers such as taxes, customs, etc. The same success however, may not be affirmed with regards to social achievements. When it comes to social matters, Europe is not as elastic and the pace is slow. It appears very difficult to achieve a joint and unified system of social contributions, health insurance, educational system, vocational training or other elements of social cohesion. Also, it also must be said that there is a negative reaction to immigrants in general. Let us only mention in this instance the referendum in Switzerland against the opening of mosques, the laws against the Muslim head covering for women in public spaces in France, the immigration critical attitudes of the political party "Lega Nord" in Italy (governing coalition), etc.

What is the model to be drawn next for a united Europe where economic and social cohesion travel together? Nature may be protected, its values preserved, but also it may be used in the interest of the human society, if society acts in unison, in joint long-term programs.

The globalized world where we live is a world of movement, exchange, competition and value complementation. Europe may become a factor in such a world only if it is effective in the above mentioned indicators. This will happen if Europe is larger and shares a programmed education, experiences and professional knowledge. For these reasons Europe must move towards enlargement with a programmed mobility, well distributed in its territories.

Present and future mobility within the European Union territory

Currently and in the nearest perspective the direction of the social mobility is from non-members or new members towards the *nucleus* EU countries, that have higher social and economic standards.

In European history, however, the direction of social mobility has never been one-sided. The Greeks established colonies in the Mediterranean basin, the Romans moved widely across different continents and so did the British, the French, the Spaniards, the Dutch and the Portuguese, who occupied and colonized territories on different continents of the globe. Considering social mobility as a historical phenomenon, we may not exclude the fact that the European society of tomorrow will want to conduct a two-sided movement, i.e. people of the Anglo-Saxon, Slavic or Nordic societies may wish to live in the Turkish area of Asia Minor or the Mediterranean coast.

How would this phenomenon be named in this case? Would there be clashes between the social groups in reference to social behaviour and cultural background of the groups concerned?

Will Turkey be accepted in the European Union?

The question may as well be: Would Turkey accept Europeans within its territory? The question may seem misplaced if we only examine the present mobility trends, however, on second consideration it appears obvious that the European society must not only work for the present welfare of its members, but also for that of future generations. What does Europe have to offer to future generations with its policy of closure towards other cultures?

Also, if the economic trends tend towards freedom of movement and communication of goods and services, may the movement of people who move with those or their coexistence be excluded?

Therefore, the present European society must ask itself an important question. It must ask itself what it is that it is seeding for future generations preferring closure to openness and enlargement, division to unification, isolation to integration and exchange.

It is a slightness of judgment to think that Europe may be only opened for countries such as Turkey, the Ukraine or the Western Balkan Countries merely for commercial and economic relations, leaving out of the European boundaries the human resources.

"Veni, vidi, vici" is quite outdated in the present society. In the times of global markets and capital flows, with such exchange of goods and services, social mobility may not be prevented and it is quite naïve to even think that it may. Each product or service bears social relations and that is why the Europe of the economic and commercial relations will also become a Europe unified by a relation between people.

Examining the tendencies of the movement of goods and trade in the EU from now to the year 2025, two trends can be noticed: towards Russia and Turkey. How can we neglect that the political class of Europe ignores these tendencies?

There may be no freedom of economic relations without that of the social relations. When the social mobility is handcuffed, so are the economic relations. A society that is mobile and fluid is competitive, for it is exceedingly superior in efficiency to a society that is not in motion. It is not a question therefore, whether the people of Turkey, for instance, must be free or not to move about Europe. The answer is undoubtedly positive. The true question that arises, therefore, is not if there should be mobility, rather how must this mobility be in terms of size, time and other indicators. What are the social and economic consequences that the movement of this population will bring to the European Union? What are the perception and the reaction of the "hosting" community towards the newcomers?

How can the EU society maximize and minimize respectively the good and not so good impacts by programming the perspective development of relations with Turkey, Russia and other countries that are willing to become members of the Union?

By answering these questions we may arrive at some conclusions about the future of the EU, the enlargement processes and its output.

How should the Community respond, in times when the global crisis has affected many countries of the EU, where growing xenophobia shows in old and new ways (different opinions among the EU population believe that their principal danger comes from foreigners)?

The USA have organized their influx through a lottery and Canada as well, though it only accepts professionals. Europe must choose another way. Mobility must not be casual, but programmed for all categories. There must be professional and language training, civic and cultural preparation involved, as well as acceptance of the hosting community. Such a development does not affect employment, yet it fills the gaps.

The future of EU under the enlargement process

In order to estimate the trends and wishes of the European citizens in relation to the future and the enlargement, we must consider their present attitude. How do they perceive their everyday professional and social life?

"Despite the gloomy picture portrayed in certain media, Europeans are happy. They are unanimously happy with both their family life (90%) and their current occupation (84%)". (Eurobarometer 2006)

If Europeans are happy with their lives, why should they include other countries in their midst? This is the question that springs up every time the future of Europe is discussed. From the same source: "European citizens are once again unanimous in declaring that they are happy living in their country".

At present, there are three social groupings with reference to the future of the Union: the Eurosceptics, the optimists and the moderates.

According to the sceptics, there is apprehension in the "host" societies towards the incoming social groups. Among other things, they see the newcomers as competition in the labour market. This fear is a particular trend that is more visible among unqualified working forces that feel directly threatened by the influxes. This problem, however, may be resolved through the selection and the professional training of the incoming categories in order to meet the market demands.

Since the enlargement process is programmed, it may be controlled by the establishment of relations between the local governments and professional authorities of the "host" and "home" countries. This process will ensure that the supply meets the demand in the labour market. At the same time this process will orientate the social, cultural and civic training of the categories willing to move from the integrating countries towards those already in the Union.

Professional training and civic education

The professional training and the civic education of the categories in motion of the integrating societies will enable the programming of mobility through the selection of the social and professional categories be they "highly skilled" or "unskilled" that are to move towards the EU countries. This process will enable the "host" and "home" countries to see each as collaborators.

These steps are essential considering that the "host" European Union states already have a well defined social, cultural and religious profile as well as a particular life style within their geographical and social area. Each massive and natural inflow would stagger the natural order of such societies. When social phenomena happen spontaneously and in an uncontrolled manner, far from consciousness, they resemble the natural phenomenon. Many are examples in nature and just as a meeting of tectonic plates would lead to disastrous earthquakes, so would the in-block meetings of different societies. The developments of the human societies however, have a great advantage in comparison to natural phenomena. They are conscious and as such they may be controlled, programmed and may become the successful result of the social communication of different and diverse groups.

The communication between the social groups of the European Community and the "Mobile" Europe must be understood as exceedingly positive, beneficial and necessary for a competitive Europe in a global dimension. The communication between the social groups of the future Europe will be an exchange of social values and human resources.

Must Europe fear the diffusion of values from Western Balkan Countries, Ukraine, Turkey etc. and particularly if these human resources are offered gradually, professionally trained to meet the market demand and civically educated? Certainly not. Such organized communication enables a mutual and natural acquaintance of the social groups and they receive information about each other's cultures.

As the "host" society selects the persons or the social groups interested in such mobility, educates them with the language and culture of the country they are to move to, it has selected resources that the society needs that will be sent exactly where needed, thus avoiding the informal competition. On the other hand these categories will benefit social contribution, health insurance, proper residences and therefore a social and professional profile and identification in the hosting country.

Let us examine the case of Albania as a country of the Western Balkans that aspires to become a member of the European Union.

The population of the Republic of Albania amounts to 3.5 million inhabitants (source INSTAT). At least a million Albanians live, work or study abroad. The rest of the population is divided as follows: 25 per cent at school age, 13 per cent retired, 7 per cent investors, 5 per cent have state jobs and 15 per cent are agro-businessmen who do not wish to leave the country.

According to the above only 0.5 million may have the inclination towards leaving the country to look for better life conditions in the EU.

What would be the model that will enable their mobility without creating professional, social and religious clashes? Such a thing would be possible through the enlistment of these categories: selection, professional and language training as well as civic education in order to facilitate their integration in the hosting communities. This is an organized education process that must be articulated in local preparation centres that would offer all the above, from professional training to life style details.

As this process shapes a new kind of category of population *in motion*, private and public institutions would cooperate towards mutual acceptance and furthermore, harmonious coexistence, offering an entirely different view of the whole process not only as a necessity, but also as mutually beneficial: a new set of values for the Europe of the future where diversity is richness.

Nuri Ali Tahir

After Turkey's Full Membership – The Role of the European Union as an Actor to Democratize its New Neighbourhood

Introduction

One of the most discussed issues in today's Europe is the Turkish membership since the negotiation process officially started on the 3rd of October 2005. It can be easily seen that the Europeans are also divided among themselves whether to admit Turkey as full member of the European Union or not. Opponents of Turkish membership argue that Turkey's is not an entirely European state and Europe might need some buffer states to protect its borders and civilization from countries like Iran and Syria. Meanwhile, proponents of the Turkish membership defend the idea that as a key actor situated along the conflictual points like the Balkans, the Caucasus and the Middle East, Turkey will be a major contributor to the peace and security in the region and will be able defend to European principles better as an EU Member State.

On its way towards Europeanization and democratization, Turkey has made significant changes in key areas like foreign policy and minority rights. Especially after 2002, when AKP[1] came to rule, Turkey began to follow more assertive policies toward regions like the Middle East, the Balkans, the Caucasus and Central Asia, which turned it into a clear regional power. Globalization, the caricature crisis, the US invasion in Iraq and Western ignorance regarding the tragic events, which took place in Palestine strained East West relations. Exactly in that moment Turkey was perceived as a bridge between the Eastern and Western world and a tool to keep open the dialogue between Christian and Muslim civilizations.

Nevertheless having such a role does not mean that Turkey is free from every kind of problem. Indeed, Turkey faced and continues to face struggles with its Kurdish minority though there were some democratic changes made recently. There is still a belief that Europeanization will help Turkey to reshape its national identity within the structures of a modern state and hence this positive progress would be a good example for neighbouring countries like Iran, Syria and Iraq.

This article aims to analyze the potential effects of the Turkish full membership from the aspects of the European Union's foreign policy and Turkey's neighbours. It will examine the EU's role in democratizing its new neighbourhood as the Union tried to formulate with its European Neighbourhood Policy

[1] Adalet ve Kalkınma Partisi (Justice and Development Party).

(ENP) document in 2003. Going a step further, it will be discussed how the EU can be successful in democratizing Iran, Syria and Iraq after accepting Turkey as a member and why it is necessary for the European Union to deal with these countries.

Democratization of Turkey and problems with the rights of minorities

Democratization can be identified as a process that leads a country to a more liberal and sustainable structure, which provides all of its citizens with equal rights and fair treatment. Turkey is often criticized because of its attitude and assimilationist policies toward minorities and especially Kurds. But these criticisms are always related to Turkey's aspirations to become a member of the EU. Because of this reason democratization is also perceived as Europeanization in Turkey. But these perceptions may vary in different sections of the society and also among politicians. When EU leaders were abstaining from giving clear perspectives about the full membership of Turkey, Prime Minister Erdoğan openly stated that "Turkey will continue ahead by turning Copenhagen Criteria into Ankara Criteria" (Radikal Gazetesi, 24.02.2007).

After this statement the Turkish Government started several projects called *openings*. The one which currently is still under progress is called the *Kurdish Opening* or in other words *Democratic Opening*. Briefly, government launched this project to comply with the requirements for EU membership. Even today the exact content of the project has not been officially announced to the public. However there are statements made by the members of the government that the opening aims to integrate the Kurdish minority into the structures of the modern Turkish Republic.

Despite the fact that the opening was first discussed in 2009, some reforms were made well in advance. There is no doubt that the current government did much more for the Kurdish minority than any other government in the past. This is no coincidence though. Because currently, Turkey is striving to become a stable regional power and, if possible, a global power in the future. Therefore the government is well aware that the Kurdish question is an obstacle in the way of Turkey becoming a super power in the region.

On the way to satisfy the needs of the Kurdish population, government decided to start Kurdish language broadcasting on radio and television during 2005 (McLaren 2008, p. 239). In the beginning, it was offered twice a week, each session lasting 35 minutes, provided by the TRT, which is the Turkish national channel funded by the government. In 2009 the government launched a new channel, which broadcasts 24 hours in the Kurdish language. Developments since 2001 are very impressive; in the southeast of Turkey and elsewhere Kurdish music, publications, festive days, radio and television all became legal at first, then tolerated and finally broadly accepted (Second Report of the Independent Commission on Turkey 2009, p. 21).

Kurdish language courses are offered by some foundations and other non-governmental organizations but they lack local demand especially from the side of Kurdish youth. Meanwhile each Kurdish festival in Turkey ends with some violent protests against the police or other civilians living in the neighbourhood, which raises the tension between Turks and Kurds. Because of this reason, the Turkish government is now eager to solve the Kurdish question in a peaceful way in order to pursue its goal and become a global actor.

In the past, Kurds were not active in the political life of Turkey in the form of having their own party. Mostly citizens from Kurdish ethnic background were elected from the lists of other major political parties. But after the elections in July 2007, Kurds had the chance to become actively involved in the political life of Turkey. They had 20 deputies among the Turkish Parliament members of the DTP[2]. The DTP has been perceived as an opportunity from both the Turkish and the Kurdish side to solve peacefully the Kurdish question and prevent the Kurdish youth from joining PKK[3].

The developments that took place after July 2007 showed that the DTP would not be a tool for the solution of the Kurdish problems since its members were accused of supporting terrorist activities in the southeast of Turkey. The DTP has been the subject of a court case attempting to close it down since 2007 and it has been charged with organizational links to the PKK. However, it was shut down by the Turkish Constitutional Court in December 2009, having been declared unconstitutional and accused of acting against the unity of Turkey. In fact by looking at the actions of the performance of the DTP it can be said that despite all the opportunities it had, the DTP could not manage to distance itself from the PKK, which was criticized even by Kurds. Furthermore, the DTP never officially described the PKK as a terrorist organization. The closure of the DTP caused some protests and violent actions in Turkey, where some people were killed. Nevertheless, Turkey showed that it can handle this crisis and keep its internal order stable.

Of course party closures are not positively evaluated by the European Union but Turkey still continues to make reforms in this area. During the last two years Turkey has started to negotiate directly with Northern Iraq's Regional Government in relation to the activities of the PKK and bases in Northern Iraq's empty mountains. Turkey is the key trading partner for Iraq and mostly Turkish goods are sold in the supermarkets of Northern Iraq. Turkish involvement in Northern Iraq is also helpful to reduce the problems related to drug trafficking and illegal immigration (Second Report of the Independent Commission on Turkey 2009, p. 23). Turkey has successfully launched and now operates projects in

---

2 Demokratik Toplum Partisi (Democratic Society Party).

3 PKK (Kurdistan Workers' Party). Officially recognized as a terrorist organization by the United States and the European Union.

the southeast of Anatolia to reduce poverty and to improve the living standards of citizens living in the area. Including EU in such process would assure a bigger success in this process and spread the peace to countries like Iran, Iraq and Syria, which will share borders with the EU in the case of Turkey's full membership.

Modern Turkey and its neighbourhood

Turkey has been a secular state from its foundation in 1923; it took the French model of secularization and tried to remove religion from any role in government and politics. Nevertheless, Turkey faced several army takeovers in its history but all these events showed that secularism is a very strong pillar of the Turkish state. Recently there were several republican demonstrations in Turkey protesting against the decision of the government to allow headscarves at the universities.

Turkey has been labelled a *pivot state of excellence* by the US because of its population, location, economic and military potential (Winrow 2004, p. 25). This definition was also affected by the fact that Turkey is in a position to influence the regional international stability. With the end of Cold War, the Western World needed Turkey as a bridge to reach Central Asia and other countries in the Middle East. But as soon as they realized that the perceived threat from Iran's regime was exaggerated, all western countries tried to get involved individually in the region. Dramatic changes like globalization enhanced the cliff between western and eastern civilizations, which made it necessary to have some tools for indirect involvement. Now Turkey is once again perceived as a bridge between east and west. Being a bridge between both poles defines Turkey's strong and weak points as it requires devotion toward both parties. That is why the Turkish Prime Minister Erdoğan stated that Turkey's close relationships with the Muslim world should not be perceived as Islamization of the country, because Turkey is trying its best to prevent a clash of civilizations between east and west.

Turkey is surrounded by states from different religious and cultural backgrounds and has some problems with almost all of its neighbours. The most discussed were the problems with Armenia. Turkish and Armenian relations suffered too much from the post-Cold War developments and from the Armenian claims that the tragic events that took place in the last years of the Ottoman Empire should be recognized as genocide. Especially after the Karabakh Conflict between Azerbaijan and Armenia, Turkey closed its Armenian border, cutting diplomatic relations.

The Europeanization and democratization process also made it possible for Turkey to rethink its ties with its neighbours and solve all the problems coming from the history. After mutual visits made by the presidents of Armenia and Turkey some progress was achieved in normalizing the relations. In October 2009 an important historic agreement was signed between Turkey and Armenia in Zürich to establish diplomatic relations and reopen the borders[4]. Meanwhile this agreement also enhanced the hopes that the dispute between Azerbaijan and Armenia over Karabakh will also be resolved in the near future since Turkey has reiterated several times that this agreement does not ignore Azerbaijani interests in the region.

Georgia is also one of the most important countries for Turkey in the region. After the problems in bilateral relations with Armenia and the closure of the border, Turkey and Azerbaijan continued to use Georgian territory and space for transport, communication and trade purposes. The Bakü-Ceyhan pipeline also crosses Georgian territory, which places Georgia in a very important position. Georgia's problematic relations with Russia put it in a search for an ally in the region and Turkey is the only choice for Georgia in this respect as the biggest western power in the region and a bordering country. During the war in 2008 between Russia and Georgia, Turkey tried to reduce the tension by urging conflicting parties to keep the dialogue open through the Stability Pact for Caucasus.

Despite all these efforts Turkey's capabilities itself are very limited by comparing the potential it has. Turkey and Russia are the main powers who shaped the region in the past and Turkey continues to increase its role in the region. Back up from the European side would trigger development in the Caucasus region. Generally, Brussels and other European capitals are perceived as weak players in the South Caucasus compared to the United States and Russia (Coppieters 2004, p. 214). Thus, the EU's capabilities of assisting the post-communist countries during the transformation process into a modern democracy are restricted. Turkey would be a good opportunity for the European Union to overcome this deficit. Also, both Russia and the US are likely to perceive each others' activities as a threat while for the EU such a perception might not exist. The European Union as a whole can deploy very powerful economic resources and support more political programs for stabilizing Georgia and the region than any single member can afford.

Turkey could be a good basis for the activities of the European Union to support the democratization processes in Georgia and Armenia and to enhance the role of civil society in the region itself. Because, if civil society forces are able to develop in the form of stable political parties and supported by a broad network of public and private organizations, then they will be able to apply pressure to the regime for a change to the better (Gill 2000, p. 126). Powerful civil society organizations can make minor changes with major consequences, which can turn into democratization.

The same situation could also be valid for Iran and the Middle Eastern countries. Most US activities are connected with potential projects of the American hegemony over the energy sources while there is not such a common per-

---

4 The New York Times [http://www.nytimes.com/2009/10/11/world/europe/11armenia.html] retrieved on 5.1.2010.

ception for the European Union. The EU has never considered the Middle East as a single area or actor like the United States and Russia have done. Besides, there are no contractual relations with countries in the region apart from low level political relations (Aliboni 2006, p. 165). This situation is a result of the individual involvements of EU Member States like France, England and Germany, which also shows clearly the deficit of the Common Foreign and Security Policy.

Once again, Turkey could help the EU to overcome its deficit in this area, since Turkey is fully engaged with the developments in the area. For instance, after the US invasion in Iraq, Turkey helped to reconcile Sunni Muslims to the new Iraqi order. Turkey also created friendly relations with Iran after 2002. Although Turkish-Iranian relations were not too problematic, there is a gradual increase in key areas like trade, tourism and cultural exchange as a result of the Turkish Government's initiatives. Turkey has a level and frequency of access to the Iranian leadership that is "greater than that of EU countries and consistently supports the EU position on Iran's nuclear programme and on halting any weaponisation" (Second Report of the Independent Commission on Turkey 2009, p. 26). Turkey is a good example for the EU to show that bordering with Iran is not bad, as is commonly assumed. After all, the border between Iran and Turkey is one of the oldest frontiers in the world. It has not changed since the last war between two countries in 1639. Therefore stability and mutual trust in bilateral relations is in place. As a European Member State Turkey would be more confident with its future activities and could contribute better to European Security.

Turkey would be a gate toward Central Asia for the European Union. Soon after the collapse of the communist bloc, Turkey created close relationships with the Turkic Republics in Central Asia through cultural and economic agreements. Turkey also has linguistic kinships with these countries, which puts it in a more advantageous position than Russia and the United States. Besides, Turkish businessmen are the main economic actors and alone in some Central Asian countries.

Today Turkey is accepted as a regional power in this area. However there is a question of whether Turkey will seek to become a hegemonic state or not. The status of the relations between the USA and Turkey will be a good indicator (Erickson 2004, p. 40). But the most important indicator will be Turkey's full EU membership. Because as a non-EU Member State, Turkey would seek to become a hegemonic power in order to balance US, Russia and the European Union. If Turkey joins the EU, then it would strive for the realization of the EU's common interests. Recent discussions about the resurgence of the Ottoman Empire show that Turkey would really become a hegemonic power.

Europe's energy security and Turkey's strategic position

The enlargement of the European Union did not only bring different countries to the Union but also brought several international issues related with the new Member States. Energy is one of them. The winter of 2008 showed the EU how important it is to have secure energy sources. During the crisis between Russia and the Ukraine, countries like Romania and Bulgaria were deeply affected by the suspended gas flow. Especially Bulgaria, which is dependent on Russian resources to one hundred percent, made the EU critically think about diversifying its gas supplies. Before then, unlike the US, most of the EU Member States had not focused on Turkey's strategic importance. Nonetheless, since Brussels started to think about developing an East-West gas transportation corridor for its long term energy security, Turkey has become the focus of the agenda (Winrow 2004, p. 27). Nabucco was the first project officially signed after this process, for which energy supply is still a problematic issue.

The Bakü-Ceyhan Oil Pipeline was built with the strong support of the United States, though it does not have the capacity to satisfy the needs of the European market. Of course it is true that Europe's long term energy security needs could be met if Turkey becomes a key gas transit state (Winrow 2004, p. 23). But this does not change the reality that Russia will be a dominant actor in the market. Including Turkey in such projects and transporting the energy through Turkish territory will reduce the European dependency rate, because Turkey can be used to transfer the gas from North Africa, Middle East and Central Asia to the European market.

Iran should not be forgotten at this stage. Iran was intentionally excluded from all the energy projects led by the United States (Winrow 2004, p. 26). When Turkey concluded an agreement with Iran on gas sales, the US blamed Turkey for serving Iranian interests. Making such an agreement with Iran would be a good solution also for the European Union. Moreover this would enhance the level of interactions between the Iranian and European officials, which would be an occasion for broader cooperation.

Turkmen gas was the other discussion topic in Turkey when the problem with restricted gas supplies arose. Building such a pipeline is costly and the Turkish government could not afford such project. With the economic support of the European Union this could be realized and Europe could start to use Turkmen gas in the future. Also, several times Turkmen officials stated that they are ready to offer cheaper prices than Russian ones.

Turkey is trying to secure its position in the region as an energy transport basis. Turkey's stable political life, its democracy, national pride and Muslim traditions continue to be an inspiration for the countries in the region. Turkey is a good example of a stable state living alongside the conflict lines. But its success will be limited or the progress will be slow in the next ten years without European membership. EU membership will trigger Turkish leadership in the region and would play a key role in the democratization process of countries like Iran, Armenia, Syria and Iraq.

Citizens of the European Union will decide whether they want an EU as a global actor in world politics and able to influence the shift of international relations or an EU without the decisive ability in key international developments (Keyman/Öniş 2004, p. 178). It is certain that an EU claiming to become an international actor needs Turkey to pursue its goals further.

Conclusions

Turkish foreign policy changed dramatically after the end of the Cold War. Turkey is still negotiating with the EU for full membership. But the EU and its Member States have to know that Turkey is trying to find its place in the region with or without the European Union. Of course, both Turkey and its neighbours will benefit from the Turkish membership, as it will attract foreign investments and stabilize the region.

Turkey, of course, is not a country free of problems. There are still serious issues with the Kurdish minority and social conflicts in the southeast region. Meanwhile it has to be underlined that the Turkish Government gives priority to solving the Kurdish question in order to direct more energy to other regional conflicts and to enhance Turkey's role in the international fora.

The recent Turkish-Armenian agreement to establish normal diplomatic relations is a very good indicator that the Caucasus is getting ready for Turkey's EU membership. European countries could benefit from such an agreement because Armenia would be the next country to transport Central Asian energy resources.

After the long Cold War period and time spent with the transition in the 1990s, it seems that Turkey is tired of searching for its real ally, which means it is now searching for another alternative, such as focussing on its own dynamics and history, to rise again.

References

Aliboni, Roberto (2006), 'Globalization and the Wider Black Sea Area: Interaction with the European Union, Eastern Mediterranean and the Middle East', in *Southeast European and Black Sea Studies*, 6:2, pp. 157 - 168.

Coppieters, Bruno/Michael Emerson/Michel Huysseune/Tamara Kovziridze/Gergana Noutcheva/Nathalie Tocci/MariusVahl (2004), *Europeanization and Conflict Resolution: Case Studies from the European Periphery*, Academia Pres, Gent.

Erickson, Edward (2004), 'Turkey as Regional Hegemon – 2014: Strategic Implications for the United States', in *Turkish Studies*, 5:3, pp. 25 - 45.

Gill, Graeme (2000), *The Dynamics of Democratization: Elites, Civil Society and the Transition Process*, St. Martin's Press, New York.

Keyman, Fuat E./Ziya Öniş (2004), 'Helsinki, Copenhagen and Beyond: Challenges to the

New Europe and the Turkish State', in M. Uğur/N. Canefe (eds.), *Turkey and European Integration: Accession Prospects and Issues*, pp. 173 - 193.

McLaren, Lauren M. (2008), *Constructing Democracy in Southern Europe: A Comparative Analysis of Italy, Spain and Turkey*, Routledge, London.

Second Report of the Independent Commission on Turkey (2009), 'Turkey in Europe: Breaking the Vicious Circle', [http://www.eliamep.gr/wp-content/uploads/2009/12/ICT-report.pdf] retrieved on 30.12.2009.

Winrow, Gareth M. (2004), 'Turkey and the East-West Gas Transportation Corridor', in *Turkish Studies*, 5:2, pp. 23 - 42.

Chapter V

Reality Difficult To Grasp

Anna Mattila

Debate Europe – Analysis of an Online Forum

Introduction

Following the negative votes in France and the Netherlands on the European Constitution in 2005, the European Council called for a *"period of reflection"* to enable a broad debate to take place in all European Union countries, involving citizens, civil society, social partners, national parliaments and political parties. The European Commission, which continued to strongly support the ratification of the "Constitution", then introduced the Plan D for Democracy, Dialogue and Debate to encourage a wider debate between the EU institutions and citizens. The purpose of Plan D was to envision a new future for Europe, building it on a clear view of citizens' needs and expectations. (Commission of the European Communities 2005, p. 2).

"Plan D is about debate, dialogue and listening. It is a means of harnessing political ideas to generate change. Faced with the challenges of globalization, people are asking tough questions about job security and pensions, about migration and living standards. Europe must renew so it is part of the solution to those challenges. Plan D aims to inject more democracy into the Union, to stimulate a wide public debate and build a new consensus on the future direction of the European Union. Now Member States must bring this process alive. My appeal today is for national governments to seize this opportunity, to kick start the debates and to act as a motor for European change." (Margot Wallström, Vice-President of the European Commission)

The European Commission aimed at creating a European public sphere, where citizens would be given information and tools to actively participate in the decision making process. As public confidence in political systems was declining, the Commission believed that it was necessary to let people feel that Europe provides added value and that citizens have the ability to affect the way decisions are taken. (Commission of the European Communities 2005, p. 3) On March 27th 2006, the European Commission launched *Debate Europe*, an online platform for discussing the future of the European Union. According to the Commission report on Communication, the Internet had become an important forum of political debate and should be used as an interactive communications medium that can facilitate the debate on the Future of Europe. This was a part of Plan D. The forum was designed to gauge public opinion, as it is open to all interested citizen in the hopes of drawing people from all walks of life[1].

---

[1] Debate Europe forum [http://forums.ec.europa.eu/debateeurope] retrieved on 13.10.2009.

Purpose and structure of the study

Despite the new European Commission agenda on building more communication among European Union citizens and its institutions using the Internet as the medium, *Debate Europe* is not first of its kind. In fact, a similar Future of Europe (*Futurum*) debate website was set up in 2001 by the European Commission as a gateway to information on the constitutional process. Beside information sharing, *Futurum* was meant to "help bring the European Union closer to its citizens and reduce the perception of a democratic deficit", a goal very similar to that of *Debate Europe*. *Futurum* was closed after the constitution process had failed in 2005, some time before the new and improved debate forum was opened up.

Futurum has since been analysed *inter alia* by Wright (2007) and Danet & Herring (2007). Wright's analysis concentrates on *Futurum's* purpose as a public sphere, its impact on policy making, its users, used languages and the nature of its debate. Danet & Herring on the other hand worked on the linguistic analysis of the forum, describing in more detail the evolution of one such discussion, the creation of dialogue and like Wright, they studied the demographic profile of the users in their quantitative analysis.

Hence, using the work of Wright and Danet & Herring as a starting point, this study is going to analyse the quantitative dimensions of *Debate Europe* in a similar fashion to the *Futurum* studies: user demographics, user activity and choice of language will be analyzed.

Debate Europe consists of eight different topical forums, each available in 24 European languages. Our study concentrates mainly on the forum Future of Europe, as it was by far the most discussed topic, consisting of over 70 per cent of all posts in *Debate Europe*. However, due to time and language limitations of this study, in-depth analysis of the 4541 discussion topics in all 24 languages was not possible and thus full qualitative dimensions such as Wright's policy impact of the forum or nature of debate will not be discussed here. However, to analyse the *Debate Europe* topics and their relevance to the agenda set by the European Commission, we search out the posts that have been posted in the past six months[2] on the English, lingua franca forum and compare the issues with those brought up in the same time span in the widely popular blog run by Margot Wallström, the vice president of the European Commission.

First, methods of study and data-collection are outlined, to give a better understanding of how information was gathered, and what problems exist in such a study of ongoing online debate. After that, quantitative analysis of *Debate Europe* will be conducted introducing analysis of used languages and user demographics. In the fourth chapter a short qualitative analysis of the forum topics will take place, and finally a summary and conclusions will be presented in the last chapter.

---

[2] Future of Europe topics from the previous 6 months, retrieved on 18.11.2009.

Methods of the study

Debate Europe is an online debate that continued to grow at the time of writing this contribution. In regard of this study, this posed a minor problem to the cohesiveness and thus reliability of the data. Unlike previous studies on *Futurum*, where online discussion had ceased before data collection, *Debate Europe* would literally expand in scope every time the browser refreshed. As collection of all relevant data at exactly the same point in time was in practice nearly impossible, data for *Debate Europe* is not entirely cohesive. As different parts of data were collected on altogether different dates, this suggests that from the time of earlier data collection, more users and more posts could have been created, decreasing data reliability. However, such an increase in users and posts was considered minor and thus not of relevance to final results.

Data collection

In this study, to obtain an overview of the forum, each discussion group, that is to say the Future of Europe forum for each language, was regarded individually. Total number of topics and posts were observed, but more importantly, relevant topics with actually following discussion were discovered by manually counting the so called spam[3] and troll[4] topics of every discussion forum. This was done to differentiate relevant discussions from topics and posts that often occur on online forums, but are not regarded as real posts. And indeed, spam and trolls constituted a staggeringly high amount of all posts, as an average of all languages it was close to 75 per cent, often stemming from the self-same user accounts. For example, we found that user Giovanni Battista Sonzogn opened topics within every forum, apparently translating his messages with an internet translator to match the language in question. The user often posted multiple topics at the same time, resulting in a substantial amount of traffic on the discussion forums. However, such topics appear to have been left without response by other users, and thus can be regarded as trolls. Hence, in this study, topics with less than two subsequent posts are regarded as spam or trolls.

0-1 posts after original poster of the topic = spam or trolls
>2 posts after original poster of the topic = real discussion

Due to such generalisation of default values, the result of non-relevant discussion topics is naturally only an estimation of the absolute amount, but serves the

[3] Spam = Forum spam is the posting of advertisements, abusive, or unwanted messages on Internet forums. (Wikipedia, 19.10.2009)

[4] Troll = a troll is someone who posts controversial, inflammatory, irrelevant or off-topic messages in an online community, such as an online discussion forum, chat room or blog, with the primary intent of provoking other users into an emotional response or of otherwise disrupting normal on-topic discussion. (Wikipedia, 19.10.2009)

purpose, as study of each individual topic was not possible due to the limitations of this research.

Figure 1 Proportion of spam/trolling in comparison to relevant topics on the forums

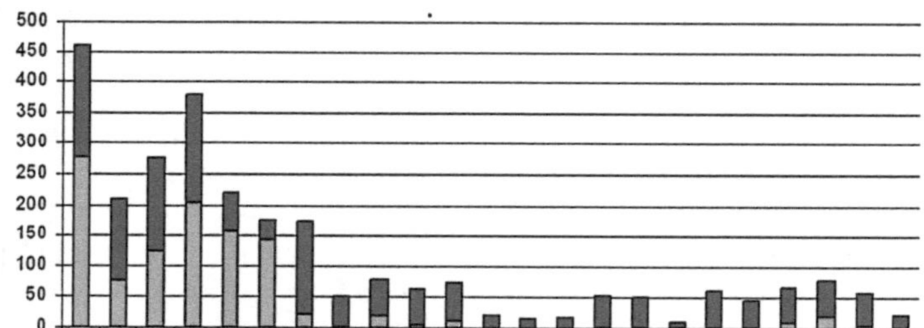

	FR	DE	IT	ES	EL	CA	PT	FI	SV	DA	NL	ET	LT	LV	BG	CS	GA	HU	MT	PL	RO	SK	SL
Spam /trolls	180	131	150	174	63	34	149	49	59	60	62	19	14	18	51	47	9	58	44	56	58	52	20
Relevant topics	279	77	125	205	157	142	24	3	20	5	12	1	1	1	3	3	2	2	2	10	21	6	2

The above Figure illustrates the division of relevant topics (lower section) and spam or trolls (upper section) on the forums. It is important to notice that though discussion in some languages hardly exists, all forums had significant amount of irrelevant topics. In the further analysis of topics, only relevant topics were regarded, and spam and trolls were no longer taken into account.

The *Debate Europe* discussion forum had 6233 registered users at the time of data collection[5]. The forum has a function, where users can be browsed and classified according to certain criteria, and in this study this was used to find out both the amount of posts that each individual user had posted, as well as to determine certain user demographics, such as user location. Furthermore it is possible to search posts from a specific forum in a certain timeline, and this was later used to determine the topics that were the most discussed in the Future of Europe forum.

Analysis of the Debate Europe forum

Use of languages

Multilingual discussion in the Internet has been widely promoted by the European Union, as such discussions have the potential to bring citizens closer together and closer to the European institutions themselves. As such, multilingual discussions have been seen as one possibility to improve decision making in the

[5] Member list: Debate Europe [http://forums.ec.europa.eu/debateeurope/memberlist.php] retrieved on 17.11.2009.

EU, as well as a possibility to reduce the democratic deficit perceived by many EU citizens. (Danet/Herring 2007, p. 385)

Similar to its predecessor discussion forum *Futurum*, *Debate Europe* also provides online discussion opportunities in all official EU languages. Since the acceptance of new Member States in 2004 and 2007, a total of 24 languages are available now, whereas *Futurum* was only provided in ten different languages (Danet/Herring 2007, p. 388). According to Wright (2007, p. 1176) language usage has important implications for the character of discussions, and who can participate: If one language dominates the discussion, it could create a linguistic barrier, excluding those who are not capable of understanding and communicating in that language.

Previous analyses of language use on *Futurum* (Wright 2007; Danet/Herring 2007) showed that though multilingual interaction existed and a wide range of languages were spoken by users, threads starting in English were by far the most discussed, compared to those started in other languages. In fact, all authors agree that English was chosen the lingua franca for communication. In case of *Debate Europe*, the same phenomenon can similarly be observed. Although the major languages English, French, Spanish, Catalonian, Greek, Italian and German constituted over 97 per cent of all the posts on the topic, over three fourths (77.73%) of all these were on the English language forum. In other words, multilingual discussions did take place, but by far the largest group of users were using English as the common language, *lingua franca*, just like it was in the case of *Futurum*.

Figure 2 below illustrates number and percentage of topics discussed in various European languages, showing the notable asymmetry between topics that were created on the English language forum in comparison to those of other languages. Furthermore, it is significant to note that besides the mentioned seven major languages, the rest of the 17 European Union languages contribute to less than a tiny three per cent of all discussed topics. These 17 message boards had an average count of 6.9 topics per forum, whereas the top six languages after English, had an average of 164.2 topics per forum.

Such major differences in use of languages on a discussion forum that was particularly designed to fill the needs of all European Union citizens, regardless of nationality and spoken language, however, should not be simply ignored and pushed aside with the justification of *lingua franca*. It may be that English rose above the other languages being the common language among EU citizens, but that does not yet explain the near to absolute lack of discussion in languages such as Finnish, Estonian, Hungarian, Bulgarian etc. Figure 3 below shows the number of discussion topics in the 17 less used EU languages trying to illustrate this unfortunate state of some forums

Figure 2 Debate Europe – Future of Europe: languages

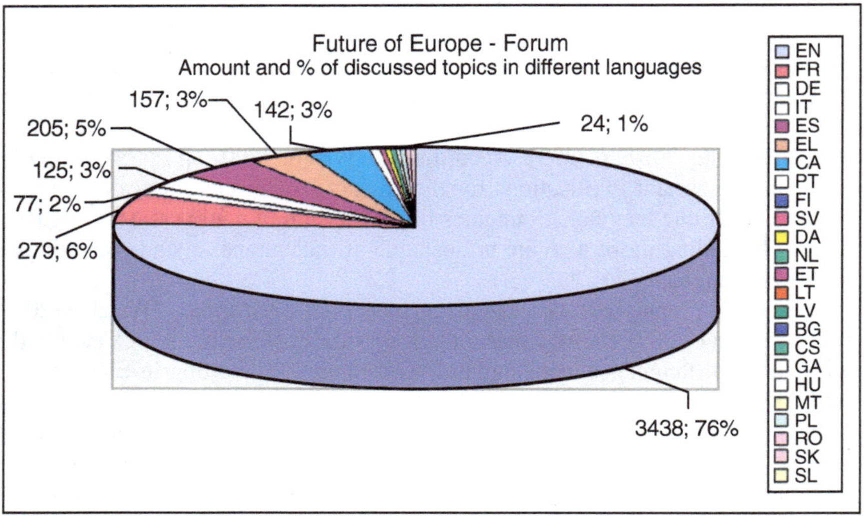

Figure 3 Number of discussed topics in the 17 "minor" EU languages

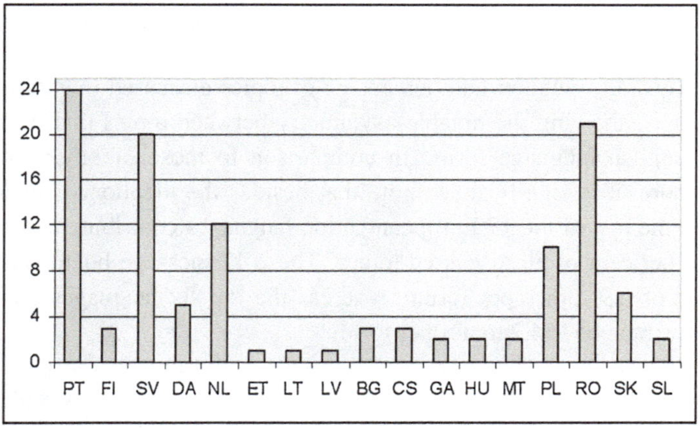

When asked about the lack of Finns participating, the moderator of the Finnish language forum assumed that *Debate Europe* was seen as too "official" by Finns. True or not, with a quick look at discussion forums of local newspapers and media companies, it can be discovered that the discussion culture that the *Debate Europe* site lacks in Finland, does however exist and even flourishes elsewhere. Kaitatzi-Whitlock (2007, p. 692) finds more refined reasons, why the EU and its policies might seem uninteresting in the eyes of an EU citizen. She argues that for national media the EU *per se* and its policies do not constitute a newsworthy topic and furthermore points out that news items that do get covered in the media, are often represented solely from national perspectives deforming the reality and nature of EU politics. Citizens of the European Union thus lack the required information and fail to perceive the EU from a *common European interest* scenario that, according to Kaitatzi-Whitlock, is the worst possible situation for communicating European politics to EU citizens.

However, coming back to the forum and the lack of interest displayed by Finns: Image, whether of Euro politics or the debate itself might be one key issue here. The Finnish forum had 52 topics at the time of data collection, of which only three were relevant, and most of the other 49 were badly translated into poor Finnish. Such an overwhelming amount of spam and troll topics – mostly posted by one person – would inevitably offer limited and weak debate possibilities to any viewer, and would as such deter users from using particular forum.

Users[6]

User activity

The *Debate Europe* forum does not require registration for viewing and reading discussions, but only registered users are allowed to participate in discussions as well as open new topics or polls. On November 3rd 2009 the *Debate Europe* forum had 6291 registered users – out of almost 500 million European Union citizens. More than half (55%) of these users had never posted a single message on the discussion boards, the number of users with 0 posts being 3452 on the day of data collection. Similarly, 20 per cent of all users (1267) had only posted one message on the forum. The following graph shows the diminishing trend of users per posted messages, suggesting that most users are rather inactive in discussions. Users that posted 0 - 20 messaged on the boards make up over 96 per cent of all users, but contribute to only 4.4 per cent of total posts on the forum. Coupled with the fact that the 100 most active users contributed to almost 80 per cent (78.29) of all posts, it can be said that the *Debate Europe* forum is dominated by a small number of users. Wright (2007, p. 1175) came to a similar conclusion when analyzing the discussion forum *Futurum*, and stated that a minority of users influenced the overall shape of the discussion. Further comparison of the two discussion forums is unfortunately not feasible, as Wright used a slightly different method to reach his conclusions, only analyzing user posts on the General Debate, whereas this study did not specify the forums where users had posted. However, 71 per cent of all posts in *Debate Europe*, were posted on the Future of Europe forums, making that the "General Debate" of *Debate Europe*.

6 User statistics: Debate Europe [http://forums.ec.europa.eu/debateeurope/memberlist.php] retrieved on 3.11.2009.

Figure 4 Amount of forum users per posted messages between 0 - 20

	0	1	2	3	4	5	6	7	8	9	10	11	12	13	14	15	16	17	18	19	20
Nr.of users	3452	1267	411	239	3166	93	83	54	36	39	39	28	22	19	19	15	19	12	13	13	13

Participants' gender – analysis of usernames

In his study of *Futurum*, Wright (2007, p. 1176) developed further the understanding of debate participants by evaluating the sex of the users. He analyzed the usernames that participants had adopted and if a username was not obviously male or female, it was marked as uncodable. Naturally there is no way of determining the sex of a user, as female users could take men's names and vice versa. In this study, analysis of all 6291 users was not possible due to time and resource limitations. To enable a rough representation of the user demographics we chose the 150 most active usernames to be analyzed. Though the top 150 users do make up only 2.8 per cent of all users, they contributed at the date of data collection to 85 per cent of all posts, thus making this group relevant when evaluating user demographics of the forum discussions.

The analysis showed that 69 per cent of evaluated users had chosen a username that was not clearly female or male, but uncodable. Of the rest, 28 per cent were male and only 3.3 per cent were female. Though most users were uncodable and could thus be either male or female in reality, the results do show a tendency of females being unrepresented in the debate. Wright (2007, p. 1178) came to similar conclusions in regard of *Futurum*, stating that discussions were male dominated and unrepresentative. His analysis showed that the majority of respondents were male, 37 per cent uncodable and 5 per cent female.

Users' location

The Internet penetration rate[7] varies from country to country inside the EU. According to the latest statistics (Internet World Stats), the EU has an internet pene-

[7] The Internet Penetration Rate corresponds to the percentage of the total population of a given country or region that uses the Internet. (Internet World Stats 2009 [http://www.internetworldstats.com/stats9.htm] retrieved on 16.11.2009.

tration rate average of 64 per cent of the population. In comparison, the EU candidate countries have an average of 36 per cent and the rest of the world that of 23 per cent. Inside the EU countries the penetration rate varied from Sweden's 89 per cent to 31 per cent in Cyprus. Such significant differences in Internet penetration rates mean that even inside the EU a great amount of people simply do not have access to the Internet and to public spheres such as *Debate Europe*. In a previous study by Kaitatzi-Whitlock (2007, pp. 697 - 698) Internet penetration in the EU25 Member States was an average of 47 per cent. She pointed out that if half of the EU population is not networked, the Commission is actively excluding those citizens from valuable information, which should be accessible by every European. Though the Internet penetration rate has increased since Kaitatzi-Whitlock's study, the citizens of countries like Cyprus (31%) and Bulgaria (37%) are still poorly represented in the Internet forums.

In his study of *Futurum*, Wright (2007, pp. 1175 - 1176) analyzed the users' country of origin, taking advantage of a 193-country drop-down list provided by the forum to identify users' location. He found out that there were significant variations between countries, not necessarily related to Internet access. Though his results suggested that a broad range of nationalities participated, Wright came to the conclusion that the participants were not representative of the European population.

Debate Europe forums allow users to locate themselves freely, thus adding extra complexity to analyzing the country of origin/location of participants. Most users (67%) had chosen no location at all, and though the majority of users that had chosen a location chose an existing one, there were also some who used locations such as the "universe" or "terra" etc. It is obvious that *Debate Europe* participants come not only from Europe, but rather from all over the world. However, due to the complexity of the issue in the *Debate Europe* forum and the obvious lack of user location statistics, further analysis will not be conducted. Nevertheless, the assumption that forum participants are not representative of European population, similar to Katiatzi-Whitlock and Wright's findings, is valid in our study as well.

Debate themes

Debate Europe's future forums had a total of 7055 topics at the time of data collection. As mentioned earlier, 35 per cent of those were spam posts or trolling. And, of those remaining 4541 relevant topics, 75 per cent were on the English language forum.

In his study of *Futurum*, Wright (2007, p. 1175) analyzed the General Debate, the largest debate on the discussion forum to find out more about the debate issues. Similarly, this study will only concentrate on the issues and topics within the largest and most popular debate – the Future of Europe debate in English. However, because *Debate Europe* has been up and running for over three and a half years since its launch in 2006, the forum contains more information and diversity of topics than can be analyzed in the limited scope of this study. Thus, only *relevant* topics from the past six months will be studied and analyzed. Furthermore, this study will present and compare the main discussion topics with those that appeared during the same timeline in the blog of Margot Wallström, the European Commissioner for Institutional Relations and Communication Strategy.

In the past six months, Margot Wallström discussed little more than a dozen varying themes in her blog. The common topics that kept reappearing in her posts were:

- Climate change
- Lisbon Treaty and referendum in Ireland
- Women and security
- Sexual violence in conflict areas
- EU communication and
- Gender equality

In comparison, most discussed themes at the Future of Europe discussions were:

- Lisbon Treaty and its ratification process (both in Ireland and in the Czech Republic)
- Anti-UK membership
- Issues regarding China
- Issues regarding Islam and Muslims
- Immigration
- Turkey's potential membership

Clearly, themes introduced by European Commission vice-president Wallström and those introduced by the citizens of EU did not greatly overlap. There are many possible explanations for this. First of all, it is important to notice, that *Debate Europe* has its own forums for 'climate change' and 'women and politics', two issues important to Wallström. Though some discussion topics at the Future of Europe forum did cover both issues, it can be assumed that most issue-relevant discussions took place within their specific forums, and only occasionally found their way into the most popular discussion forum. Secondly, Wallström is an individual with her own agenda and hence she writes about topics where she wants a difference to be made. On the contrary, *Debate Europe* consists of many individuals, posting and responding to various topics created either by users or by moderators. Individual agenda setting is less obvious and many of the most frequent discussion topics stem from the more general, common interests of the users. Lastly, some influential top posters at the Future of Europe forum seem to have a tendency of promoting their own agenda. A perfect example of such behaviour is user Shuimo with 3281 (1.7% of all) posts on the *Debate Europe*.

Shuimo, located in Lhasa, Tibet according to his (her) own definition, seems to be responsible for nearly all China-related topics created in the forum in the past six months. China-related topics would hardly be among the most discussed on the forum, if it wasn't for Shuimo intentionally raising the appearance and density of such issues and provoking discussion.

Thus, most discussed topics at *Debate Europe* consist of issues that are both topical for European Citizens, e.g. Lisbon Treaty, immigration, but also important for the users that dominate the forum. Wright (2007, p. 1175) similarly concluded in his study of *Futurum*, that a minority did greatly influence the overall shape of the discussion. Hence, this raises questions about *Debate Europe* forum's purpose and reliability as the overall platform for European citizens. If a small number of users can strongly shape the nature of conversation, will there be enough substance for the European institutions to search for an advice from such forums, and can the European citizens feel that they have a chance to affect the way decisions are taken?

Summary and conclusions

Debate Europe is an online platform that was created after the negative European Constitution votes to enable a broad discussion on the European future. It was designed to bring together European citizens and institutions, decrease perceptions of democratic deficit and to evaluate public opinion.

Taking previous studies by Wright (2007) and Danet and Herring (2007) as an example, this contribution analyzed *Debate Europe* mostly in its quantitative dimensions, looking at languages in use, participant demographics and user activity. To study the qualitative aspects of the forum, the most substantial topics were analyzed and briefly compared with those that European Commission vice president Margot Wallström respectively handled during the same time span.

Though *Debate Europe* offers discussion possibilities in 24 different European languages, English proved to be the most commonly used language, even if users were not native speakers. French, German, Spanish and a few other languages also provided active discussions, but in many minor languages discussion hardly existed at all. This could be seen as a sign of lack of interest about the subject in those language groups, but more probably it was a simply a case of lack of participants and topics to make discussion seem interesting on a non-major language forum.

In light of this study, *Debate Europe* does not serve its purpose as the common medium between citizens and institutions in EU, not only because it lacks the power to attract citizens from all parts of Europe in all languages, but also because it has been shown to be a medium of a very small user group dominating the discussions. Despite the massive potential of 500 million EU citizens, *Debate Europe* has only slightly over 6000 users participating in the discussions. Most of these users have never posted a single message on the forum, sadly decreasing the real amount of participants to half of the original number. Even more importantly, the forum is dominated by a very small group of active users, who might not even be of European origin. This study showed that the 10 most active users made up over one quarter of all posts on the forum, hardly leaving any room for doubt about their power of influence on the discussions. As users can freely choose their country and location of origin, there is no way of finding out, whether the participants come from inside or outside of Europe.

Though this contribution concludes that *Debate Europe* has not reached the goals that were given to it by the Commission, it is important to point out that *Debate Europe* has nevertheless inspired broad discussion on many important issues and brought interested, motivated and different people together. As the debate is by far not over yet, we suggest that results from this study should only be seen as guiding assumptions and findings of its own time in the ongoing process. The forum and its purpose as a common medium should hence be further studied on a bigger scale and with more in-depth analysis.[8]

References

Commission of the European Communities (2005), 'Communication from the commission to the council, the European Parliament, the European Economic and Social Committee and the Committee of the Regions: The Commission's contribution to the period of reflection and beyond: Plan D for Democracy, Dialogue and Debate', pp. 1 - 12, Brussels.

Danet, Brenda/Susan C. Herring (2007), *The multilingual Internet: language, culture, and communication online*, Oxford University Press US, pp. 1 - 443.

Kaitatzi-Whitlock, Sophia (2007), 'The missing European public sphere and the absence of imagined European citizenship: Democratic deficit as a function of a common European media deficit', in *European Societies,* pp. 685 - 704.

Wright, Scott (2007), 'A virtual European public sphere? The Futurum discussion forum', in *Journal of European Public policy,* pp. 1167 - 1185.

Margaret Wallström blog [http://blogs.ec.europa.eu/wallstrom/] retrieved on 17.11.2009.

Speak up Europe [http://www.speakupeurope.eu/plan_d.html] retrieved on 20.10.2009.

[8] Note from the editor (January 2011): In the meantime, Debate Europe has been closed, but the website can still be found at [http://ec.europa.eu/archives/debateeurope/future/index_en.htm]. Visitors will find the pages stamped with "This site has been ARCHIVED ON 28/02/2010".

Milan Jazbec

The European Union: An Empire in Search of a Joke

Introduction

Subtitling reality

This contribution focuses on analyzing, contemplating and generalizing the experience of the Slovenes in former Yugoslavia[1] through the eyes of political jokes. It means that our intention is not to look at the country from a directly dry and serious point of view, but to try to uncover it by paying attention to details from daily life. With such an approach, though, we would nonetheless like to arrive at dry and serious conclusions about our research topic.[2] This experience will be briefly compared with the period from Slovenia's independence in 1991 till the EU membership in 2004, as well as with the period after joining the EU, all the time having in mind the appearance of political jokes and the impact of their instrumentalization.

We would start our research effort from a general impression that the first period was full of political jokes, while the next two are marked by either their absence or only with a minor number of political jokes, which are, more or less, the repetition of old samples, adjusted to a new political framework. This proposition stems from the personal experience of the author. Additionally, we share the opinion that political jokes not only reflect the political, social, security etc. atmosphere in a certain country, but also express more or less hidden criticism towards its regime as well as ideology, and might also include a hint about its possible future development or even existence, aiming towards its destruction. One could also say that political jokes share the structural complexity of the country itself.[3] This would also mean that we try to maintain a rather broad view upon jokes, understanding them as an instrument of criticizing a given system as well as a tool to upgrade identification with the same system. From both of these aspects one could also find out possible marks of how a system could develop in the future (namely, is it sustainable or not).

---

1 Here we have in mind the Socialist Federal Republic of Yugoslavia, which is a *de facto* synonym for Yugoslavia after World War II. Although the country changed its name a few times following World War II, time-wise this name dominated the whole period, till its dissolution in 1991.

2 From this point of view, see also the collection of essays by Drakulić Ilić Slavenka, How We Survived Communism and Even Laugh at the Same Time (Zagreb, 1994).

3 Here, the understanding of a joke is close to that of an aphorism, which is supposed to be a universe in a raindrop.

For the purpose of this contribution we would present a random sample of nine political jokes, which the author remembers from his personal experience, and divide them into three groups. The first one would focus on jokes about socialism as a system and ideology, the second one on jokes about Yugoslavia and the third one on jokes about Slovenia[4] as a part of Yugoslavia at that time. Consequently, we discuss these groups of jokes from three points of view: firstly, we seek criticism of a system (regime, ideology); secondly, we look for possible hints about the future of the system, and thirdly, we search for aspects of relaxation (identification with the system). The jokes here presented, analyzed and commented upon are a selection of those known to the author since his secondary school years in the first half of the Nineteen Seventies. All the jokes quoted here and the majority of others, remembered by the author, were originally told in Slovenia and in the Slovene language, although some of them included words or phrases from the then Serbo-Croat language; some of them were told in that language also in Slovenia (some of them are still being told in it today, for the specific context and their essence, although neither the former state nor its most widespread language, primarily an artificial linguistic combination, exist anymore).

Finally, we would briefly dwell on the question of what the situation is with regard to political jokes in Slovenia after its independence and in the EU as well as what their presence or absence, having in mind the Slovene experience from Yugoslavia, could mean for the future development of the EU.

Theoretical framework

From unconscious to intention

Jokes accompany us in our daily life. Most probably it would be difficult to find a person who has not heard (and laughed about) at least a single joke in their life. Although some people do not have any affiliation towards jokes and humour, listening to jokes and re-telling them would be nice as well as pleasant (cf. Freud 1992, p. 258).

The joke is a *playful* judgement[5], where the aesthetic attitude is *playful* in contrast to work (Freud 2002, p. 5). In the conceptual definition or description of the joke, they are also a '*contrast of ideas*', '*sense in nonsense*', '*bafflement and light dawning*' (ibid.). People listen to jokes, remember and re-tell them, but also invent them; however, few people are capable of the joke-work (Carey 2002, p. xi). While laughing at jokes, a certain amount of pleasure is released in us, which makes us feel better, perhaps even happy. We briefly forget hard things and times, feel familiar and closer to the object of the joke and are pre-

---

[4] Slovenia was one of the six socialist republics, which according to the federal constitution from 1974 also had some attributes of a state.

[5] Fischer (1871, p. 51) quoting from Freud (2002, p. 4).

pared to (or even do so) lower our dissatisfaction with, or criticism of, the object in question. One could say that the pleasure released by a joke touches upon the aesthetical attitude, while criticism touches upon the political. But perhaps, it would be better to say that criticism is hidden behind pleasure, which minimizes criticism and raises acceptance of the object of a joke. We can laugh at a joke since it is funny *per se,* or since it retains a certain point addressed to, or targeted at, somebody. This would mean there are two kinds of jokes, generally speaking: "Sometimes the joke is an end in itself and serves no particular purpose; at others, it does put itself in the service of such purpose: it becomes *tendentious*. Only the joke that has a tendency or intention runs the risk of coming up against persons who do not want to listen to it" (Freud 2002, p. 87).[6] These jokes hit the objective, i.e. "pin-point the places where problems are hiding" (Freud 2002, p. 90); even more, "they touch on the solution to problems" (ibid.).[7] We tend to call this kind of joke *political jokes*.

If it is in the nature of a joke to release what has been inhibited, what we otherwise would not have been able or allowed to express, then political jokes are suitable for transferring hidden messages. They reach the surface, from our unconscious, since the form of a joke enables us to say what we want to but would otherwise not dare to for internal (education, culture) or external reasons (authority): "… the obstacle to the aggression that the joke helped to get round was internal – an aesthetic objection to the insult – in other cases it may be purely external" (Freud 2002, p. 101). With this kind of joke we have an appropriate tool at our disposal, which enables us to express our annoyance, dissatisfaction or even aggression while not risking a harmful reaction from the target.[8] "The joke then represents rebellion against such authority, liberation from the oppression it imposes" (Freud 2002, p. 102). That is the reason why "the tendentious joke is so well suited to attacking disparagement by internal inhibitions or external circumstances" (ibid.). Additionally, such a joke may well have "one side for show, a façade (…) while another may try to look behind it" (Freud 2002, p. 103). Hence, the "suspicion may begin to stir that this façade is meant to dazzle the probing eye, that stories of this kind have something to hide" and "to hide not only what they have to say, but also that they have something – forbidden – to say" (ibid.). Forbidden, because it could open the listener's eyes,

[6] In his famous book on jokes (2002), first published in 1905, Freud develops a complex and detailed theory of jokes, relating them to dreams and links both to processes, which go on in our subconscious. He categorizes various types of jokes and techniques for joke-producing as well as listing numerous jokes, with which he supports his elaborations. For our discussion we find most interesting section III, The Tendencies of the Joke (pp. 87 -114).

[7] Freud (2002, p. 94) says that these jokes put themselves "at the service of two tendencies only, which can themselves be merged into a single viewpoint; it is either a *hostile joke* (used for aggression, satire, defence) or it is an *obscene joke* (used to strip someone naked)."

[8] However, expression via the use of political jokes does not prevent this, in any case.

reveal the true intention of the joke-maker as well as the joke-teller and aim to disrupt, dismantle its object.

Here we arrive at perhaps the most important reasoning of political jokes: "But the joke's object of attack could just as well be institutions, persons in so far as they are representative of the institutions, moral or religious precepts, philosophies of life enjoying such great respect that any criticism of them can only make appearance masked as a joke, that is, as a joke hidden by its façade" (Freud 2002, p. 106). The joke would then try to uncover what should remain covered, while the process of uncovering should be "able to say it outright, by not saying it at all" (Freud 2002, p. 7), avoiding with this a possible reaction of the addressed authority. Political jokes as well as those who invent, tell, re-tell and listen to them appear to be dangerous for those regimes and ideologies, which see themselves as the only possible and right option (Južnič 1996, p. 553). Dealing with political jokes therefore demands sharp mind, courage and capability for witty articulation.[9]

So people invent and tell jokes about high authorities, criticizing them and trying to hint at what they really think, in secrecy or even in their unconscious about them. They laugh while doing this, but at the same time a sharp eye on the object of criticism could be *via facti* softened. It is also in the nature of a joke to establish a relationship between both sides, which at the end of the day could serve in favour of the criticized object. It may easily happen that with an expression of criticism, which reveals itself through a joke, releasing pleasure, the object of a joke looks less critical and more acceptable. Political jokes have a kind of two-faced appearance like the ancient mythological Greek god *Janus*. But which side is the right one? Which interpretation of this two-faced nature could one rely on? Should one rely on it at all? Do the authorities and the joke-consumers have in mind the same face?

It may well be that regimes and ideologies need jokes and laughter. The negative attitude that lies in the very centre of a joke is compensated for by strengthening the relationship between the two parties, the joker and the target: "The ironical distance and laughter could work also as an inner condition of each real ideology, which is characterized exactly by the fact of avoiding direct diction of dogmas and psychical repression, attacking us precisely there where we feel most safe and independent" (Zupančič 2004, p. 10). This stream of thought continues: "Laughter is a condition of ideology. Only laughter gives us that distance, that space, in which ideology could outburst. Only with laughter we materialize as ideological subjects [...]. What at first glance destroys dogma actually very efficiently establishes it."[10]

---

[9] It demands, of course, also an audience, since jokes materialize within a social context only, this being the difference to humour as such.

[10] Dolar (1986, p. 307) quoted in Zupančič (2004, p. 10).

Since it is not our intention to dwell broadly and deeply on theoretical aspects of jokes, the above-presented characteristics as well some dilemmas, however narrow and limited they might be, should be sufficient for our further elaboration of the researched topic. In any case, during our later contemplation on the selection of political jokes from former Yugoslavia we would here and there return to some additional theoretical observations.

Selected empirical reconstruction

Three circles of targeting

What follows in this part of the text is the already mentioned selection[11] of nine political jokes from the former Yugoslavia, clustered in the three mentioned groups.[12] Our ambition here is to offer to the reader a collection of jokes and to provide the necessary material for further discussion. The examples are accompanied only by brief information, referring to their origin and specifics, without any further elaboration.[13]

Group No 1: Socialist system

Joke No 1: *Forgive*[14]

When the occasion of the one hundredth anniversary of the October Revolution was coming closer, a special Organizing Committee was formed in Moscow to prepare the official celebration. After everything had been arranged, the question of a guest speaker remained to be resolved. There were many ideas, but all were rejected as not suitable. Then the youngest member of the Committee, who kept silent more or less all the time in the presence of higher authorities, suggested that it should be Karl Marx in person. The suggestion was rejected almost unanimously at first. But after a period of deliberation it became apparent that this was indeed the best option. Hence they contacted the late leader. He was not willing to appear at first, but was somehow persuaded to do so. However, he put forward one condition: His speech would amount only to five words. His condition came as a shock to the Committee, but in the end, they decided to accept it. So, the ceremony started and it came to the turn of the keynote speaker. He appeared on

---

11 As Carey claims for Freud's collection of jokes: "Any selection illustrates aims present before the selection was made." (2002, p. xxviii).

12 They were translated for the purpose of this contribution by the author, who is aware of the following question, namely "how to translate the jokes – both word-play dependent on the configurations of their language, and social jokes exploiting the peculiarities of their culture – and still keep them even remotely funny; [...]." (Crick 2002, p. xxix) Here, the author would like to express his thanks to his son Luka for polishing the translation.

13 For the latter, later parts are instructive.

14 The author was told in a private chat in spring 2009 in Tirana, which he had with one of the former prime ministers that this joke was also told in socialist Albania.

the podium, cleaned his throat and said with a strong voice: "*Proletarians of all countries, forgive.*"

Joke No 2: *Ideas*

Comrade Edvard Kardelj, a Slovene and the ideological master of the Yugoslav socialist system, who wrote the majority of all of the most important party manifestos, documents and theoretical works, used to spend his holidays at home. Once chatting with his closest neighbour and a long-time friend, the latter complained that his cow had been ill for days and no medicine could cure the disease. Kardelj suggested to try with huge amounts of fresh cut grass in the morning and in the evening, both on a daily basis, and promised to come around again in a week's time to see how the therapy is going. Since he was told at their next meeting that the medicine did not work, he suggested the same approach, but with two-week-old cut grass, each time complemented with a handful of fresh wheat. The next time it was a mixture of fresh corn, wheat and grass. When they met again a week later, Kardelj asked his friend how the ill cow was doing. He told him that the poor creature had died the other day. Kardelj was highly surprised and replied sincerely: "*Oh, what a pity, I had so many more ideas*!"

Joke No 3: *Membership*[15]

Once upon a time the application trend for membership in the Communist Party appeared not to be increasing at the usual rate. That fact started to worry the leadership and hence they decided to meet at a special closed session. After a long and deep discussion, they took the decision to open a country-wide contest for gaining new members. Citizens were broadly encouraged to participate. The organizers managed to win huge support for the project among the population, since at the end three awards were supposed to be delivered. The third among the best was given the suspension of paying the membership fee for the next ten years. The second received the suspension of paying the fee for the next twenty years. And the winner was given a special written confirmation that he never was a member of the Communist Party.[16]

---

[15] The author has a friend, who on one occasion did receive written official confirmation that he never was a member of the Communist Party (although he was). However, this is already an anecdote and not a joke anymore. Perhaps on a highly sophisticated and symbolic level it could also serve as a joke, in particular since the friend, employed at the Federal Secretariat for Foreign Affairs (the Party Organization, which lost his documentation), asked the Party Organization of the Armed Forces in the place, where he – while serving the duty – was accepted to the Party membership, to send him the confirmation that he was a member (and not, of course, asking for a paper, that he was not a member). Luckily, there were no consequences for him, when the authorities received the document stating that he was not a member.

[16] As far as the author can recall, this joke did not include a geographical location, which

Group No 2: Yugoslavia

Joke No 1: *The Hammer*

At the Olympic Games the representative of Yugoslavia, a Bosniak[17], took part in the discipline of the hammer throw. He achieved a record result and increased the distance by more than two meters, which was an incredible achievement. The media immediately surrounded him and the first question he received was what his next goal would be. The answer was straightforward: "*Well, the hammer has been thrown away, the sickle comes next, and that's it.*[18]"

Joke No 2: *The Drive*

One Sunday afternoon Marshall Josip Broz Tito, the lifetime President of Yugoslavia, decided to take a relaxed drive. After a while the driver arrived at a countryside street crossing with only two ways ahead. The left sign showed the way to communism and the right one towards capitalism. The driver was hesitant about what to do, hence he asked the President politely for instructions, about which way to drive. The response was immediate, brief and clear: "*Indicate to the left and turn to the right.*"

Joke No 3: *Disappearance*

Junior privates, who had just entered Army Service in the Yugoslav Peoples' Army, were listening to the political speech of the commander during the regular weekly political hour. At the end, as was usual, a questions & answers session followed. One of the privates, sitting in the last row, asked the question, where did Savka Dapčević Kučar disappear to?[19] The private was promised by the lecturing officer to receive the answer at the next session. At their next meet-

---

could probably mean that it happened in Yugoslavia. This impression was supported by the existence of a similar joke, saying that there was a contest for the best political joke, organized by the Communist Party of the Soviet Union. The third award was twenty years of prison, the second award was a life term in prison, and the first was to meet comrade Marx in person.

[17] In Yugoslavia, the stereotype for Bosniaks was that they were simple, rather uneducated, psychically strong, open-minded and generous people, who always said what they thought, in a harmless manner. Therefore, they could afford to say more than others, sometimes also what others had in mind but didn't dare to say. Hence, they were also forgiven for saying what they occasionally said in that manner. One can, of course, never be sure …

[18] The hammer and the sickle were the most obvious and known elements of the Yugoslav, socialist, coat of arms. Some other states also had these in their state symbols.

[19] Ms Kučar was the leader of the Croat Nationalistic movement, which together with the same stream in Slovenia and Serbia, emerged in Yugoslavia at the beginning of the 1970s. The movement was cracked down upon rather soon and the leaders removed from public life, some for decades (like the later and late first Croatian President Franjo Tudjman) and some forever (like the Slovene Prime Minister at the time, Stane Kavčič).

ing, the usual Q & A session followed at the end of the presentation. This time, one private, again from the last row, addressed the lecturer with two questions: firstly, where did Savka Dapčević Kučar disappear to, and secondly, where did the private, who asked the same question last time, vanish to?

Group No 3: Slovenia

Joke No 1: *The Speech*

Two eminent Slovene and Yugoslav communist leaders, Sergej Kraigher and Stane Dolanc, once took part at a big people's meeting in Kozjansko, a remote hilly part of Slovenia, for an event commemorating World War II. While preparing himself for the speech, Dolanc asked Kraigher: "What would you say, am I allowed to finish my speech with God bless you?" The reply from the senior was immediate and clear: "*For Heaven's sake, no*."

Joke No 2: *The Cat*

In the Old Town of Ljubljana, at the very riverbank of the Ljubljanica, there is a restaurant called "Maček" (The Cat). In the late 1960s the president of the Slovene Parliament was one of the best known and for sure the most feared Slovene communist leaders, an old partisan, Ivan Matija with the nickname Maček.[20] Soon after he became elected, a joke started to circulate among the citizens of Ljubljana and was slowly (and carefully) disseminated across Slovenia. It went in the form of a brief dialogue. A person, going to the Parliament, was asked: "Where are you going?" The answer was: "To Maček." And the person, going to the restaurant Maček, was asked the same question: "Where are you going?" And the answer was: "To the Parliament."

Joke No 3: *The Sava River*[21]

One of the most popular political jokes, retold in a form of a questions game, was this one. The question: "What would be the colour of the river Sava[22] if the

---

[20] The afore-mentioned Edvard Kardelj married Matija's sister Pepca, whom he met during World War II.

[21] This joke was taken as an example for joke analysis for the first time in Jazbec (2008). Highly positive reactions to this approach as far as political and social analysis of former Yugoslavia is concerned, encouraged the author to dwell deeply and seriously on this matter.

[22] The Sava flows from the very northwest of Slovenia through Slovenia, Croatia to Serbia, and at Belgrade merges with the Danube River. For the most known and best Slovene poet France Prešeren that was in his poem "Povodni mož" (the Underwater Man) the place where Turkey begins: "It's not close, it's not close the way, which to Turkey white goes, where Sava blue in the Danube flows" (i.e. at Belgrade). Translated by the author.

Russians[23] attacked Slovenia?" The answer: "Red." The question: "And why?" The answer: "Because the Slovenes would fight till death." The next question: "And what would be the colour of the river Sava if the Americans were to attack Slovenia?" The answer: "Red, as well." The question: "And why this time?" The answer: "Because everybody would be throwing away their Communist Party membership cards."[24]

Crosscutting structural analysis

Dwelling under the surface of reality

The above-presented selection of political jokes illustrates a specific view upon the discussed country, its system as well as its reflection in daily life. We would try to uncover some of the hidden meanings and messages as well as to understand their purpose. This would mean that we try to explore reflections of reality, i.e. searching for reflections of the reflection (of the reality). As we have seen, releasing pleasure through jokes brings about also other aspects of social positioning, like criticism, appreciation, speculation regarding hidden problems as well as their possible solutions etc. This could be presented in a rather direct or indirect, i.e. hidden form (wording, suggestion, slight hint etc.).

Firstly, our attention goes to the intensity of messages carried by the jokes and which we understand as criticism (targeting the system and its attributes), as hints about the future of the system and as expressions of relaxation (or affiliation towards the system or even raised sympathy). According to what we have learned about jokes so far, there is a presumption that all of these could be found in (these) jokes, so we measure the intensity of these characteristics. In addition, let us stress that we are, on a general level, discussing political jokes about a country that no longer exists, and that these jokes are recalled by the author, who has a long personal experience of listening to them as well as sharing them. This would from one point of view show deep insight into the understanding of jokes and their reflection of the then-reality, but could from another point of view also raise a subjective approach to their understanding and elaboration. We measure the intensity of the researched views in three different levels (low, medium, high).[25]

---

23 It is interesting that these are Russians and not Soviets, whose attack was to be feared. Perhaps this illustrates that Soviets *de facto* did not really exist as a nation (like the Yugoslavs) and were an artificially created term and form for political purpose only (with historical background). It could also stem from the fact that when the Soviet Union intervened in Czechoslovakia in the summer of 1968, the majority had in mind (and spoke about) Russians and not Soviets. However the case (and the joke in question), Slovenes and Russians have always had good mutual relations.

24 Their colour was, of course, red.

25 Indicator of scale: low - ○, medium - ●, high - ◙. The measurement criteria reflect the author's own reasoning of these jokes.

One could say that the level of *criticism* in the selected jokes is rather strong (in five high and four low, out of nine altogether). Possible *hints* about the future of the object of jokes (generally, the system) are dispersed between high (three) and low (five), with one for medium, which could most probably be the measured level in this view. The *affiliation* seems to be well positioned as medium (in two cases high and in five medium, with two low). High criticism corresponds to low affiliation in two cases and in three to medium, while low criticism corresponds in two cases both to medium as well as to high affiliation. High – low relations between the two extremes correspond quite well, while there seems not to be a strong offer about the future, generally speaking.

Table 1 The Intensity of the Researched Views

Group	Joke	View		
		Criticism	The Future	Affiliation
The System	Forgive	◙	◙	●
	Ideas	○	○	●
	Membership	◙	○	●
Yugoslavia	Hammer	◙	◙	○
	Drive	○	○	●
	Disappearance	◙	●	○
Slovenia	The Speech	○	○	◙
	The Cat	○	○	◙
	The Sava River	◙	◙	●

The general impression would be that both criticism and appreciation are rather strong, something above the average. At the same time, possible hints remain something below the average level. As it looks, we deal with seemingly strong criticism and not much less strong affiliation, with a lower level of hints. Since the object of these jokes existed at the time of their producing and sharing, one could speculate that the effect, exercised by affiliation, was practically stronger as far as the future existence of the system is concerned, than the effect of criticism. One would need a stronger dose of criticism than of affiliation to try to dismiss what already exists; hence in this case the former had less effect than the latter as far as only jokes are concerned. However, obviously a more or less combined effect was produced by these jokes in the discussed case.[26] This would most probably speak in favour of lowering the dose of the then-criticism, while releasing it through jokes.

[26] Two methodological remarks should be added here. Firstly, the sample is too small for a broader generalization (but it could serve as a possible matrix for further research), and secondly, it would be useful to know and compare the level of criticism of political jokes in other socialist countries, since it is known, that the Yugoslav system appeared different in some, not unimportant nuances from the others.

The presence of political jokes as well as the awareness of this from the side of the political elite was producing (or strengthening) social context, which with an indirect expression of criticism through political jokes was also simultaneously producing an affiliation with the same target. We may speculate that the former was less damaging for the system than the latter was useful.

Secondly, our attention is also addressed to the concrete targets (the system itself) of these jokes. We search to uncover in what forms they appear, namely whether they are institutions directly or illustrated by individuals representing them, as well as whether the message (criticism and affiliation) is expressed directly or in a hidden manner (indirectly).[27]

Table 2 The Form of the Target and of the Message of the Jokes

Group	**Joke**	**Target**		**Message**	
		Institution	Individual	Direct	Hidden
The System	Forgive	+	–	+	–
	Ideas	–	+	–	+
	Membership	+	–	–	+
Yugoslavia	Hammer	+	–	+	
	Drive	+	–	–	+
	Disappearance	+	–	+	
Slovenia	The Speech	+	–	–	+
	The Cat	–	+	–	+
	The Sava River	+	–	–	+

A brief overview would tell us that the institution (i.e. the system directly) appears primarily as a target of jokes and that the message of the joke is primarily expressed in a hidden (i.e. an indirect) manner. This would correspond with the finding that the target is the institution (the external barrier) and that the message should be hidden and not direct for a joke to be efficient. If the joke is too direct, then it becomes plausible and may lose its effect, but it could also become dangerous (cf. Južnič 1996). The purpose of a joke is to tell the truth we feel but do not dare to express, other than masked.

Additionally, one could speculate that when the institution is targeted directly, the expressed criticism is served with a harder note. In this case the effect of the joke may well lie only in the fact that it (the criticism) was expressed and the pleasure released, while it is a question, to what extent this would bring sympathy for the target and upgrade the affiliation with it. Consequently, one may speculate that when the individual (who represents the insti-

[27] We measure this by simply detecting if the searched form appears in one way or another (+ or -).

tution) is the target of the joke, this would mean less criticism for the system and more affiliation to it. When the individual serves as a means of criticizing, then the level of criticism is perhaps lower, but through sympathizing with the authority, which appears as a normal person, the affiliation with the system is upgraded. A political joke that directly targets the system is serious but also funny, while a joke that targets the system through individuals that represent this very system is funnier, producing more laughter. It brings criticism, but it is masked by our appreciation of the leader, who appears as a normal human being, like one of us, so to speak.[28] Such jokes produce hidden[29] messages and may well be of use for the target that they are actually addressing. They work more in favour of its object than against it. They are more sophisticated, hence the question – which we would not be able to fully answer in this contribution – who is being served by these well thought-out jokes?

Judging from the content of the political joke, one could find out what the problem is and where it is hidden. The problem is the target addressed by the joke: Communism is a problem, Marx finds out a century later, while Tito does so still in office. The former announces this at the anniversary to a vast audience, the latter signals this message only to his driver in a code, which he surely understands. The first one does not need its benefits anymore, having been dead for a century; hence he announces this in public. The second would obviously like to enjoy its benefits, since he is still alive; therefore he announces it just to his driver, between four eyes only and through an attractive code, which is yet so plain that it is understandable by everybody.

The problem could also be too much experimenting with the system, as Kardelj did, or the fact that the party membership is declining. But why experiment if the system is not good? Would it not be easier to simply change it? Or this – that the system was not changed by its stakeholders, as jokes teach us – is perhaps a reflection of the fact that Kardelj (and Tito) truly believed in socialism, but only in a softer, milder nuance in comparison with the much tougher Stalin? The solution to the problem, as jokes continue to teach us, could also be its dismissal, or simply to bypass it; but the solution could as well be an unconventional way of tackling the problem (trying to get more members with a confirmation of non-membership as an asset). But why would

[28] We could even admire him/her for finding the way out even better than we would have done it. This is the very point where we feel that the leader is equal with us – we both try to bypass the system. But there is, of course, also the question if we too feel equal with the leader.

[29] However hidden, these messages are actually still very obvious, but due to a different form of expression, they also work differently. Perhaps hidden would in such cases mean they are masked so well that we like criticism in these messages so much that we do not understand or see it as criticism anymore, but only as a sympathy with the target. At the end of the day, we are all made of "flesh and bones", are we not?

the authority try to use a spin-doctor approach in attracting new members if the very same move actually proves that real value lies somewhere else (non-membership as such)?

Nevertheless, the question of increasing affiliation with the target, while expressing criticism on its account, remains open. Such an affiliation could transform not only the listener but also the re-teller, a kind of laughter in the rain: we got wet, but still feel fine, to a certain extent. The pleasure was released, but the defined frame remains.

Three dilemmas for the empire

Survival without political jokes

Former Yugoslavia, being a kind of an empire in itself, not that much by size but by its internal complexity, did not survive. There was an infinite number of political jokes circulating, some of which we have presented and analyzed. Many of these jokes expressed criticism of the system, and hinted in a certain way towards its collapse. These jokes were primarily dispersed around by sharing in closed circles of friends or acquaintances. They also reflected, as we have seen, sympathy with the system, which would mean they were also functioning in favour of their target.

From the dissolution of Yugoslavia in 1991 till 2004 Slovenia was established, then gained international recognition and was operating on its own, for the first time in history as an independent state. From spring 2004 onwards, Slovenia has been an EU member state, which also means that it follows the *acquis communautaire* as its main legal framework; *de facto* it would mean that Slovenia is again a part of the empire.[30]

Generally speaking, there are hardly any political jokes to be noticed in Slovenia after 1991.[31] The same goes for political jokes about the EU in Slovenia after 2004.[32] One could also say that those that do circulate are mostly repetitions of old samples along new premises, composing rather un-innovative adaptations, but lacking an original, innovative and sparkling message.[33] This is

---

30 For a comparison of some selected aspects between the two empires (former Yugoslavia and the EU) see Jazbec, 2008.

31 A purely personal observation would say that the author now hears fewer political jokes in ten years, than back then in one year.

32 Again, the author stems from his personal experience and could not at the moment offer any other empirically more reliable proof.

33 As an exemption (which proves the rule?) one could present the following two political jokes, heard on Radio Slovenia (the first one in spring 2008 and the second one in spring 2010). The first one goes: "A child, coming home from primary school in Slovenia, asks the father: Daddy, were communists really red? The father's reply: No, my son, golden." And the second one: "The government has enriched the pension reform package with the following two amendments: firstly, persons, reaching the age of 58, are allowed to cross

not necessarily the same as re-telling old jokes, but close to it: the older audience, who remembers such jokes from previous times, already knows the context and the frame, while the younger audience, who does not have a personal experience from previous times, hears those renewed jokes for the first time, adapted to new circumstances. An impression of a shortage of political jokes arises. If this is true, one could try to explain it from at least three points of view.

First, the EU is a democratic structure and institution, not an authoritarian one, which would mean that it hardly produces any political jokes needed for the system to be sustained.[34] If a joke or even laughter within such a context were really a *conditio sine qua non* for the ideology to function, then the EU as a post-modern phenomenon, which does not rest upon ideology, would either not need political jokes for its survival or even produce them.[35] It would most probably have other means of reflection and possibly also functional equivalents of jokes, like other media, blogs etc.[36] However, one should add a certain reservation here, asking the question of whether there exists a system that would be de-privileged by producing jokes. If there would be a correlation between political jokes and the nature of the system, focused on the essence of this relation, could it be that democracies would not provoke political jokes and only dictatorships would?

Second, the EU is an artificial structure, far away from the daily life and perception of its citizen, who hardly find regular, constant and strong identification with it. This could mean there are not many reasons to produce jokes for either criticizing or defending it. This unique superstructure would hardly deserve any such reflection since its habitants bother with closer, more concrete issues of their interest or devote their attention to other topics (i.e. related to national political elites etc.). Would perhaps their absence mean that the EU is still a kind of a success story and most probably does not need either a higher level of identification from its citizen or to fear failure?[37] Could one, additionally, speculate that there is enough satisfaction with the system in a democracy

---

the street at the red light, and secondly, persons, reaching the age of 63, have to."

34 This view was encouraged by comments during the discussion after the author presented his paper at the Klagenfurt 2009 Symposium.

35 However, if party combinations and groupings not only within the EU Parliament but also, for example, for the composition of the EU Commission would continue to play an increasingly important role, then it would for sure attract (and deserve) more attention from joke-makers.

36 Here we, of course, do not want to say that humour is absent from daily life within the EU. As Freud distinguishes between (political) jokes and humour, we also try to focus our intention on political jokes only. This too means that we do not deal with, for example, many ways of ridiculing the EU through various humorous ways.

37 Political jokes in the socialist system were indicating its failure. Looking back now, one could claim that hadn't it been for jokes, it would have failed anyway.

so as not to provoke political jokes anymore? Furthermore, would there not be enough dissatisfaction with the regime as such that this could provoke political jokes, which would hint to a necessity for a system change?

Third, a certain, perhaps not small, reservation as to why there seems to be a shortage of jokes about Slovenia and the EU should fall upon the author. A few decades have passed between the time when the jokes in question were produced and the present. The international environment has changed dramatically, other important media of communicating jokes appeared and the author is no longer part of young social (-ist) networks, which were (are) circulating jokes by sharing them. We compare at least two different (political) times and (social) places in which jokes have been made and re-told. One should still, maybe not only for theoretical reasons, presume that there are plenty of political jokes circulating and that the author simply does not get in touch with them (or hardly).

Understanding the way political jokes are being produced and their messages decoded, one could gain some knowledge to dwell on the issue of this shortage of jokes and, furthermore, to try to compare the case of former Yugoslavia with the EU from this point of view. Could the excess of political jokes in former Yugoslavia tell us anything useful about the shortage of jokes in the EU and advise us on the political consequences of this comparison? This might help us to reach lessons learned from the former to understand the latter from a specific point of view. However, it would be rather difficult to speculate on this, since it would take much empirical work to possibly prove any correlation between the appearance of jokes and the future of a given system. Besides, there would be a need to explain whether the shortage of jokes speaks in favour of either of the two empires, as well as whether their absence would have any meaning, any messaging at all. Still, it would be at least interesting to find out if a political joke brings anything to the decommissioning of its target.

Conclusion

To search or not to search

Our aim in this contribution was to analyze and contemplate political jokes in former Yugoslavia (primarily in Slovenia) as well as to compare findings on a general level with a similar situation in independent Slovenia, including the current period of its EU membership. Throughout this research endeavour we kept in mind the appearance of political jokes and their impact on the system in question (satisfaction or criticism). Our approach, as far as the methodology and concept were concerned, rested on the personal experience of the author. This was primarily determined by the fact that our inquiry started from a random sample of nine political jokes, which the author remembers, among many others, from his personal experience from his secondary school years in the early Nineteen Seventies.

Dwelling on the way political jokes are produced and shared as well as what their content means, tested through the presented sample, has basically proven our proposition that jokes reflect the social complexity of a country (system). This offers at the same time both satisfaction with the target and criticism towards it. Which aspect prevails depends on the joke itself and the way the message is constructed, wrapped up and released.

Here, our most important finding would be that the institution appears primarily as a target of jokes and that the message of the political joke is primarily expressed in a hidden conduct. Understanding the content of the joke brings us to the problem, this being the target of the joke. Surrogating the institution by its leader, who appears as a normal human being, often shows this serious message in an attractive way. This type of joke produces advanced hidden messages, works more in favour of its object than against it and is more sophisticated. One could say that replacing the institution with an individual helps to bring the target closer to the listener, raises his/her affiliation with it and reduces the criticism towards it. Furthermore, one could even say that having the individual as the target of a political joke helps to redirect the message of a joke from formal criticism to the *de facto* affiliation, where the former loses importance and the latter gains.

Looking at our sample of political jokes we could claim that they express: first, rather strong criticism towards the target; second, they point out medium strength hints about the future destiny of the target; and third, they produce a medium level affiliation with the target. When the target is the institution, strong criticism could be noticeable as well as weak affiliation. This takes the target away from the listener. However, when the target is an individual (as a replacement of the institution), less strong criticism could be noticeable, but affiliation is strong. This fact at least partially transfers the target, i.e. the individual into a kind of "our hero" as well as bringing the target close to the listener. In both cases the message is hidden: in the former not to reveal criticism to the extent that it would already be dangerous, and in the latter not to reveal the purpose of raising the affiliation with the target. This could be the most important concrete finding of our research, which, however, should be tested on a larger sample of jokes, namely: political (tendentious) jokes work in favour of the target, when the target is an individual, i.e. the person who symbolizes the system and with whom listeners are able to sympathize. The real nature of such a message should most probably be even more hidden than that with an aim of pure criticism. But at the same time it should be plain enough to raise spontaneous sympathy.[38]

---

[38] After Tito's death in 1980 the institution of the collective Presidency was put to test. There were eight members in it, from each of the republics and both autonomous provinces one; they all personified gerontocracy and *status quo*. One of the oldest was the Serbian representative, Petar Stambolić by name, who was well over eighty. For this, immediately when his presiding turn came, the following joke was in circuit on his account: Once he was

Perhaps we could then also say that political jokes reflect and measure the political atmosphere in a given country. They serve as a mirror demonstrating the scope of criticism as well as of praise, both presented in a hidden, masked manner. They most probably indicate the future of the target, too. However, it would not be easy to say they, if at all, contribute to the dismissal of the target. But they contribute to a subtle understanding of the target and the way it functions. Additionally, it would be even more difficult to explain what the absence of political jokes, if proven, would mean.

Nevertheless, having the EU without political jokes (provided this is the case) would at least signify the absence of both criticism and praise,[39] expressed through such a way, which brings around mirroring messages, hiding their true meaning and pointing at a specific characteristic of the target. The political joke as a result of political contemplation would be appreciated and perhaps the EU should launch a quest for good political jokes. If not for other reasons, then that this should not be interpreted as a sign of despair.[40]

References

Carey, John (2002), 'Introduction', in S. Freud, *The Joke and its Relation to the Unconscious,* Penguin Books, London, pp. vii - xxviii.

Crick, Joyce (2002), 'Translator's Preface', in S. Freud, *The Joke and its Relation to the Unconscious,* Penguin Books, London, pp. xxix - xlii.

Dolar, Mladen (1986), 'A Shot in the Middle of a Concert', in Th. W. Adorno, *Uvod v sociologijo glasbe (Introduction to Sociology of Music)*, DZS, Ljubljana.

Eco, Umberto (2004), *Ime rože (The Name of the Rose)*, Mladinska knjiga, Ljubljana.

Fischer, Kuno (1871), *Über die Entstehung und Entwicklungsformen des Witzes,* Heidelberg.

Freud, Sigmund (1992), 'Der Humor', in S. Freud, *Der Witz und seine Beziehung zum Unbewußten*, Fischer, Frankfurt a. M., pp. 253 - 256.

---

taken to the airport for state reasons. While sitting comfortably in the car, he turned to his Chief of Protocol, addressing him with the following question: "Are we departing for somewhere or are we receiving somebody?" Who could not laugh at such a joke and feel sincere sympathy with the old man, behaving so naturally? Who would not find this relatable? But, of course, who could not be horrified by having such a President, obviously not capable of performing the most simple of the responsible state duties? Here, sympathy serves as a strong material to hide the real message of the joke.

39 Linguistic barriers must also be noted; whereas in former Yugoslavia, the similarity of the languages – as well as one official language – meant that jokes were easily transferred, the linguistic gap in the EU could mean that even if there are plenty of jokes about it in one of its official languages, this may not translate well (if at all) to others, and thus we may not be aware of it. This aspect was brought to my attention by my son Luka.

40 Dr. Milan Jazbec is the Ambassador of the Republic of Slovenia in Ankara, Turkey, and Associate Professor of Diplomacy at the Faculty of Social Sciences, University of Ljubljana. The views expressed here are solely those of the author.

Freud, Sigmund (2002), *The Joke and its Relation to the Unconscious*, Penguin Books, London.

Gay, Peter (1992), 'Einleitung', in S. Freud, *Der Witz und seine Beziehung zum Unbewußten*, Fischer, Frankfurt a. M., pp. 7 - 22.

Gilli, G. Antonio (1974), *Kako se istražuje: vodič u društvenim istraživanjima (How to Research in Social Sciences)*, Zagreb.

Hafner, Fink Mitja (1994), *Sociološka razsežja razpada Jugoslavije (The Sociological Aspects of the Dissolution of Yugoslavia)*, Faculty for Social Sciences, Ljubljana.

Isaacs, Jeremy/Taylor Downing (2008), *Cold War*, Abacus, London.

Jazbec, Milan (2001), *The Diplomacies of New Small States: The Case of Slovenia with some comparison from the Baltics*, Ashgate, Aldershot.

Jazbec, Milan (2006a), *Ein Slovene in Belgrad: 1987 - 1991,* Hermagoras Verlag, Klagenfurt.

Jazbec, Milan (2006b), *Slovenec v Beogradu: 1987 - 1991 (A Slovene in Belgrade: 1987 - 1991)*, Second Slovene Edition, Pohanca: Self-published.

Jazbec, Milan (2008), 'Slovenia: the Long March from Belgrade to Brussels', in J. Langer (ed.), *Forces shaping the EU,* Peter Lang, Frankfurt a. M./New York, pp. 241 - 257.

Južnič, Stane (1996), 'Antropologija humorja (The Anthropology of Humor)', in *Teorija in praksa,* 33 (4). pp. 545 - 557.

Lorenz, Konrad (2002), *On Aggression*, Routledge, London/New York.

Repe, Božo (2002), *Jutri je nov dan: Slovenci in razpad Jugoslavije (Tomorrow is a New Day: The Slovenes and the Dissolution of Yugoslavia),* Modrijan, Ljubljana.

Sulzberger, C. L. (1980), *Sedem celin in štirideset let: Izbrani memoari (Seven Continents and Forty Years: Selected Memoirs),* Globus, Zagreb.

Toplak, Cirila (2003), *Združene države Evrope: Zgodovina evropske ideje (The United States of Europe: the History of the European Idea),* Faculty for Social Sciences, Ljubljana.

Zupančič, Alenka (2004), *Poetika. Druga knjiga (Poetics. Second Book),* Analecta, Ljubljana.

Index

List of Authors

AIGNER, Birgit
School of Management, Carinthia University of Applied Sciences, Villach/Austria

DÖRING, Thomas
School of Management, Carinthia University of Applied Sciences, Villach/Austria

JAZBEC, Milan
Ambassador of the Republic of Slovenia in Ankara/Turkey; Faculty of Social Sciences, University of Ljubljana/Slovenia

KNAPPITSCH, Eithne
School of Management, Carinthia University of Applied Sciences, Villach/Austria

KRPAN, Tomislav
Department of Information and Communication Studies, University of Zadar/Croatia

LANGER, Josef
Department of Sociology, Alpen-Adria-Universität Klagenfurt/Austria

MALI, Franc
Faculty of Social Sciences, University of Ljubljana/Slovenia

MATTILA, Anna
Graduate Student of International Business at the Turku School of Economics, Turku/Finland

MEIER-DALLACH, Hans-Peter
Institute for Social Science Research "cultur prospective", Zurich/Switzerland

MULITA, Reis
University "Marin Barleti", Tirana/Albania

NIŻNIK, Józef
Institute of Philosophy and Sociology, Polish Academy of Sciences, Graduate School for Social Research, Warsaw/Poland

OLGIATI, Vittorio
University of Macerata, Faculty of Law, Macerata/Italy

SOČAN, Lojze
Faculty of Social Sciences, University of Ljubljana/Slovenia

SUŠAC, Vlado
Department of Information and Communication Studies, University of Zadar/Croatia

TAHIR, Nuri Ali
International University Institute for European Studies (IUIES), Gorizia/Italy

Josef Langer (ed.)

Forces Shaping the EU

Social Science Approaches to Understanding the European Union

Frankfurt am Main, Berlin, Bern, Bruxelles, New York, Oxford, Wien, 2008.
265 pp., num. tab. and graph.
ISBN 978-3-631-57401-0 · pb. € 45.50*

This book investigates the European Union as an object of the social sciences. Although its main direction is to discuss different dimensions of the EU project and the direction of its development, it also reflects the state of the social sciences in this development. Accordingly, the book is structured to take into consideration "modernist", "critical" and "culturalist" perspectives. Given this frame the contributions by individual authors deliver a wide range of insights into the EU project, insights which often point to aspects hidden, rarely mentioned or not at all recognized in the official discourse about the EU. Besides, attention is raised for the precarious cognitive situation of the social sciences in times of rapid societal transformation.

Contents: Inspired by Modernity – The European Union in a Global Context · On Uncertain Ground – A New Global Power or a New Civil Community? Path Dependence, Future Scenarios for the European Union · Ambiguous Cultures – Legal Fictions as Constitutional Sociotechnics, The Tower of Babel Revisited, Notes for Another European Culture · Legitimacy from the Periphery – Perspectives of Borders

Kolibri 360 GmbH
Ferdinand-Jühlke-Straße 7
99095 Erfurt, Deutschland
produktsicherheit@kolibri360.de